Dead Theory

Also available from Bloomsbury

Literary Criticism in the 21st Century, Vincent B. Leitch
Alienation After Derrida, Simon Skempton
Deconstruction without Derrida, Martin McQuillan

Dead Theory

Derrida, Death, and the Afterlife of Theory

Edited with an introduction by
Jeffrey R. Di Leo

Bloomsbury Academic
An imprint of Bloomsbury Publishing Plc

B L O O M S B U R Y
LONDON · OXFORD · NEW YORK · NEW DELHI · SYDNEY

Bloomsbury Academic

An imprint of Bloomsbury Publishing Plc

50 Bedford Square	1385 Broadway
London	New York
WC1B 3DP	NY 10018
UK	USA

www.bloomsbury.com

BLOOMSBURY and the Diana logo are trademarks of Bloomsbury Publishing Plc

First published 2016

© Jeffrey R. Di Leo and contributors, 2016

British Library Cataloguing-in-Publication Data
A catalogue record for this book is available from the British Library.

ISBN: HB: 978-1-4742-7435-7
ePDF: 978-1-4742-7437-1
ePub: 978-1-4742-7436-4

Library of Congress Cataloging-in-Publication Data
A catalog record for this book is available from the Library of Congress.

Typeset by Newgen Knowledge Works (P) Ltd., Chennai, India
Printed and bound in Great Britain

... after my death *there will be nothing left.*

Jacques Derrida (2007)

Contents

Acknowledgments   ix

Introduction: Notes from Underground: Theory, Theorists, and Death   1
Jeffrey R. Di Leo

Part 1   Theory, Theorists, Death

1   The Heirs to Jacques Derrida and Deconstruction   25
    W. Lawrence Hogue
2   The Humanists Strike Back: An Episode from
    the Cold War on Theory   53
    Herman Rapaport
3   The Afterlife of Critics   73
    Henry Sussman

Part 2   Derrida, Death, Theory

4   Thanatographies of the Future: Freud, Derrida, Kant   101
    Jean-Michel Rabaté
5   Ghosts in the *Politics of Friendship*   111
    Paul Allen Miller
6   Death, Survival, and Translation   133
    Brian O'Keeffe
7   Theory's Autoimmunity   155
    Zahi Zalloua

Part 3   Politics, Death, Theory

8   Eclipse of the Gaze: Nancy, Community, and the
    Death of the Other   173
    Kir Kuiken
9   Deleuze, Kerouac, Fascism, and Death   191
    Hassan Melehy

10   Theory's Ruins   205
     Nicole Simek
11   Undying Theory: Levinas, Place, and the Technology of
        Posthumousness   217
     Christian Moraru

Notes on Contributors   233
Index   237

Acknowledgments

My primary debt of gratitude goes to the contributors to this volume for sharing their thoughts on death, theory, and theorists. I have benefitted greatly from my conversations with them about this topic and others, and appreciate their willingness as theorists to work on a subject that brings to the fore difficult issues relating mortality and an area of inquiry near and dear to us all.

I am also grateful to Vikki Fitzpatrick for her administrative assistance and to Keri Farnsworth for the help she has given me in preparing this manuscript for publication. At Bloomsbury, I would like to thank David Avital for his help in steering this manuscript through the peer review and publication process.

Finally, I would like to thank my wife, Nina, for her unfailing encouragement, support, and patience.

Introduction: Notes from Underground: Theory, Theorists, and Death

Jeffrey R. Di Leo

High or grand theory was exemplified through the work of figures such as Jacques Lacan, Jean-François Lyotard, Gilles Deleuze, Michel Foucault, and Jacques Derrida—each of whom is, alas, no longer among the living. Others though, such as Julia Kristeva, Luce Irigaray, and Hélène Cixous, are still very much among us. These structuralist and poststructuralist thinkers set an impressive agenda for theory in the late twentieth century though were met with opposition from many different quarters. Vincent Leitch of the University of Oklahoma, the pre-eminent historian of theory of our generation, contends that it came "from not only conservative scholars, but also a broad array of contending liberal and left theorists, indicting it (particularly deconstruction) for philosophical idealism, nominalism, obscurantism, and quietism, charges early made famous by certain Marxists, feminists, critical race theorists, and cultural studies scholars."[1]

The kind of high or grand theory exemplified by the work of Deleuze, Foucault, and Derrida was eclipsed by both low theory, which found its form in a multitude of "studies," and posttheory, "a pragmatic approach to theory which leads them to assess various theoretical models on the basis of the socio-cultural and political understanding that these models bring about."[2] Since the ascent of high theory (or the even higher, so-called sky-high theory or "theoreticism"[3]) and the emergence of various forms of opposition to it, rumors of and statements about its death have persisted well into the new century. Even today, closure regarding the issue seems remote. Again, just consider the work of Leitch, who recently published one of the most robust and enthusiastic defenses of the continuing presence of theory in the twenty-first century.[4]

Leitch acknowledges that word on the street is that theory is dead—superseded by a multitude of studies. Gone are theory stalwarts such as deconstruction, Marxism, and feminism. They have been replaced by studies of everything and anything from Barbie dolls and Beyonce to biopolitics and books. Leitch maintains that there are "94 subdisciplines and fields circling around 12 major topics" in literary and cultural theory today, which he notes are "reminiscent of planets and satellites."[5] Of these ninety-four subdisciplines, fifty include adjectives followed by the noun "studies": patronage, subaltern, working-class, debt, object, technoscience, animal, food, postcolonial, border, diaspora, new American, resistance, surveillance and security, body, cyborg, gender, disability, age, leisure, new Southern U.S., whiteness, indigenous, ethnic, women's, queer, masculinity, sexuality, celebrity, fashion, sport, gaming, sound, visual culture, TV, film, periodical, archive, professionalization, canonization, academic labor, literacy, composition, reception, performance, narrative, trauma, memory, and holocaust.

Another twenty clearly imply the noun studies, but for some reason it is not stated. For example, the field media studies has eight subdisciplines. All but three (new media, social media, and book history) include the noun studies— and for at least two of these (new media and social media) the noun studies is clearly implied. The final one, book history, is probably more accurate with studies replacing the noun history. Among the ninety-four subdisciplines, the noun "theory" is only used twice: in cognitive theory and affect theory.

Clearly, if Leitch is even somewhat accurate in his universal mapping of literary and cultural theory in the twenty-first century, there is little or no room in the new millennium for the more dominant mapping of literary theory and criticism, namely, one that divides it into schools and movements. For Leitch, designators of the theory and criticism universe such as Russian formalism, New Criticism, psychoanalysis, feminism, Marxism, structuralism, poststructuralism, queer theory, New Historicism, and postcolonial theory are strictly a twentieth-century phenomena. Though these designators were important to the emergence of theory in the last quarter of the twentieth-century, they have outlived their usefulness for mapping literary and cultural theory in the twenty-first century. The explosion of "studies" in the first quarter of the twenty-first century leaves little opportunity for organizing literary and cultural theory into the older matrix of schools and movements. Or, alternately stated, studies as a subspecies of the "twentieth-century" schools and movements makes for very messy and confusing mapping. Hence, why bother? Better to just leave it to the historians of theory to trace the legacies of theory amid the studies multitude.

What then to do with theory, that is, the sum body of the twentieth-century's schools and movements in the wake of the explosion of twentieth-first century studies? Leitch's answer is surprising. Namely, dub the first quarter of the twenty-first century a "theory renaissance." This is the somewhat counter-intuitive task of his book—a task which as difficult as it may sound, is one for which he makes an incredibly strong case. In a nutshell, his argument is that all ninety-four subdisciplines and twelve major topics "stem directly from recognizable contemporary schools and movements of theory."[6] Therefore, because there is no other term that adequately captures the "proliferation" charted into ninety-four subdisciplines and twelve major topics, we need to just continue to use the designator: theory.

Leitch's approach to theory in the twentieth century is right on the mark and represents the most energetic response to the so-called death of theory. Not only is theory not dead, it is undergoing a "renaissance" of sorts. Still, what is overlooked in these and other conversations of late about the death of theory is the related topic of the death of theorists.[7] Sure, there have been obituaries and legacy volumes—and even some biographies of theorists—but not much discussion about what the death of theory's progenitors means for the institution of theory. And even when the topic is broached, there seems to be efforts to avoid it. Take, for example, a recent work by Alain Badoiu.

A few years ago, the founder and publisher of Editions La Fabrique approached Badoiu about putting together a book of tributes to some of the philosophers who are no longer with us. Badiou says he "agreed almost without thinking about it, mainly because it seemed to me to be a tonic and far removed from death"[8] Among the fourteen individuals that Badiou addressed are many of the progenitors of high theory: Lacan, Lyotard, Deleuze, Foucault, and Derrida. However, after completing the book, he said, "Now, I hold the view that neither death nor depression should be of interest to us."[9]

In this volume, however, death *is* of interest to us. Not though in the form of tributes or obituaries, but as a means of understanding how the deaths of the high priests of theory have affected the life of theory and our relationship to it. Badiou himself gives us some insight into this when he speaks on the death of Derrida. His first feeling, he says, was "not a very noble sentiment." "I actually said to myself," writes Badiou, "We are the old ones now."[10] But he continues:

> So, we . . . We . . . who are we? Well, to be quite specific, it means we who were the immediate disciples of those who have passed away. We who were aged between twenty and thirty in those years from 1962 to 1968, we who followed the lessons of those masters with passion, we who, as they grew old and died, have become the old ones. Not in the same sense that they were the old ones, because they were the signature of the moment of which I speak, and because the present moment probably does not deserve any signature. But we are the

old ones who spent our entire youth listening to and reading such masters, and discussing their propositions day and night. We once lived in their shelter, despite everything. We were under their spiritual protection. They can no longer offer us that. We are no longer divorced from the real by the greatness of their voices.[11]

Badiou's comments here are both enervating and empowering. The death of the masters of theory calls for us to engage the present moment without their shelter and spiritual protection. The real is now our charge and will ultimately come to define who we are and our signature to those who follow in our path. Question is, will we rise to the task or hide behind the voices of our masters?

Applied theory

Theory has always struck me as being a *living* entity. Perhaps it was because its major figures always seemed so full of life and lively—most of all in their writing. Not staid and static creatures like the philosophers,[12] but dynamic and dangerous individuals who by the power of their personalities and enchantment of their intellect brought to life a body of thought that straddled but was never at home in any of the traditional humanities disciplines.

This disciplinary homelessness created a continuous institutional anxiety about theory. Departments who allowed it entry did so at their own peril—a peril fraught with the potential of disrupting their traditional self-identity. But they also opened up their department to a continual sense of new possibilities and knowledge formations as well as to closer ties with other areas of knowledge and academic disciplines.

Through the eyes of theory, traditional disciplinary lines such as philosophy, English, comparative literature, and foreign languages blur via elegant readings that continuously ignore disciplinary stop signs. Moreover, theory always seemed to have a different relationship with history than its associated disciplines.

From the vantage point of theory, the institution of philosophy always appears to be unfolding backward into the call and response of its history, whereas theory always appears to remain in the present—and, in effect, resist the pull of history. It might even be said that efforts to map out "the history" of theory or to capture it "in history" are merely attempts to normalize it, that is, to bring it in line with the histories of more traditional areas of inquiry such as philosophy or science. Most certainly, when history finally gets a grip on theory it will be history—in the same way that alchemy and philology are history.

But, the distinction here is not between the historical and the ahistorical—the drama the institution of philosophy still plays out over and over again, namely, is philosophy a historical or an ahistorical enterprise? Choosing sides here leads to very different types of philosophical discourse. Rather, in the case of theory, the distinction is between the historical and the present—or, more precisely, the contemporary.

For many, to call philosophy *contemporary* is an act of diminishment. Why? Because philosophers like to believe that their work is either solving problems that transcend time and place, or, alternately, that the problems of philosophy are historically situated and contingent. Even today, areas of philosophy that deal with contemporary social and political issues are often viewed within the institution of philosophy as "soft"—philosophy that is more akin to sociology than physics.

However, to call theory *contemporary* has always been a badge of honor. Though the theory of the 1960s and 1970s did not directly deal with contemporary issues (such as the Vietnam War or the Equal Rights Movement), its anti-establishment approach to the traditional disciplines and formations of knowledge rang well with the progressive politics and political activism of the time. Perhaps it is not a coincidence that the birth of applied ethics within the institution of philosophy in the late 1960s and early 1970s coincided with the rise of theory—for both are heavily invested in the contemporary.

But the legacies of applied philosophy were never directly linked to the work of particular individuals in the same way that the legacies of theory are linked to their progenitors. And, applied philosophy never sought to become interdisciplinary even though it called upon work in legal studies and sociology.

Applied philosophy took up social and political issues such as abortion, capital punishment, euthanasia, and animal rights—and read them through the framework of mainstream philosophical analysis. In the United States, this amounted to conceptual analysis and metaethics turned loose on the social and political issues of the day.

Though figures such as Judith Jarvis Thomson from MIT and Peter Singer from Princeton distinguished themselves a bit from the pack of philosophers writing on applied topics, their separation from the rest of the field is not great. And while their contribution to applied ethics will be missed when they die, no one would ever maintain that they will carry applied ethics with them to their grave.

This seems to be the fear though among theorists. Namely that when the last of the great theorists from the final quarter of the twentieth century pass on, so too will theory. The belief seems to be that theory as an institution is not strong enough to withstand the death of its leading figures.

And to some extent there is already some evidence for this in the cases of Paul de Man, François Lyotard, Michel Foucault, and Roland Barthes. While their work is still discussed and used, if the sessions of the Modern Language Association or, to a lesser extent, the American Philosophical Association, are any indicator of contemporary relevance and institutional import, then the work of these folks is already merely history and textbook fodder—or worse.

In the case of de Man, questions about his past continuously threaten to enervate his contemporary status and theoretical legacy. A recent biography by Evelyn Barish, *The Double Life of Paul de Man* (2014), for example, throws gasoline on the de Man character fire by accusing him of forgery, embezzlement, anti-Semitism, bigamy and Nazi-sympathy among other moral transgressions. Fair or not, even if one is able to regard his theoretical work outside of questions regarding his moral compass, the specter of such questions still haunt his work in the same way that they do the work of similarly morally disparaged figures such as Richard Wagner, Ezra Pound, and Martin Heidegger.[13]

But what, if anything, died in their theory when they changed tense? Or why does their death seem to coincide with the changing tense of their theory? Why does death seem to have such a profound effect on their legacies, whereas in other new areas of inquiry, such as applied ethics, the death of its major progenitors leaves the area of inquiry virtually unscathed? To be more direct, whereas psychology did not die along with William James, Sigmund Freud, and Jacques Lacan, why does theory feel like it is dying with the deaths of Barthes, Foucault, and, especially, Jacques Derrida? Is "applied theory," whatever that may be, the only way to save theory from imminent death?

Double death

In many respects, the issue of "the death of theory" and the issue of "the death of the theorist" are two very different and distinct issues: questions about the death of theory are ones about the continuing relevance of theory—or, one might say—its *contemporaneity*; questions about the death of theorists are ones about the loss of lives that were instrumental to the rise and dominance of theory—or, one might say—its *life force*.

The fact that we seem to be more concerned with the death of theory than the death of theorists may stem from the dominance of theory itself. Just as it is taboo for many theorists to recall the life of the author in the reading of their texts, so too is it taboo for the *post-* or *after*-theory generation to hinge the death of theory to the death of theorists. Theory transcends its theoreticians in the same way that philosophy transcends the work of individual philosophers. Or does it?

I recall a point in the composition of my doctoral dissertation where one of my committee members became irked with my constant reference to "philosophy" as though it were a noun or proper name. His comment was that there is no such thing as "philosophy"—only the work of "philosophers"—and had me correct the manuscript accordingly.

At the time, I was embroiled in the debates between "philosophy and literature"—debates that the theorists of the 1970s and 1980s awakened for an idealistic group of students like me who dreamed of a dialogue between them rather than disciplinary fights. And then into the room walked the Cassius Clay of the scholarly world: theory.

He was yelling and screaming that he was the King of the Humanities; that his readings of philosophy and literature floated like a butterfly and stung like a bee. He even changed his name lest we confuse him with the "mere" institutions of philosophy or literature. But after a while, his butterfly float looked more like a root-beer float—and his bee-sting lost its zing. The post-theory and after-theory generations had moved on to a new King of the Humanities: *studies.*

Like theory, studies floats among disciplines and departments. However, unlike theory, it is linked more to key concepts related to contemporary social and political issues than to a pair of the perennial pillars of the humanities, "philosophy" and "literature." The post- and after-theory generations salvage parts from theory for their studies, but do not rely on it for relevancy.

In a way, studies have much more in common with "applied" philosophy than theory ever had with it. Though both studies and theory share a preoccupation with the present, studies connect more directly with contemporary social and political issues. For example, theory reads the violence of language, whereas "race studies" considers both the violence of language and the actual violence done on the racially divided streets of Los Angeles, New York, and Chicago.[14]

I point this out not to belittle the work of theory and theorists on violence; rather to show the difference between these two modes of inquiry. Both do "readings" though studies work backward from contemporary social and political events to conclusions about them, whereas theory works within the context of social and political events though rarely deals directly with them.[15] Perhaps there is some insight on the fate of theory vis-à-vis the current successes of *studies* in a recent example from the world of applied ethics.[16]

In her John Dewey lecture delivered at the American Philosophical Association meeting in December of 2012, Judith Jarvis Thomson reflects back on a long career in applied ethics—and looks forward to work in philosophy she would like to see be done. Looking backward, she notes how different philosophical ethics was in the 1950s before the applied turn started to take on steam in the 1960s. "Philosophers interested in ethics began publishing papers on topics that the standard philosophy journals never published papers on before," says Thomson. "[W]e wrote on topics such as abortion, just war, the right to privacy, self-defense, and affirmative action and preferential hiring and the rights of women and minorities more generally." "It was remarkable!"[17]

And just as with theory, new journals formed to welcome new areas of inquiry. "Much of that material was at first published in *Philosophy and Public Affairs*," comments Thomson, "which was founded by Marshall Cohen in 1971: it invited lawyers and political theorists to join moral philosophers in dealing with concrete moral issues and was an immediate success."[18] However, by Thomson's estimation, "by the mid-eighties . . . enthusiasm for attending to concrete moral issues began to abate."[19] Sound familiar? I recall talk of the death of theory in the early 1990s—though I'm sure it was losing steam well before then.

But what Thomson does not say is that while applied ethics as a sub-species of metaethics and conceptual analysis did fade out in the mid-1980s, it was replaced by race, class, gender, and later, sexuality studies-based methodology. In other words, the rainbow of race, class, gender, and sexuality brought color to the grey conceptual analyses of first-generation applied ethics. And, even though Thomson lost interest in applied ethics, the field went on albeit with a new focus, direction, and energy. In short, the applied ethics of the 1990s became more the activist lesbian ethics of Sarah Hoagland and Chesire Calhoun, and the radical ethics of Angela Davis or even Peter Singer, than the staid and conservative ethics of Thomson or even John Rawls.

Looking forward, Thomson would like to see work on two questions: "Why do we care about philosophical theories?" and "Why do some philosophical theories seem safer against counter-cases than others do?"[20] These are good questions for theorists as well, particularly the first one—questions I'm not sure even theory has fully addressed.

Now to my ear, these two questions are as far from applied ethics as theory is from studies. Does asking metaphilosophical questions make Thomson any less of an applied philosopher? Does it somehow detract from her philosophical legacy? I don't think so.

The advent of applied ethics in philosophy was as revolutionary and disruptive to the institution of philosophy as theory was to literary studies. New journals formed around applied ethics just as they did around theory. However, even leading figures in the field of applied ethics such as Thomson felt that its life cycle had gone its course long before their careers were over. Finding oneself late career, like Thompson, asking questions more akin to ones asked at the start of her career should not be viewed as the failure of applied ethics. Rather it should be viewed as its success as it opened the door to the rainbow colors of second-generation applied ethics. Why not view the fate of theory in the same way? Specifically, why not view studies as an extension of the heterodox vision and contemporary focus of theory?

Alone together

So, if the death of theory and the death of the theorist are really two distinct issues, why does it not feel that way? Moreover, why *shouldn't* we see the two issues as intertwined and interrelated, namely, the death of theory and the death of theorists? The main reason is probably that to do so *belittles* the status of theory. To hinge the life of theory to the life of the theorist is to assume a fragility for theory that is similar to saying that Socrates's arguments lose their value when he is no longer around to continue them.

But still, theory always seemed to reside in a realm where theorists were ageless and could never die—a realm similar to the one occupied by Bowie and the Stones in the music world—an eternal present. Nevertheless, their fates have been similar. Aging and a lack of public performance has arguably diminished the relevancy of these musicians to the contemporary music scene. Their performances now are all nostalgia—and no danger. They are reminders of a time when the music industry was a different place. So too is it with our dying and dead theorists. While the theory industry continues to release archival and greatest hits volumes from Derrida, Barthes, and de Man, their impact is more to remind of days gone by than serious engagements of the issues of the day.

Sean Gaston, in his excellent recent book, *The Concept of the World from Kant to Derrida*, echoes this sentiment in the case of Derrida's posthumous publications:

> Almost ten years after the death of Jacques Derrida, Derrida studies finds itself
> in the strange temporality of the posthumous publications, of waiting for the
> forty years of seminars and lectures to appear. Looking backward into a steadily
> receding and fixed point, these works are hardly contemporary, but they will no
> doubt be given a contemporary status or be equally condemned for their lack of
> relevance or acuity for the pressing issues of the day.[21]

Perhaps though the most scathing recent indictment of theory comes from Tom Cohen of Albany, who works on climate change and its connections with critical theory. "The eco-catastrophic logics disclosed in the past decade," comments Cohen, "were not addressed by the master thinkers of the 20th century, whose idioms form different guilds and extensions today."[22] For Cohen, existing theory—including the work of Derrida or Deleuze—cannot "account" for anthropogenic climate change. Therefore, concludes Cohen, contemporary critical thought on climate change demands a new kind of "theory." For Cohen, climate change "opens to an exteriority irrecuperable by the current tropological order"—and is "in a sense unrepresentable" within it.[23]

But none of this is the fault of the theorist or theory. The contemporary is ever-changing and shifting, and it is unreasonable to expect newly published posthumous work always to be responsive to it, or, worse yet, to expect theory's past always to be responsive to present concerns. However, the opposite can also be the case: namely, that posthumous theory publication can be responsive to contemporary concerns. It has surely been the case with the recent publication of Foucault's lectures at the College de France from December 1970 until his death in June of 1984. Not only do they show a different side of his thinking, but these forty-year-old lectures, particularly the ones on governmentality and neoliberalism, are extremely relevant to contemporary concerns.[24]

How then should we view the legacy of theorists?

Double feeling

In his final interview, published in 2007 under the title *Learning to Live Finally*, Derrida said that he was preoccupied with questions of inheritance. "Who is going to inherit, and how?" asked Derrida. "Will there ever be any heirs?"[25]

In some ways, these questions seem odd given the range and impact of his lifework.

Internationally recognized, widely anthologized, and the author of some seventy books during his lifetime—and many more that have appeared after his death— the last thing on his mind should be inheritance. Is not every contemporary theorist an heir to Derrida's legacy? Is there any way to think about the intersections of philosophy and literature without at least acknowledging an inheritance from Derrida? Isn't all contemporary theory (to crib Whitehead's quip about Plato) a footnote to Derrida? But this does not seem to be what Derrida means.

In some ways, the mere history of ideas is the most trivial dimension of thought. Trivial in the sense that there is no way to look back at philosophy and literary studies in the latter part of the twentieth century, particularly in the United States and on the continent, without also coming into contact with Derrida's many contributions. This is the mere literary or philosophical—or even theoretical—history noted earlier. What Derrida is preoccupied with though seems to be something more "living" and in the present. That is, whether his "thought" will die when he dies.

"When it comes to thought," reflects Derrida, "the question of survival has taken on absolutely unforeseeable forms."

> At my age, I am ready to entertain the most contradictory hypotheses in this regard: I have simultaneously—I ask you to believe me on this—the *double feeling* that, on the one hand, to put it playfully and with certain immodesty, one has not yet begun to read me, that even though there are, to be sure, many very good readers (a few dozen in the world, perhaps, people who are also writers-thinkers, poets), in the end it is later on that all this has a chance of appearing; but also, on the other hand, and thus simultaneously, I have the feeling that two weeks or a month after my death *there will be nothing left*. Nothing except what has been copyrighted and deposited in libraries. I swear you, I believe sincerely and simultaneously in these two hypotheses.[26]

Elsewhere, he states his feelings about his legacy even more directly: to wit, that he will be forgotten as soon as he dies. If Derrida—whose impact on theory is comparable to Freud's on psychology, namely both theory and psychology are unthinkable without these respective individuals and their work—has this "double feeling," then the legacy of the rest of the theory world is in even worse shape.

The first feeling though, that "one has not yet begun to read me," seems to me to be about contemporaneity, specifically, posthumous contemporaneity.

Namely, without active or living readers to draw his works into an engagement with contemporary concerns, "there will be nothing left" after his death but his published writings and his remaining manuscripts, namely, the second feeling. And without readers these texts are nothing—they are merely *dead theory*.

However, the possibility of theory living on—and of legacies being built—depends on the ability of theoretical writing to be responsive to present and future concerns. Nonetheless, just like literature, which upon the death of the author is embalmed in history, so too is theory. It becomes another chapter in the history of theory—or perhaps even the dual histories of philosophy and literary studies. Though it loses its "life" in the passage into history, it forever awaits a reader to make it "undead" theory—in much the same way that Foucault and Derrida often brought the ancient world and its history and philosophy and literature "back to life" as "theory" in their heyday.

The tasks of theory today are much different than they were forty or even twenty years ago. Climate change, debt culture, the specter of terrorism, and the assault on the humanities haunt the present. So too do the ghosts of theory. The legacy of theory is thus contingent on its ability to be responsive to the contemporary and its issues. We need to worry less about the deaths of theory—and more about the individuals who are going to guide us through the process of thinking through the present not in theory—but *with* theory.

Dead theory

Given then the role of Derrida in the formation of what has come to be known as theory, and his recent death and self-reflections on it, it is fitting that a volume dedicated to the topic "dead theory" begins with an assessment of his legacy and heirs. Opening the first part of this book, "Theory, Theorists, Death," is a wide-ranging and provocative essay, "The Heirs to Jacques Derrida and Deconstruction," by W. Lawrence Hogue. In his essay, Hogue shows us some of the multifaceted legacies of the work of Derrida in areas within philosophy, anthropology, theology, postcolonialism, feminism, and literary criticism. For Hogue, these multidisciplinary appropriations of deconstruction and poststructural theory affirm and relaunch them for a new generation of theorists. In effect then, for Hogue, "they keep Derrida and theory alive."

If Hogue's essay is forward-looking in that it is an assessment of how Derrida and theory have stayed alive in spite of the theory wars, then the next essay is backward-looking in that it is an account from the front lines of one of the battles from these wars. "The Humanists Strike Back: An Episode from the Cold War on Theory" by Herman Rapaport takes us back to a period beginning in the late 1990s—a time when theory was alleged to have died. He terms this period the "cold war" on theory because it deals not so much with "outright opposition" to theory, but is characterized by a "general neglect" of it, that is to say, "a lack of recognition, interest, and support that disqualifies theory as a legitimate and worthwhile enterprise." "Whereas the hot war on theory relied quite heavily upon the staging of affairs, scandals, and/or uncomfortable confrontations at symposia," writes Rappaport, "the cold war on theory has been waged seemingly by way of tacit agreement less as a matter of negative reinforcement than of no reinforcement at all."

If there is an analogy from applied ethics to Rappaport's account of the theory wars, it is the one illustrating the moral difference between active and passive euthanasia, that is, killing someone versus letting them die. The difference is often illustrated by using the examples of pushing someone's head down in a tub in order to drown them versus watching them drown in a tub without reaching in to help them. The cold war on theory was a lot like the latter. In spite of watching it drown, no one seemed to be coming to theory's rescue during this period. In this episode from the cold war, Rappaport shows us the role of humanism and humanists like Martha Nussbaum in allowing theory to drown. Though this cold war has other episodes, the role of humanism serves to exemplify one of the accounts of how theory came allegedly to meet its demise in the last decade of the twentieth century.[27]

In many ways, Hogue and Rapport are tilling the same wartime soil, and both are trying to come to grips with the complex legacies of the so-called death of theory albeit from different angles. If this is the case, then so too is Henry Sussman, who in his essay, "The Afterlife of Critics," provides an intriguing account of how the casualties of the theory wars live on. Using cybernetic theory grounded in the work of cognitive scientist Douglas Hofstadter, Sussman brilliantly provides us with one perspective of how critics can persist far after "their active practices of inscription and their biological lives" end. Sussman concludes that he does not see "Blanchot, Deleuze/Guattari, or Derrida, railing too vehemently against the charge that they opened up, by means of their ingenious devices and phrases, 'points of incompletion' in systems otherwise too stratified, frozen, blind, or complacent to recognize lapses, that always compromise . . . opportunities." Indeed, though very different from the historically situated accounts of Hogue and Rappaport, there is a compellingness and power in using theory to discuss its own afterlife; one that always already has the effect of short-circuiting any and all calls for the death of theory.

The transition from the essays in Part One to those in Part Two is a movement from considerations of the death *of* theory and theorists to considerations of death *in* theory. This next part, entitled, "Derrida, Death, Theory," gravitates around the theoretical work of Derrida on death and its philosophical and poetic context. In sum, they make a strong case for the continuing relevance of theory.

The first essay, "Thanatographies of the Future: Freud, Derrida, Kant," by Jean-Michel Rabaté situates Derrida's work on death in relationship with that of Freud and Kant. In the process, Rabaté not only provides us with a greater understanding of Derrida's work on death (and the death drive), but also deepens our knowledge of the psychological and philosophical foundations of Freud's systematic confrontation with death in his book, *Beyond the Pleasure Principle* (1920), as well as provides insight into the role of death in Kant's considerations of the future. "A consideration of death," writes Rabaté, "is a good spot to try and think both a priori conditions of human psyches and the general question of the future"—including that of theory.

In "Ghosts in the *Politics of Friendship*," Paul Allen Miller deepens our understanding of the relationship of death and theory in Derrida through a close examination of one of his major philosophical works. Published immediately after *Specters of Marx* (1993), Derrida's *Politics of Friendship* (1994) is for Miller "a text haunted by the ghosts of friends past, both those who have died and those who are no longer friends," which Miller does an excellent job demonstrating. However, as Miller shows, *Politics of Friendship* is not simply a memorial volume. Rather, it is also one with a deep and significant political dimension, that is, "a text whose wager on a democracy to come is predicated on the force of those friendships and the loss they necessarily entail."

Questions concerning how theory addresses itself to matters of life and death in Derrida continue through the lens of his thoughts on translation in Brian O'Keeffe's contribution, "Death, Survival, and Translation." Through pursuit of how the idea of translation squares with his work on life, death, and "living-on," O'Keeffe comes to pursue a set of important questions: "Can literary texts die? Can they anticipate their impending demise and do something about it? Is doing something about it a matter of asking us to respond to the text which senses its imminent death, and which appeals for rescue, or for translation?" Derrida's most significant response to them however, for O'Keeffe, is not found in mammoth and monumental texts like *Specters of Marx* or *Politics of Friendship*, but rather is a most unlikely and little-known text, namely, an interview he did for the Italian journal *Poesia* in 1988. In the end, O'Keeffe's essay shows that "translation is a work of mourning because it is concerned with the afterlife of a literary text"—and how, specifically, poetry gets "into all things that risk death."

The final essay in this part, Zahi Zalloua's "Theory's Autoimmunity," examines the ways in which Derrida's notion of "autoimmunity" makes more visible the difference between philosophy and theory. He reminds us, drawing on Fredric Jameson, that philosophy "is always haunted by the dream of some foolproof, self-sufficient, autonomous system, a set of interlocking concepts which are their own cause." In other words, philosophy is timeless—and never dies. Theory, on the other hand, says Jameson, "has no vested interests as it never lays claim to an absolute system . . . it has only the never-finished task and vocation as such, of unraveling affirmative statements and propositions of all kinds." Or, in other words, theory is not timeless like philosophy, but rather always suffering "deaths" through its never-ending "unraveling of affirmative statements and propositions." Zalloua uses Jameson's comments as a gateway to examine skepticism's relation to philosophy and theory, and finds that "skepticism functions as a *pharmakon* . . . as a remedy and poison for conceptualization and thinking. As such, Derrida's notion of autoimmunity can be seen to make "the differences between philosophy and theory all the more visible."

Unlike the essays in Part Two, which all explicitly revolve around the work of Derrida, essays in the last part follow the interrelationship of death and theory into a related but decidedly different direction. Part Three, entitled "Politics, Death, Theory," opens with Kir Kuiken's "Eclipse of the Gaze: Nancy, Community and the Death of the Other." In his essay, Kuiken examines the "motif of a 'death' that lodges itself at the heart of contemporary critical theoretical questioning about some of our most basic (political) concepts, including the concept of community."

"Theory," comments Kuiken, "has *always* been dying, one could say from the moment of its birth," and as such should be regarded as internal to theory, rather than external to it. "If death is not just a figure for the limit, but also the result of (twentieth-century) attempts to radically refound collective life," argues Kuiken, "the question of what is at stake politically, ethically, or otherwise, in trying to rethink the concept of community through the motif of death becomes imperative." Drawing on George Bataille, Jean-Luc Nancy, and Maurice Blanchot, Kuiken elegantly demonstrates the way in which the figure of death is central to their notions of community.

The next essay, Hassan Melehy's "Deleuze, Kerouac, Fascism, and Death," deepens the connections among politics, theory, and death. Building from the work of Deleuze and Guattari, which has been viewed as "a powerful affirmation of life against the domination of death," Melehy shows how a critique of fascism can be found in the creative work of Jack Kerouac. The work of Deleuze and Guattari, at least in the eyes of Michel Foucault, writes Melehy, "stems entirely from the antifascist energy that drives it." For them, fascism is defined "in its historical manifestation as very precisely a domination of death, which carries the people who embrace it to an inevitable and violent end." The spontaneity of Kerouac's writing, its "willingness to live in the moment and not be concerned with definitions in order to find or produce something new," squares well with Deleuze's notion of the kind of writing that should be seen as a critique of fascism—or at the very least, should be seen as advocating anti-fascism.

In "Theory's Ruins," Nicole Simek continues the political engagement of literature as a means to gain further insight on the relationship between theory and death. Her essay takes us to the Caribbean and the writings of Derek Walcott, Patrick Chamoiseau, and Jean-Luc de Lagarigue. For Simek, "dead theory is also a theory *of* the dead, of an object that prompts reflection on theory's temporality and ethical commitments." Her essay examines "theory's relationship to enchantment and disenchantment, to affective investment and critical distance," a topic she believes the site or figure of "the ruin" highlights particularly well. "Theory's ruins," writes Simek, "are those transient objects, those historical fragments or material traces that seem to call out for theorization, that present an alluring hermeneutic puzzle."

The final essay in this part—and the collection—is Christian Moraru's "Undying Theory: Levinas, Place, and the Technology of Posthumousness." It is a coda to all that has been done in this volume under the name "dead theory." Moraru sees the topological triangulation of theory's "place," that is, its renewed lease on life, alleged death, and zombie-like state, as a form of "sublime violence done to, or transactions imposed concurrently on, place and life." He says that this violence or these transactions should be considered as "an *ethic beyond the ethnic*: an ethic that neither erases nor discounts ethnic background and all backgrounds, grounds, and *Gründe*, but, to the contrary, one that acknowledges and honors them by working with, through, and over their contested geography, their territorially circumscribed and ethno-culturally demarcated spaces, turfs, and discourses." For Moraru, this ethic (re)values death and "sponsors a certain posthumousness"; it is one that "weaves together theory, place, life, and death, and then, self and other as their condition of possibility." In sum, death is viewed by Moraru as both "an environment and supreme test for theory, for what we do, and for the doers themselves," and as "life's paradoxically energizing *memento mori*."

In sum, the essays in this collection provide a wide range of insight on the relationship between death and theory. Not only do they explain some of the ways in which theory takes on a different "life" after the death of the theorist or even has a life of its own, but essays like Moraru's provide a rich context on the very question of what does it mean to say that theory is living or dead? They extend from literary historical engagements of the topic to rich and inventive examinations of the relationship between politics, theory and death. In a way, calls for the death of theory as seen through the essays in this volume seem only to strengthen and deepen the stature and importance of theory for a new generation of philosophers and critics.

At the center of the volume though is the work of Jacques Derrida, the philosopher whose work on death in the last decade of his life has been the centerpiece of so much recent interest. Derrida was certain that he would be forgotten as soon as he died, but he also thought that he would live on in cultural memory. Additionally, he promised himself that he would never write "following the death" of his friends, yet he still wrote about Paul de Man, Emmanuel Levinas, Roland Barthes, and others after they passed.[28] If nothing else, the essays in this volume help us understand how and why these contradictory statements are not only possible, but meaningful. They encourage us to see death in relation to theory not as its end, but rather as the very condition of its possibility.

Derrida is dead, long live Derrida!

Theory is dead, long live theory!

Notes

1 Vincent Leitch, *Living with Theory* (Malden, MA: Blackwell Publishing, 2008), 10.

2 Jeffrey R. Di Leo and Christian Moraru, "Posttheory Postscriptum," *symplokē* 3.1 (1995), 120. For us, posttheorists both critique extant theory as well as use it to position their work both on and off campus. See also, Jeffrey R. Di Leo and Christian Moraru, "Posttheory, Cultural Studies, and the Classroom: Fragments of a New Pedagogical Discourse," in *Class Issues: Pedagogy, Cultural Studies and the Public Sphere,* ed. Amitava Kumar (New York and London: New York University Press, 1997), 237–246 and Jeffrey Williams, "The Posttheory Generation," *symplokē* 3.1 (1995), 55–76.

3   See, Dominic LaCapra, *History in Transit: Experience, Identity, Critical Theory* (Ithaca, NY: Cornell University Press, 2004), 156.

4   Vincent Leitch's *Literary Theory in the 21st Century: Theory Renaissance* (New York: Bloomsbury, 2014).

5   Ibid., first recto. This page of the book contains figure 1, "Twenty-first Century Literary and Cultural Theory Renaissance," a chart of the current state of "theory."

6   Ibid., viii.

7   See, for example, Terry Eagleton, *After Theory* (New York: Basic Books, 2003), Nicholas Birns, *Theory after Theory: An Intellectual History of Literary Theory from 1950 to the Early 21st Century* (Buffalo, NY: Broadview Press, 2010), *Theory after "Theory,"* eds. Jane Elliott and Derek Attridge (New York: Routledge, 2011), and, most recently, Vincent Leitch's *Literary Theory in the 21st Century*, for a representative sample.

8   Alain Badiou, *Pocket Pantheon: Figures of Postwar Philosophy* (London and New York: Verso, 2009), vii.

9   Ibid.

10 Ibid., 123.

11 Ibid., 123–124.

12 The tensions and distinctions between "analytic" and "continental" temper my use of the term "philosopher." The "philosophers" from the continent such as Deleuze, Foucault, and Derrida, came to be known as "theorists" in the American academy and the battles to include or exclude their work in US philosophy departments are legendary. My use of the term reflects here my American educational background.

13 See, for example, the recent controversies over the release of Heidegger's "Black Notebooks" in Paul Hockenos, "Release of Heidegger's 'Black Notebooks' Reignites Debate over Nazi Ideology," *The Chronicle of Higher Education* (February 24, 2014).

14 A strong case may be made that social and political events such as the Gulf War, but especially those of September 11, 2001, decidedly turned the academic momentum from theory to studies, or, alternately, from critique to criticism. French theorist Jean Baudrillard's responses, for example, to these two particular events in works like *La Guerre du Golfe n'a pas en lieu* (Paris: Éditions Galilée, 1991), and "L'esprit du terrorisme" (2002) and "Requiem pour les Twin Towers" (2002) (both of which are translated and collected in Jean Baudrillard's *The Spirit of Terrorism* [London: Verso, 2012]) were widely criticized and the subject of much debate. See, Jeffrey R. Di Leo, "The Ruins of Critique" in *Criticism after Critique: Aesthetics, Literature, and the Political*, ed. Jeffrey R. Di Leo (New York: Palgrave, 2014), 1–4.

15　Journals that combine both modes of inquiry, that is, "studies" and "theory," ultimately make the most valuable contributions to understanding complicated and contemporary topics such as "violence." Moreover, the best work in theory avoids doctrinaire approaches. The charge of thinking through the present with, through, and in theory is perhaps its most important role today. For a good example of the intermingling of "studies" and "theory" approaches to violence, see *symplokē* 20.1-2 (2012), a special issue on the subject edited by Jeffrey R. Di Leo and Sophia McClennen.

16　Again, there is perhaps no more robust defense of the success of studies than Vincent Leitch's *Literary Theory in the 21st Century* (2014), where he shows the current state of "theory" as consisting of ninety-four subdisciplines and fields circling around twelve major topics. For an assessment of Leitch's volume, see my review in *The Comparatist* (2015).

17　Judith Jarvis Thomson, "How It Was," in *Portraits of American* Philosophy, ed. Steven M. Cahn (Lanham, MD: Rowman & Littlefield, 2013), 55.

18　Ibid., 55.

19　Ibid., 55.

20　Ibid., 60.

21　Sean Gaston, *The Concept of World from Kant to Derrida* (Lanham, MD: Rowman & Littlefield, 2013), 160.

22　Tom Cohen, "A Labyrinth of Exanthropies: 'Climate Change' and the Rupture of Cultural Critique," *Telemorphosis: Theory in the Era of Climate Change, Vol. 1*, ed. Tom Cohen (Ann Arbor, MI: Open Humanities Press, 2012), i.

23　Ibid., ix.

24　See, for example, Jeffrey R. Di Leo, "A Dog's Life: Austerity and Conduct in Neoliberal Academe." *symplokē* 22.1-2 (2014), 59–76, which uses Foucault's work in his lectures on the Cynics to elaborate issues in neoliberalism in higher education today.

25　Jacques Derrida, *Learning To Live Finally: The Last Interview: An Interview with Jean Birnbaum* (Hoboken, NJ: Melville House Publishing, 2007), 32.

26　Ibid., 33–34.

27　The bathtub cases with respect to active and passive euthanasia were first proposed by James Rachels in a 1975 article from the *New England Journal of Medicine*. See, James Rachels, "Active and Passive Euthanasia," in Jeffrey R. Di Leo, *Morality Matters: Race, Class, and Gender in Applied Ethics* (New York: McGraw Hill, 2002), 198–202.

28　See, for example, Jacques Derrida, *Memoires for Paul de Man, Revised Edition* (New York: Columbia University Press, 1986), *Adieu to Emmanuel Levinas* (Stanford, CA: Stanford University Press, 1999), and "The Deaths of Roland Barthes," *The Work of Mourning*, eds. Pascale-Anne Brault and Michael Nass (Chicago and London: The University of Chicago Press, 2001).

Works cited

Badiou, Alain. *Pocket Pantheon: Figures of Postwar Philosophy*. Trans. David Macey. London and New York: Verso, 2009.

Barish, Evelyn. *The Double Life of Paul de Man*. New York: W. W. Norton, 2014.

Baudrillard, Jean. *La Guerre du Golfe n'a pas eu lieu*. Paris: Éditions Galilée, 1991.

Baudrillard, Jean. *The Spirit of Terrorism*. Trans. Chris Turner. London: Verso, 2012.

Birns, Nicholas. *Theory after Theory: An Intellectual History of Literary Theory from 1950 to the Early 21st Century*. Buffalo, NY: Broadview Press, 2010.

Cahn, Steven M., ed. *Portraits of American Philosophy*. Lanham, MD: Rowman & Littlefield, 2013.

Cohen, Tom. "A Labyrinth of Exanthropies: 'Climate Change' and the Rupture of Cultural Critique." *Telemorphosis: Theory in the Era of Climate Change, Vol. 1*. Ed. Tom Cohen. Ann Arbor, MI: Open Humanities Press, 2012.

Derrida, Jacques. *Adieu to Emmanuel Levinas* [1997]. Trans. Pascale-Anne Brault and Michael Naas. Stanford, CA: Stanford University Press, 1999.

Derrida, Jacques. "The Deaths of Roland Barthes." *The Work of Mourning*. Eds. Pascale-Anne Brault and Michael Nass. Chicago and London: The University of Chicago Press, 2001.

Derrida, Jacques. *Learning To Live Finally: The Last Interview: An Interview with Jean Birnbaum*. Trans. Pascale-Anne Brault and Michael Naas. Hoboken, NJ: Melville House Publishing, 2007.

Derrida, Jacques. *Memoires for Paul de Man, Revised Edition*. New York: Columbia University Press, 1986.

Di Leo, Jeffrey R. *Corporate Humanities in Higher Education: Moving Beyond the Neoliberal Academy*. New York: Palgrave Macmillan, 2013.

Di Leo, Jeffrey R. "A Dog's Life: Austerity and Conduct in Neoliberal Academe." *symplokē* 22.1–2 (2014): 59–76.

Di Leo, Jeffrey R. *Morality Matters: Race, Class, and Gender in Applied Ethics*. New York: McGraw Hill, 2002.

Di Leo, Jeffrey R. "Review of Vincent Leitch, *Literary Theory in the 21st Century*." *The Comparatist* 39 (2015): 412–415.

Di Leo, Jeffrey R. "The Ruins of Critique." In *Criticism after Critique: Aesthetics, Literature, and the Political*, ed. Jeffrey R. Di Leo. New York: Palgrave, 2014. 1–12.

Di Leo, Jeffrey R., and Sophia McClennen, eds. *Violence*. Special issue. *symplokē* 20.1–2 (2012).

Di Leo, Jeffrey R., and Christian Moraru. "Posttheory Postscriptum," *symplokē* 3.1 (1995): 119–122.

Di Leo, Jeffrey R., and Christian Moraru. "Posttheory, Cultural Studies, and the Classroom: Fragments of a New Pedagogical Discourse." In *Class Issues: Pedagogy, Cultural Studies and the Public Sphere*, ed. Amitava Kumar. New York and London: New York University Press, 1997. 237–246.

Eagleton, Terry. *After Theory*. New York: Basic Books, 2003.

Eagleton, Terry. *Literary Theory: An Introduction*. Malden, MA: Blackwell Publishing, 1983; 2nd ed., 1996; 3rd ed., 2008.

Elliott, Jane, and Derek Attridge, eds. *Theory after "Theory."* New York: Routledge, 2011.

Gaston, Sean. *The Concept of World from Kant to Derrida*. Lanham, MD: Rowman & Littlefield, 2013.

Hockenos, Paul. "Release of Heidegger's 'Black Notebooks' Reignites Debate over Nazi Ideology." *The Chronicle of Higher Education* (February 24, 2014). http://chronicle.com/article/Release-of-Heidegger-s/144897/forceGen=1.

LaCapra, Dominic. *History in Transit: Experience, Identity, Critical Theory*. Ithaca, NY: Cornell University Press, 2004.

Leitch, Vincent. *Literary Theory in the 21st Century: Theory Renaissance*. New York: Bloomsbury, 2014.

Leitch, Vincent. *Living with Theory*. Malden, MA: Blackwell Publishing, 2008.

Leitch, Vincent, ed. *The Norton Anthology of Theory and Criticism*. New York: W. W. Norton, 2001; 2nd ed., 2010.

Rachels, James. "Active and Passive Euthanasia." In *Morality Matters: Race, Class, and Gender in Applied Ethics*, ed. Jeffrey R. Di Leo. New York: McGraw Hill, 2002. 198–202.

Thomson, Judith Jarvis. "How It Was." John Dewey Lecture delivered at the American Philosophical Association meeting, December 2012. Reprinted in Steven M. Cahn, *Portraits of American Philosophy*, 47–62.

Williams, Jeffrey. "The Posttheory Generation." *symplokē* 3.1 (1995): 55–76.

Part One

Theory, Theorists, Death

1

The Heirs to Jacques Derrida and Deconstruction

W. Lawrence Hogue

In his last interview, Jacques Derrida was certain that he would be forgotten soon after his death, certain that he and Deconstruction would live on in cultural memory, in the archives, but not a part of the lived experience. This situation worried him until the end. The questions poised for this article are: What is the relationship between death and theory? Does theory take on a different "life" after the death of the theorist? Is the life of theory dependent upon the life of the theorist? I will respond to these questions within the context of Derrida's life and death and in the examination of what he thought would happen to his deconstructive propositions after his death. In an interview with Jean Birnbaum in *Learning to Live Finally*, recorded just weeks before his death, Derrida expressed an interest in survival. "To survive," he states, "in the usual sense of the term mean[s] to continue to live, but also to live after death . . . like a book that survives the death of its author."[1] Derrida was fully aware that his traces would live on after his death, that they would be rethought, revised, and rearticulated by different individuals for different audiences. The problem is he is not sure how or to what extent. In that same interview with Jean Birnbaum, he stated,

> when one writes books for a more general audience: you do not know to whom you are speaking, you invent and create silhouettes, but in the end it no longer belongs to you. Spoken or written, all these gestures leave us and begin to act independently of us . . . Each time I let something go, each time some traces leave me . . . unable to be reappropriated, I live my death in writing. It's the ultimate test: one expropriates oneself without knowing exactly who is being entrusted with what is left behind. Who is going to inherit, and how? Will there even be any heirs?[2]

From the above quote, we can deduce that Derrida believes that the "life of the theory" is independent of the life or death of the author. Derrida's death in October of 2004 changes nothing about the status of his traces. But in the above quote, he is also concerned with who is being entrusted with his traces, who will be his heir.

Derrida uses the word "heir" in the sense that he, as an heir, belongs to and shares a common (mostly male) western European heritage with others, one that includes Marx, Freud, Nietzsche, Heidegger, Lyotard, Deleuze, Foucault, Blanchot, Sarah Kofman, Levinas, Lacan, Barthes, Althusser, and others. But he thinks that our current "techno-culture" has radically changed this tradition of heirs. Again, in the interview with Jean Birnbaum, he concluded,

> The people of my "generation," those of the previous ones, had been accustomed to a certain historical rhythm: one thought one knew that a particular work might or might not survive, based upon its own qualities, for one, two, or perhaps, like Plato, twenty-five centuries. Disappear, then be reborn. But today, the acceleration in the forms of archivization . . . are transforming the structure, temporality, and duration of the legacy . . . I have the feeling that two weeks or a month after my death there will be nothing left. Nothing except what has been copyrighted and deposited in libraries.[3]

He thinks he will be in the archive but not a part of the lived experience. This is his concern.

With changes in culture and in the duration of legacy today, particularly in France, Derrida understands the difficulties of having heirs. I think this explains why, as he is sick and dying, he is still travelling the world, to Rio de Janeiro, to London, to the United States, and to other places, because he sees what he calls "media intellectuals" in France such as Bernard Henri-Levy, Pascal Bruckner, and Andre Glucksmann who appear on television or in the newspaper, advising French governments, rising up against "French theory," filling up the nonfiction best sellers' lists, and repressing or erasing the common heritage, the Sixties Era, that he shares with Foucault, Barthes, Deleuze, Levinas, Sarah Kofman, Cixous, Lyotard, and Blanchot.[4]

With Derrida, we are not talking about someone who is rejected after his death; rather, we are talking about someone who is rejected in life, compounding his fears. Derrida and his ideas have been consistently meet with resistance. In addition to being misappropriated by scholars who did not read him and certainly did not understand him, he was labeled an enemy of truth, justice, reason, and the university, both in France and the United States. In the United

States, New Critics and traditional American critics such as Allan Bloom, E. D. Hirsch, George Steiner, Roger Shattuck, and John Hollander immediately rejected Derrida and deconstruction because it challenged their logocentric perceptions. Many, if not most, American intellectuals, particularly in English and Comparative Literature departments, are uncomfortable with or they outright reject Derrida's deconstruction. He is perceived as a threat to their American way.

But ironically, Derrida, near his death, was more popular among certain individual scholars and intellectuals in US humanities departments than he was in France, where his theories are scarcely taught, even in philosophy departments, which have long distrusted his global vision of politics and art and the world. "Around the beginning of the 1980s, right when the works of Foucault, Deleuze, Lyotard, and Derrida were being put to work on American campuses," writes Francois Cusset in *French Theory*, "those very names were being demonized in France as the epitome of an outdated 'libidinal' and leftist type of politics."[5] (Of course, this is not to say that certain individual scholars and intellectuals in France did not continue to read and write about Derrida and other post-structuralist theorists.) In 1997, Alan Sokal and Jean Bricmont published *Impostures intellectuelles*, rejecting French theory and defending "the canons of rationality and intellectual honesty that are . . . common to all scholarly disciplines."[6] In France, Derrida is defined by many in the academy as an enemy of and a danger to the status quo.

By the late 1990s, some prominent, Western critics had pronounced deconstruction as passé. Marxist theorists such as Slavoj Žižek, Alain Badiou, and Terry Eagleton critiqued deconstruction, deeming it not universal. Cornel West minimized deconstruction because "it tends to preclude and foreclose analyses that guide action with purpose."[7] In one of her intellectual moments, Camille Paglia, who essentializes paganism in her work, calls Foucault an "arrogant bastard" and denounces French theory, demonstrating how much she needs a basic course in deconstruction.[8] Under these circumstances, it becomes difficult for Derrida to ascertain who his heir would/could be.

But Derrida was perceived as a threat everywhere. He was falsely arrested in Prague for the possession of drugs and the French government had to intervene. When he was offered an honorary doctorate at Cambridge University in the United Kingdom, faculty members protested, claiming "despite occasional disclaimers, the majority preoccupation and effect of his voluminous work has been to deny and to dissolve those standards of evidence and argument on which all academic disciplines are based."[9] Upon his death, obituaries in the *New York Times* and the *New Criterion* welcomed his death and hopefully the end of deconstruction, referring to Derrida's death as the departure of an "abstruse theorist."[10] Despite his innovation and influences, Derrida was never wholly received by the mainstream academy.

But as the attacks on him and deconstruction continued, Derrida focused more on the ethical and the political, shifting his deconstructive acts of reading from just Western metaphysics and the Western philosophical tradition to the world's ethico-political stage, where he dealt with issues and events that are considered political. "[T]here is a progression in which [the] originally ethical and political motif in his work, deeply Levinasian in tone," writes John D. Caputo, "has worked its way more and more to the front of his concerns in the writings of the 1980s and 1990s."[11] One of the reasons for the shift was that Derrida developed a close affinity to certain political and social movements. With friends, he established the Jan Hus Association, which aided dissident or persecuted Czech intellectuals. He began to speak out against apartheid in South Africa, participating in the organization of the exposition "Art against Apartheid"; he opposed Israeli policies and supported the Palestinian cause.[12] He fought for the rights of Algerian immigrants in France and protested against the death penalty in the United States, totalitarian regimes, and forms of intellectual censorship. Speaking at the colloquium organized, in 1989, by the Cardozo School of Law in New York on "deconstruction and the possibility of justice," Derrida, declaring that deconstruction is justice, assisted in the initiation of the development of his "deconstructive" research into the theory of the law (critical legal studies) in the United States. He began to travel to Japan, Latin America, Africa, the Middle East, and to the Palestinian-occupied territories, where he met with Palestinian intellectuals, and the other takes on a more human face. And in articles like "Racism's Last Word" in Gates' *"Race," Writing, and Difference*; in books like *The Death Penalty, Specters of Marx, The Beast and the Sovereign, Of Hospitality, Acts of Religion, Monolingualism of the Other, Adieu: To Emmanuel Levinas, On Cosmopolitanism and Forgiveness*, and others; and in interviews in *Negotiations* and *What For Tomorrow*, Derrida did not cease challenging the unquestioned assumptions of the Western philosophical and metaphysical traditions. Rather he began to more overtly transgress these traditions and took his deconstruction and his democracy to come onto the world stage where he deconstructed traditional, Western ethics because it did not deal with the suppressed and concealed other, injustice, oppression, capitalism, and globalization.

In his overt shift into politics, Derrida became a prophet of the other, the oppressed, the undocumented, and the unseen. How he viewed the Western

philosophical tradition and how he viewed world politics, especially as it per-
tained to the other, came out of his own personal experience. Until he was
nineteen, he saw himself as belonging to a marginalized, oppressed community
in Algeria. In his conversation with Mustapha Cherif in *Islam and the West*,
Derrida was emphatic about the fact of who he was, saying his work had something to do with the fact that he was raised in Algeria as a French Jew who was
other both to the French and to the Algerians.

> The cultural heritage I received from Algeria is something that probably
> inspired my philosophical work. All the work I have pursued, with regard
> to European, Western, so-called Greco-European philosophical thought, the
> questions I have been led to ask from some distance, a certain exteriority,
> would certainly not have been possible if . . . I had not been a sort of child
> in the margins of Europe, a child of the Mediterranean, who was not simply
> French nor simply African, and who had passed his time traveling between
> one culture and the other feeding questions he asked himself out of that
> instability.[13]

It was his marginal status, his experience of otherness, his embrace of this
hybrid experience, this instability that caused him to discern the limitations of
the Western philosophical tradition. "One difficulty is the attitude of a West
with entrenched ideas, which refuses to admit plurality, to really listen to the
other, to recognize that there exist other completely different ways to see the
world."[14] His approach, then, to the European philosophical tradition was from
the margin where he could constantly and continually asks the ethical question: where is the other who is usually rendered invisible? Derrida belonged to
and worked within the European philosophical tradition, opening it up to the
other and revealing differences.

Since Derrida talks about dislocation, dispossession, occupation, and resistance, which are rendered invisible in mainstream society, the likely candidates
to be his heirs would be threatened, marginalized, minoritized, delegitimized,
oppressed identitarian communities in society. In "Women in the Beehive,"
Derrida alludes to fact that "it has been written somewhere that deconstruction
in the United States was successful among feminists and homosexuals."[15] But
this raises interesting questions: do you have to be a member of a threatened
identitarian community to be an heir to Derrida's deconstructive procedures?
Do you have to belong to or work within the European philosophical tradition
to be Derrida's heir? Or is there a difference between those intellectuals who are
heirs to Derrida's deconstruction and those who take Derrida's deconstruction

into other heritages and traditions, exposing us to the challenge of hitherto suppressed or concealed otherness?

This concern about the other and his heir placed Derrida in a difficult and complicated position. As he looked around him, most, if not all of others— women, racial and ethnic minorities, colonized people, religiously threatened communities in the West and the East, who have hybrid/multiple experiences (inner multiplicity)—practiced identity politics and Derrida mistrusted identitarian compulsion and communitarian logic. These are violently threatened communities who think that they need unity and solidarity to survive, that their racial, religious, or sexual identity claims make them essential groups. Derrida defined an identitarian community as a "homogeneous milieu that reproduced and in a certain way countersigned—in a reactive and vaguely specular fashion, at once forced (by outside threat) and compulsive—the terrible violence that had been done to it."[16] For Derrida, identitarian compulsion and communitarian logic tend to homogenize identities, to affirm the self, to affirm oppositions; and they also tend to exclude the different, the other. These identity groups tend to be unable to go beyond or to rethink identity and the existing community structure, which tend to reproduce the violence and hierarchies with which they organize to resist.

Yet, despite the fact that Derrida mistrusted identity politics or communitarian logic, he insisted on the other as one to whom an incalculable responsibility is owed. The other makes us human. Therefore, he felt that "he must make [the threatened community his] own, at least provisionally, whenever [he] recognize[d] discrimination or a threat."[17] He was prepared to support the causes of threatened, marginalized communities "up to the moment when [he] become[s] mistrustful, when the logic of the demand seems to [him] potentially perverse or dangerous,"[18] signaling a double gesture I will discuss later.

Still, despite the mistrusts, Derrida took his habits of deconstruction into the other, these threatened, marginalized identitarian communities, translating them into something that is not present and that is hoped for, thereby exposing the other, opening them up to suppressed differences, and keeping the future open-ended. If the future is to come, Derrida believed, then, we must ethically extend justice to the other. "There can be no future as such unless there is radical otherness, and a respect for this radical otherness. It is here . . . that justice . . . analytically participates in the future."[19] In examining Derrida's deconstructive analyses of these threatened, marginalized identitarian communities, I focus specifically on how he transgressed his Western philosophical tradition and took his habits of deconstruction into Islam (religion), feminism,

and (homo)sexuality. Then I discuss more generally how non-European scholars and intellectuals take Derrida's deconstructive procedures into race and
postcoloniality, welcoming the other and recognizing differences.

With his values of difference and multiplicity, Derrida moved into religion
and deconstructed the Islam-West binary opposition, opening it up to its other.
When Derrida wrote on religion, it was always on the "ancient" notion of the
Abrahamic. "[T]he Abrahamic," writes Gil Anidjar in the introduction to
Derrida's *Acts of Religion*, "has been considered either the original and gathering root of the three major monotheistic faiths or, more pervasively, as the
(three) branches of one single faith."[20] Abraham's name appears in all three
religions. Discussing his opposition to the Islam-West binary with Mustapha
Cherif, Derrida states, "I agree with you about the need to deconstruct the
European intellectual construct of Islam. The so conventionally accepted contrast between Greeks, Jews, [and] Arabs must be challenged. We know very well
that Arab thought and Greek thought intimately blended at a given historical
moment and that one of the primary duties of our intellectual and philosophical memory is to rediscover that grafting, that reciprocal fertilization of the
Greek, the Arab, and the Jew."[21] Here, Derrida moves into the European construction of Islam as the other to Europe and, through double gestures, transgresses its border, opening up the system to intermingling and intermixing.
First, using the ancient notion of the Abrahamic, which is at the origin of the
three religions, Derrida reclaims territorialized roots, welcoming togetherness.
He cites Spain as a place where "Greek, Arab, and Jewish thinking intimately
blended together," where they "truly fertilized each other."[22] Within what one
calls religion, states Derrida, "there are . . . tensions, heterogeneity, disruptive
volcanos, sometimes texts . . . which cannot be reduced to an institution."[23]
Second, Derrida examines Algeria, where "the Arab and Muslim or Arabo-
Muslim culture of Algeria and of Maghreb is also a western culture. There are
many Islams, there are many Wests,"[24] thus challenging essences and binary
oppositions, affirming the invention of the radical other, and bringing difference and multiplicity to both the West and Islam.

In addition, Derrida took his deconstructive critiques into Christian and
Islamic fundamentalism, especially in the United States and in those Muslim
or Arabic countries that merge politics and the theocratic. "It is not out of
respect for religion," he states, "that we must dissociate things and that we must
cease to lead politics in the name of religion, or under the authority of religion,
or sometimes under the authority of religious authorities themselves."[25] In the
United States and in Muslim/Arabic countries, he calls for the "securalization

of the political, without the need to renounce faith or religion."[26] Resisting religious communitarianism, he believes that a religious community can organize itself in a "lay space, without invading the lay space and while respecting the freedom of the individual,"[27] opening the space up to the religious person who can also act as a nonreligious citizen.

In focusing on difference and the other in Islam, Mustapha Cherif in *L'Islam: Tolerant ou intolerant?* takes the analyses of Derrida's deconstruction into Islam, opening it up to new inventions. "His thinking," Mustapha Cherif writes, "has contributed to advancing our attempt at a reflection on the destiny of Islam . . . For us, Muslim intellectuals, his thinking opens up the path to a new encounter with the West."[28] Two years after Derrida's death, Algeria, the country of his birth, pays a tribute to him, remembering and recalling the modern, living, and open thinking of Jacques Derrida. Certainly, Derrida's respect for welcoming alterity and differences had an influence on the philosophical works of the influential Swiss (Muslim) public intellectual Tariq Ramadan. Gil Anidjar, author of *The Jew, the Arab: A History of the Enemy* and the author of the introduction to Derrida's *Acts of Religion*, also takes deconstruction into Islam. Like Derrida, Ramadan and Anidjar, who come to Derrida through the European philosophical tradition, reinvent Islam, not rejecting the traditions of Islam but opening them up to the possibility for the coming of the wholly other.

Likewise, despite his distrust of the communitarian logic of the Women's Movement, Women's Studies, and feminism,[29] Derrida took his deconstructive propositions of affirming otherness into this politically threatened and marginalized community. Writing in "Becoming Woman" and thus using Nietzsche's discussion of the concept-metaphor "truth becoming woman" as his text, Derrida transgresses Nietzsche's boundaries and opens up the term "woman" to differences. He states emphatically, "There is no such thing as the essence of woman because woman averts, she is averted of herself. Out of the depths, endless and unfathomable, she engulfs and distorts all vestiges essentiality of identity, of property."[30] Associating woman/the feminine with truth, he argues that not only is the truth plural but it cannot be pinned down. Here, truth is adventurous, risky, and not reassuring. Since it is plural, truth is non-truth; the field is open. Suspicious of essentialized categories, Derrida declares, "Feminism is nothing but the operation of a woman who aspires to be like a man. And in order to resemble the masculine dogmatic philosophers this woman lays claim—just as much claim as he—to truth, science and objectivity in all their castrated delusions of virility. Feminism too seeks to castrate. It wants a castrated woman."[31] For Derrida, one can seek her, but woman is "not to be found in any of the familiar modes of concept or knowledge. Yet [it] is impossible to resist looking for her."[32] Hélène Cixous, Derrida's contemporary, in *The Newly Born Woman* agrees with Derrida that the "feminine" cannot be labeled or categorized in existing modes of knowledge.

In "Choreographies," Derrida uses the famous quote from radical anarchist and feminist Emma Goldman—"If I can't dance I don't want to be part of your revolution" —in response to a questioner who wants to know his stance on feminism. "Why must there be a place for woman? And why only one, single, completely essential place," he asks?[33] Derrida deeply resists essentialism because it assumes that there is a presence that predates the play of traces. Here, Derrida plays on Goldman's term "to dance" as a way of destabilizing and deconstructing any set notion of "place" for woman. Dancing, then, would be a way of displacing, of stepping otherwise, of "differing"/"deferring," and "différance." Woman dancing challenges a "certain idea of the *locus* . . . and the place (the entire history of the West and of its metaphysics)."[34] What he advocates in the "dance" metaphor, argues Anne-Emmanuelle Berger in "Sexing Differences," is a "relentless stepping in and out of traditional political and philosophical confines,"[35] as a way of not getting stuck in one foundational term that can easily be thematized and essentialized.

But Derrida emphasizes and argues for dance, at the same time that he points out that dancing might "compromise the political chances of feminism and serve as an alibi for deserting organized, patient, laborious 'feminist' struggles when brought into contact with all the forms of resistance that a dance movement cannot dispel."[36] This is an example of Derrida opening up the field of feminism to difference, to different, and possibly contradictory and "undecidable," positions, leaving the decision to the participants to carefully look at both gestures, take a risk, and decide which is most appropriate for a given situation.

At the conference at Brown University, Derrida is asked to respond to the question of Women's Studies, especially given the fact that it exists in an institution that has its own phallocentric rules, procedures, and guardians of the Law. "Do the women who manage these programs, do they not become, in turn, the guardians of the Law, and do they not risk constructing an institution similar to the institution against which they are fighting?"[37] Clearly aware that if he answers the question in the negative, he runs the risk of appearing "reactionary" or dangerous but refusing to capitulate to the gathered American feminist audience and holding true to his values of différance, Derrida begins with, "to remain within a department, would be a failure. On the other hand, if you give up the idea of a feminine studies program, then you will weaken the feminine cause."[38] Then, he concludes with a two-gestured approach: maintain a women's studies program and integrate women's studies into the university's curriculum. You can do both simultaneously.

But, in the discussion at Brown, Derrida returns to the issue of female subjectivity that he raised in "Becoming Woman." He states,

> If someone tries to deconstruct the notion of subjectivity within women's studies, saying "well, woman is not a subject, we no longer consider woman as a subject"—this would have two consequences: one radically revolutionary or deconstructive, and the other dangerously reactive . . . The effect of the Law is to build the structure of the subject, and as soon as you say, "well, the woman is a subject and this subject deserves equal rights," and so on—then you are caught in the logic of phallogocentrism and you have rebuilt the empire of the Law. So it seems that women's studies can't go very far if it does not deconstruct the philosophical framework of this situation, starting with the notion of subject, of ego, consciousness, soul and body, and so on. The problem with this strategy is that it's difficult to make so many gestures at the same time.[39]

This becomes another one of those instances where Derrida refuses to resolve the supposedly conflict/contradiction, thereby challenging logocentric thought. You can have two or more gestures—the radically revolutionary or deconstructive one and the reactionary conservative one, and so forth—happening simultaneously without resolution. Without a priori value or proper norm, you use the two or more in accordance with what is best for the present situation. On the one hand, he distrusts communitarian feminist demands. Yet, on the other hand, he is willing to join force and fight when there is oppression of women. It has to do with the politics of situatedness. By affirming difference, contradiction, and plurality in all of the above situations, Derrida demonstrates his distrust of a "homogeneous milieu" for the woman that can reproduce the "terrible violence that had been done to [her]." But he also commits himself to fighting the oppression of women.

Yet, despite his distrust of feminist identity politics, Derrida, in taking his deconstructive procedures into women's studies, feminism, and the women's movement, had an impact. Many feminists realized that the struggles of deconstruction and feminism are the same: to dismantle a "structure, which is called phallogocentrism, which is a whole structure, [and] which is a system."[40] Both get beyond identitarianism and recognize that it is a system that violently excludes and subordinates. After his death, *Differences: A Journal of Feminist*

Cultural Studies devotes an entire issue to "Derrida's Gift," with tributes from feminists such as Judith Butler, Elizabeth Grosz, Peggy Kamuf, Christie McDonald, Gayatri Spivak, Jane Gallop, and others. Writing in "Notes on an Unfinished Question," Christie McDonald states, "The feminist revolution questioned the accepted canon and began deconstructing gender hierarchies, challenging gender assumptions both in literature and in society; *differences* was a part of that movement."[41] "Derrida's gift to feminism," writes Elizabeth Grosz, "is the concept of difference, the very concept whose contours explain not only the relations between the sexes and the relations between sex and gender but also the relations between subjects and the relations constituting subjects."[42] Arguing that feminism shares with deconstruction a "groundless solidarity," Diane Elam in *Feminism and Deconstruction* believes that feminism and deconstruction have in common the "displacement of the subject [and] of identity politics."[43] Although Jacqueline Rose, Elaine Showalter, and Margaret Homan wrote against deconstruction, thinking it was "subjectivist essentialist" (Showalter) or that it defines "Woman" as a sign for indeterminancy (Rose), Gayatri Spivak defends deconstruction against Rose's charge. "*Différance* and 'woman' are two names on a chain of nominal displacements where, unmotivated names, neither can claim priority,"[44] arguing that if différance/woman opens up the question of symbolic possibility, deconstruction is not, as Rose suggests, a storyline suppressing sexual and cultural difference in the name of différance. Luce Irigaray in *Speculum of the Other Woman* uses Derrida's procedures to deconstruct the male/female, active/passive binaries in Freud and Lacan.[45]

Third and final, Derrida took his deconstructive analyses into sexuality. Just as he distrusted "the place of woman," he also distrusted identitarian gays and lesbians, putting (homo)sexuality within a play of differences, inscribed within différance. Derrida views terms like "straight" and "gay," "male" and "female" as fixed containers, prisons, trapping individuals in one place, one role, closing off the places of multiple sexual spacing. In "Choreographies," Derrida rhetorically asks the question: "[W]hat if we were to approach here . . . the area of a relationship to the other where the code of sexual marks would no longer be discriminating"? Then he answers,

> The relationship would not be a-sexual, far from it, but would be sexual otherwise: beyond the binary difference that governs the decorum of all codes, beyond the opposition feminine/masculine, beyond bisexuality as well, beyond homosexuality and heterosexuality which come to the same thing. As I dream

of saving the chance that this question offers I would like to believe in the multiplicity of sexually mark[ed] voices. I would like to believe in the masses, this indeterminable number of blended voices, this mobile of non-identified sexual marks whose choreography can carry, divide, multiply the body of each "individual," whether he be classified as "man" or as "woman" according to the criteria of usage.[46]

Here, Derrida transgresses or passes through the boundaries of these domi-nant, almost naturalized, sexual/gender categories, without abandoning them, exploring what they omit, exclude, expel, ignore, or scorn, translating them into something that is not present, and "dreaming" of a process of sexual differentiation—"the multiplicity of sexually mark[ed] voices"—beyond any kind of limit. Judith Butler in undoing gender and in emphasizing multiplic-ity approaches Derrida's full elaboration of différance. "Queer theory," writes Butler in *Undoing Gender*, "is understood, by definition, to oppose all identity claims, including stable sex assignments."[47] In taking his deconstructive pro-cedures into Islam, feminism, and (homo)sexuality, bringing differences and multiplicity and welcoming the other, Derrida was no longer concerned with egalitarianism, civil rights, the law, or any pre-given goal. Rather, in his ethics, justice is never equal to the law. Here, Derrida is "committed to the full elabo-ration of difference and its uncontrollable and uncontainable movements of differentiation or becoming."[48]

In the United States and internationally, non-European literary critics and writers who were exposed to critical theory in the 1980s and 1990s deploy Derrida's habits of deconstruction, his values of affirming difference and plural-ity, into their respective heritages and (literary) traditions. African American and other critics and writers of color, including this author and others such as Houston A. Baker, Fred Moten, and Gerald Vizenor, transgress identitar-ian African American, American Indian, and Chicana literary communities, canons, and cultural and political institutions and affirm differences and mul-tiplicities. Houston Baker's *Blues, Ideology, and Afro-American Literature* "is as anti-metaphysically and profoundly indebted to Derrida as anything [he has] ever written."[49] Opening up the blues to its alterity, Baker in *Blues, Ideology* uses Derrida's "always already" to define African American culture "as a complex, reflexive enterprise which finds its proper figuration in blues conceived as a matrix . . . [which] is a point of ceaseless input and output, a web of intersect-ing, crisscrossing impulses always in productive transit."[50] Baker transgresses the borders of the standardized, personalized form of the blues, inventing and affirming the radical other ("the phylogenetic recapitulation"). In my *African American Male, Writing, and Difference*, I, using Derrida's concept of difference, do not reject but transvalue the mainstream racial uplift canonical narrative, opening up the field of African American literature to multiple traditions. Writers of color like Percival Everett, Gloria Anzaldua, Gerald Vizenor, Samuel Delany, and others take Derrida's concept of difference into the formation of their fiction.

Internationally, postcolonial critics and theorists who read Derrida's and post-structuralist's texts, take Derrida's deconstructive movements into Asia, Middle East, and Africa. Although French theorists such as Derrida, Foucault, Deleuze, and others do not write specifically about colonialism/imperialism, they influence the formation of postcolonial theory as an alternative form of knowledge about modernity. In their desire to bring difference, subjectivity, and agency to Africans, Middle Easterners, and Asian Indians who have been constructed as devalued other by the West, Edward Said, Gayatri Spivak,[51] Homi Bhabha, Anthony Appiah, V. Y. Mudimbe, Achille Mbembe, and many other postcolonial critics and historians use Derrida's deconstruction, along with other French theorists such as Lacan and Foucault, to deconstruct "the symbolic forms and representations underpinning the imperial project."[52]

In using French theory to assist in the formation of his postcolonial theory, Achille Mbembe, possibly the most eminent political philosopher working on postcolonial Africa today, does not reject the heritage of anticolonial studies. Rather, he transvalues it. He states, "But added to this [postcolonial critics such as Fanon, Cesaire, Senghor, and Glissant] is the influence of French thinkers of Otherness . . . also the contribution made to postcolonial thinking by the analyses of Foucault, Derrida, and even Lacan." In the Derridean tradition, Mbembe defines African subjectivity in terms of "afropolitanism—a way of being 'African' open to difference and conceived as transcending race."[53] Postcolonial critics' desire for recognition of the other in their traditions and of their suppressed otherness makes them indirect heirs to Derrida's values of difference and multiplicity, without hierarchy.

In short, individual scholars and intellectuals at colleges and universities throughout the United States, Australia, Africa, Asia, Latin America, Europe, and the United Kingdom have been influenced by or are heirs of Jacques Derrida and deconstruction. The religious philosopher Mark C. Taylor summarizes, "No thinker in the last 100 years had a greater impact than he [Derrida] did on people in more fields and different disciplines. Philosophers, theologians, literary and art critics, psychologists, historians, writers, artists, legal scholars and even architects have found in his writings resources for insights that have led to an extraordinary revival of the arts and humanities during the past four decades." And at the personal level, Avital Ronell, a friend of Derrida, best describes his larger-than-life presence in the academy when she writes, "One cannot imagine how whited-out the academic corridor was when Derrida arrived on the American scene. There was really no room for deviancy, not even for a quaint aberration or psychoanalysis . . . Derrida cleared spaces that looked like obstacle courses for anyone who did not fit the professional profile at the time. He practiced a . . . politics of contamination. His political views . . . distinctly leftist, knew few borders and bled into the most pastoral sites and hallowed grounds of her education."[54] Derrida's influence and impact are simply unquestioned.

In identifying and displacing the oppressive structure proper to all institutions, as he invented the radical other and brought difference and multiplicity to normative institutions and categories, Derrida's full elaboration of différance culminated into a democracy to come. His democracy to come is tied not to citizenship, the nation-state, or territoriality, but operates at the level of international alliance.

> What you call the universalism of democracy, a concept that is very difficult to define, presupposes that democracy is conceived in a way other than as a fixed model of a political regime. I believe that what distinguishes the idea of democracy from all other ideas of political regimes . . . is that democracy is the only political system, a model without a model, that accepts its own historicity, that is, its own future, which accepts its self-criticism, which accepts its perfectibility . . . To exist in a democracy is to agree to challenge, to be challenged, to challenge the status quo, which is called democratic, in the name of a democracy to come . . . Democracy is always to come, it is a promise, and it is in the name of that promise that one can always criticize, question that which is proposed as de facto democracy.[55]

As a place where the "other [is] recognized as other, recognized in his alterity,"[56] the democracy to come is also an international alliance where dialogue and negotiation can open up between the so-called West and the East, "between the different cultural regions and different religious regions of the world, if such an exchange is possible through words, through thoughts, and not through force."[57] At this level of international relations, there must exist "an infinite will for coexistence and respect for [or hospitality toward][58] the other,"[59] where there exist just relations between individuals, on the one hand, and between societies, on the other.[60]

In making the relation to the other central to his democracy to come and in spreading his values of difference, plurality, and heterogeneity in multiple disciplines in Europe, the United States, and around the world, Derrida becomes a part of an emerging planetary movement. In this planetary movement, as the theoretical works of Enrique Dussel and Gayatri Spivak[61] point out and as I discuss in *Postmodern American Literature and Its Other* and Christian Moraru concurs in *Cosmodernism* and *The Planetary Turn*, the other is no longer foreign to the West. "As a result of mass migrations, diasporas, globalized mass culture, and transnational public spaces, it is impossible to say with certainty exactly where one culture ends and another begins . . . With acceleration of globalization, we get a cultural context that includes a newly felt proximity of 'the other' and simultaneously heightened concerns about 'difference,' which have intensified struggles for recognition."[62] The other is part of the West and the West is part of the other. Derrida's democracy to come is a part of this international turn toward the planetary.

There have been remarkable advances in philosophy, literary criticism, historiography, anthropology, politics, legal studies, feminism, postcolonial theory, queer theory, and religion inspired by Derrida, Foucault, and other post-structuralists, which have transformed our contemporary thinking. It was the post-structuralists who problematized everything in terms of how identities are "invented," "hybrid," "fluid," and "negotiated." The subject, argues Derrida, "is not some meta-linguistic substance or identity, some pure *cogito* of self-presence; it is always inscribed in language."[63] It is from Derrida and the post-structuralists—and in the tradition of Nietzsche—that we learned to display a gesture of suspicion with regard to any body of knowledge, to question all the assumptions, categories, and explanatory models, that we learned to critically interrogate the premises of all disciplines. It was from Derrida and deconstruction that we received the concept of difference, the awareness that the logic of binary oppositions is domination and subordination. "Derrida's deconstruction of hierarchical oppositions," writes Rapaport in *The Theory Mess*, "has been of major importance for the critique of prejudicial values and hence for underrepresented peoples and their social issues."[64] The imperative to know or engage the other comes from post-structural theories. But Derrida's ethical thinking about the other "has become foundational for contemporary thinking on self-other relations."[65] For Derrida, who believed a leap of faith was needed to engage with the other, the gift and hospitality are about loving/welcoming the other, the stranger. Derrida's "discourse on marginalization" is "central to feminism, post-colonialism, and queer theory."[66] It was Derrida and

the post-structuralists who taught us that language—in which we express ourselves and our knowledge—is not absolute, precise, or logical, that every word,
every phrase, and even the way we place them in sentences, beget blurring
and ambiguity. Derrida's deconstruction taught us to make works—literary
text, political text, movie, speech, and so on—speak from within themselves,
through their fault lines, their blanks, their margins, their contradictions, but
without trying to kill them. According to Derrida, this is how you make these
works live and speak.

Without understanding and engaging these advances in knowledge, can
one honestly move beyond Derrida and post-structuralism? Can we simply
reject these ideas because we think they are difficult? Rejecting or abandoning
Derrida and post-structuralism means going where? A "return to [a] critical
order with all the logocentric, totalitarian, [mastery, possession] and transcendental baggage"[67] of the past, asks Herman Rapaport in *The Theory Mess*? If
it means a return to New Criticism, when are the philosophical presuppositions that are at work in New Criticism's methodology exposed? In the turn
away from deconstruction toward transnationalism or orthodoxies in Empire
Studies, how will postcolonial critics deal with irreducible differences in history and intellectual genealogies as they cross national borders?[68] And if new
materialists such as Rosi Braidotti, Manuel DeLanda, and Graham Harman
want to reject the "linguistic turn," what do they want to do with the awareness that Saussure and Derrida taught us about language being imprecise and
ambiguous?[69] Finally, if the turn from theory is back to identity politics, how do
you address the violence and domination in binary oppositions? In community
structure?

For Derrida's critics such as Alain Badiou, Terry Eagleton, and Slavoj Žižek
who reject deconstruction and who advocate universalism and a return to traditional Marxism, I ask what do you do with the other—the majority of the
people in the world who have been devalued? How do you engage differences
and contradictions, which are very much a part of the current globalized world?
Are you afraid of the interruption of the self that comes with extending hospitality to the other? When do you examine the cruelty and blindness as effects
of Western reason, humanism, and universalism? Alain Badiou in *Logics of
Worlds* and *Being and Event* overlooks Derrida and the post-structuralists
of the 1960s and returns to Louis Althusser and Marxism, where he never
raises the issues of the other or of colonialism and imperialism. In his meet-
ings with Etienne Balibar, Slavoj Žižek, and others in the conferences on "The
Idea of Communism," Badiou, as he and his colleagues reimagine European

communism, not only does not mention non-Europeans but he also fails to reimagine communism in China, India, and Cuba. Is the communism that he wants to return to power the same old Eurocentric, Marxist universal that ignores, excludes, or represses the other?

To move forward and not become retrograde in our thinking, we have to deal with Derrida and post-structuralism. Deconstruction, which has its own alterity, is not about one way of reading texts but is about asking all methods of reading texts—whether it is Surface Reading, New Historicism, New Materialism, Marxist theory, Feminist theory, Object-oriented theory, or Affect theory—to be aware that they are only one way among others, that they all should be open toward their otherness, their differences, showing that there are more ways than one to read a text.

The crucial and relevant question now is: how do we institutionalize Derrida and deconstruction in a way that his values of difference, of multiplicity, and of the relation to the other are available for future American generations? During the height of theory in the 1970s, 1980s, and early 1990s, it is clear that there was very little institution building. No English department in the United States was completely theoretical, including UC Irvine and Yale. Most departments had several individuals who did theory. More importantly, at its peak, unlike Derrida who cofounded the College *internationale de philosophie* with Francois Chatelet to institutionalized his ideas, none of the high-profile experts or celebrities of theory such as Stanley Fish, J. Hillis Miller, Gayatri Spivak, Judith Butler, and others institutionalized theory by establishing journals, centers, conferences, societies, and institutes whose main focus was the teaching and dissemination of critical theory.[70]

Therefore, without much institutionalization, the anti-theory forces, which were always present, began to reemerge and assert themselves. In English and humanities departments in the United States since the 1990s, theory has fallen on hard times. These departments hired fewer specialists in French theory, if any, as they move to deemphasize the presence of theory in the department's course offerings. Graduate students are increasingly discouraged from learning and using theory. Writing in "Against Eclecticism," Joan Wallach Scott discusses how young scholars who have been influenced by post-structuralist theory minimize the "theoretical dimensions of their work" to accommodate not only an audience who is hostile to "theory" but also non-accommodating university employers who are offering jobs or granting agencies who are offering fellowships.[71] In the last several years, I have attended job talks at the University of Houston and witnessed job candidates mask their obvious use of French theory because they are afraid the audience will be hostile or because they are afraid they will not get the job. These young scholars mask their use of theory or invoke the term "eclecticism, which can . . . lead to a permanent silencing of the critique that certain theories have enabled."[72] And with the masking of theory into certain areas within the various disciplines, there is almost no recognition of who the major theorists are anymore. Furthermore, the Association of Literary Scholars and Critics (ALSC) organized a separate literary organization in 1994 because the MLA promoted "scholarship that focuses on questions of race, class and sex when analyzing works of literature" and because it placed "too much emphasis on critical theory."[73]

In addition, by the late 1990s and the early 2000s, there were other anti-theory forces operating in English departments. As more traditional creative writing programs, particularly those offering the PhD in English and Creative Writing, became influential in English departments, some joined with the anti-theory forces, encouraging their students to bypass theory. Tom Grimes in *The Workshop* writes, "For the writer, literary theory not only is of no use but is detrimental to his progress and well-being. Once a writer starts believing that theory and not literature can be his guide through the labyrinth, he's doomed."[74] I wonder what Grimes thinks of Auster's *The New York Trilogy*, Calvino's *Invisible Cities*, Coetzee's *Foe*, Brooke-Rose's *Amalgamemnon*, Vizenor's *The Heirs of Columbus*, Rushdie's *Midnight's Children*, Tsepeneag's *Vain Art of The Fugue*, Pavic's *Dictionary of the Khazars*, Montalbetti's *Western*, Evenson's *Fugue State*, and Carole Maso's *AVA*—just a few great literary texts, which are "guide[d]" by or influenced by theory. Finally, in the last ten years, I have increasingly experienced hostile or indifferent audiences in English departments around the county when I presented papers with an obvious theoretical dimension. The anti-theory forces have increased in the twenty-first century.

And now that Derrida, the last of the major 1960s post-structuralist theorists, is dead and his almost larger-than-life personality is no longer on the world stage to provoke reaction, we need to revisit theory and institutionalize Derrida and post-structuralist theory. Most of us who read and use theory came of age in the 1980s and 1990s when theory was available and vibrant in the academy. To keep theory alive, to keep Derrida a part of the lived experience, we need to do what many theorists in the 1970s and 1980s did not do: regularly teach courses and seminars in theory and build institutions such as journals, centers, societies, and institutes to maintain and promote it.[75] We must make it readily possible for students to read Derrida's and other theory texts. We must make theory a part of the undergraduate English degree and of the PhD curriculum requirements. If we do this and are successful, members of the current and successive generations would, to use Butler's words, "take it up and rethink it for their own time or for various times."[76]

Derrida, who has taken his deconstruction into philosophy, religion, literary criticism, politics, feminism, queer theory, and who, as he is dying in 2004, is worried about who will be his heir, who can he "entrust" with his traces, and who will take his deconstructive propositions and relaunch them for future generations. At the end of his life, he was fully aware of the enormous impact that deconstruction and post-structuralism have had on the world; he knew that theory had transformed much scholarship in the West. So, why was he worried? Weeks before his death, why is he granting an interview to *Le Monde*, talking about being "the final representative of a 'generation'" and the "surviving" of that generation?[77] Given the way Derrida and post-structuralist theory are currently ignored, not by individual intellectuals, but by the universities in France, including philosophy departments, Derrida's concern had to do with whether he will be institutionalized in France, whether he will exist only in libraries, whether he will be a part of the lived experience in France, and whether he will have French heirs.[78]

But let us get back to the question of what Derrida means by an heir? In *For What Tomorrow*, he recognizes himself "in the figure of the heir," "to know how to reaffirm what comes before us." To reaffirm the common European heritage means "not simply accepting this heritage but relaunching it otherwise and keeping it alive."[79] To reaffirm means to continue and to interrupt, to be faithful and unfaithful to this common heritage, to "welcome what comes before us and yet to reinterpret it."[80] So who can be Derrida's heirs, who can take his habits of deconstruction and read texts and art and the world and relaunch them for the "purpose of reinterpreting [them] and endlessly reaffirming [them]"?

To be an heir to Derrida's deconstructive propositions, operations that welcome the other, one would have to belong to or work within the Western philosophical tradition. Derrida is almost always in conversations with philosophers, linguists, and texts of his and previous generations, with whom he shared/shares a common European heritage. (As I have discussed earlier, this does not mean that intellectuals from other non-European heritages and traditions cannot work within the Western philosophical tradition or cannot take Derrida's deconstructive analyses into their respective heritages and traditions, opening them up to the other.) Therefore, his heirs would be individuals from the various disciplines in succeeding generations who will read and reinterpret Derrida and the post-structuralist thinkers of the Sixties Era in the same way Derrida, Foucault, and Deleuze revisited and reinterpreted Hegel, Kant, Rousseau, Descartes, Nietzsche, Marx, Freud, de Saussure, Husserl, Heidegger, Levinas, Levi-Strauss, and so on.[81] This would cause the heirs to speak of Derrida's work in the present tense because his work acts on them, giving them a new sense of their present time.

But more importantly, the other question is: how easy is it for members of threatened groups such as feminists, homosexuals, religious, racial, and ethnic minorities scholars who, unlike Derrida, belong to identitarian groups, to give up what they perceive as the psychological security of belonging to a group and become deconstructionists? What would bring about this change? Would it be the luxury of a certain mainstream security where they feel less threatened? Would it require a certain education? A certain awareness of their repressed otherness?

If members of threatened and marginalized communities through education are exposed to the theories of Derrida and post-structuralism, they will read and understand the texts, and become susceptible to theory. Theory speaks to their lived experiences. Thus, it is a matter of exposures, readings, and understanding. The same holds true for mainstream "white" American students, who, like threatened, marginalized individuals, also belong to a communitarian logic, albeit unacknowledged, of which Derrida would be equally as mistrusting. They too can come to understand theory, and many do, when they are exposed to it.

As an heir to Derrida's deconstructive propositions, one would have to deconstruct the hegemonic structure and also the structure of their own identity group. The heir would have to be aware of his or her own alterity, his or her division, and his or her heterogeneity. This means the heir would have to affirm and relaunch his or her community and the world, realizing that universals repress or exclude differences, that universals murder the other. And if the heir belongs to more than one heritage or tradition, he or she would have to perform the group's identity, or the Western heritage, using it only for convenience. It would have to become a performative act. And if it is a performative act, the heir will be aware that it will "arrive at a point where the opposition does not function any more."[82] As an heir, he or she will suffer but they can also be emancipated, for deconstruction allows them to interrupt dogmatic slumber, permitting them to reflect *both* on their belonging and on their not belonging to the community, to the Western heritage, or to the world. And the rupture of belonging to an identity, a community, or a heritage can give them the chance for a judgment that is more just, less unjust, on the politics of the communities and the world to which they are supposed to belong. Socially, literarily, politically, psychoanalytically, and historically, the heir can closely read the forces at work in texts that expose him or her to the other. And in their deconstruction, he or she can open the community and the world up to the other and difference in an affirmative way.

These moves will allow the heir to affirm and relaunch Derrida and these texts, keeping them alive. This is what Judith Bulter, who is obviously working with Derrida's habits of deconstruction, had in mind when she said, in honoring Edward Said, "we use Said to tell the story of his time and then take it up and rethink Said for our time." And there are feminists who are rightful heirs to Derrida. There are also philosophers, anthropologists, theologians, postcolonial critics, literary critics, and others who, we can say, are rightful heirs to Derrida's deconstructive propositions, who take up Derrida and rethink him for their time, because they work with and share with him a common heritage. And in taking him, deconstruction, and post-structural theories up and relaunching them, they keep Derrida and theory alive, they keep him a part of the lived experience.

Notes

1   Jacques Derrida, *Learning To Live Finally: The Last Interview: An Interview with Jean Birnbaum*, trans. Pascale-Anne Brault and Michael Naas (Hoboken, NJ: Melville House Publishing, 2007), 26.

2   Ibid., 32–33.

3   Ibid., 34.

4   Ibid., 27–28.

5   Francois Cusset, *French Theory: How Foucault, Derrida, Deleuze & Co. Transformed the Intellectual Life of the United States* (Minneapolis: University of Minnesota Press, 2008), xviii.

6   Qtd. in Francois Cusset, *French Theory*, 3.

7   Qtd. in Herman Rapaport, *Later Derrida: Reading the Recent Work* (New York and London: Routledge, 2003), 15.

8   Qtd. in Francois Cusset, *French Theory*, 268.

9   Qtd. in James K. A. Smith, *Jacques Derrida: Live Theory* (New York: Continuum, 2005), 4–5.

10 Jonathan Kandell, "Jacques Derrida, Abstruse Theorist, Dies at 74," *New York Times* (October 10, 2004), sec. 1:1.

11 John D. Caputo, ed., *Deconstruction in A Nutshell: A Conversation with Jacques Derrida* (New York: Fordham University Press, 1997), 127. This is not to assume that Levinas was not always present in Derrida's work. He is present in the early essay, "Violence and Metaphysics," and in "Différance," where he notes the idea of difference means a critique of classical ontology undertaken by Levinas, and in Derrida's dealing with the other in *Of Grammatology*. Here, in the shift, Levinas comes to the forefront as Derrida deals with regularly political issues.

12 Derrida was quite vocal in his condemnation of Israeli policies, going so far as to call them "the disastrous and suicidal politics of Israel and of a certain Zionism," as he supported the Palestinian cause (Jacques Derrida, *Learning To Live Finally*, 39). He also publicly criticized the fundamentalist Christians in the United States, who claimed to be authentic Zionists, and the power of their lobby. These positions taken by Derrida certainly had something to do with the vicious attacks on him during the last couple of decades of his life.

13 Mustapha Cherif, *Islam and the West: A Conversation with Jacques Derrida*, trans. Teresa Lavender Fagan (Chicago and London: University of Chicago Press, 2008), 31.

14 Ibid., 10.

15 Jacques Derrida et al., "Women in the Beehive: A Seminar with Jacques Derrida," *Differences: A Journal of Feminist Cultural Studies* 16.3 (Fall 2005): 139–157, 196.

16 Jacques Derrida and Elisabeth Roudinesco, *For What Tomorrow . . .: A Dialogue* (Stanford, CA: Stanford University Press, 2004), 111.

17 Ibid., 22.

18 Ibid.

19 Jacques Derrida and Maurizio Ferraris, *A Taste for the Secret* (Cambridge, UK: Polity Press, 2001), 21.

20 Gil Anidjar, "Introduction," *Acts of Religion* by Jacques Derrida (New York and London: Routledge, 2002, 1–39), 3.

21 Cherif, *Islam and the West*, 39.

22 Ibid.

23 Caputo, *Deconstruction in a Nutshell*, 21.

24 Cherif, *Islam and the West*, 39.

25 Ibid., 65.

26 Ibid., 72.

27 Ibid., 51.

28 Ibid., 102.

29 It is the communitarian nature of American feminism, the Women's Movement, and Women's Studies that women of color in the United States and non-European women from around the world constantly contest/deconstruct United States and

European feminisms because they do not believe that there is more than one reality for women or that there are other feminisms.

30 Jacques Derrida, "Becoming Woman," *Semiotexte* 3.1 (1978): 128–137, 128.
31 Ibid., 130.
32 Ibid.
33 Christie McDonald, "Choreographies," *Points . . . Interviews, 1974–1994* (Stanford, CA: Stanford University Press, 1995), 93.
34 Ibid., 94.
35 Anne-Emmanuelle Berger, "Sexing Differences," *Differences* 16.3 (2005): 52–67, 54.
36 McDonald, "Choreographies," 95.
37 Derrida et al., "Women in the Beehive," 193.
38 Ibid., 145.
39 Ibid., 145.
40 Ibid., 148.
41 Christie McDonald, "Notes on an Unfinished Question," *Differences: A Journal of Feminist Cultural Studies* 16.3 (Fall 2005): 35–40, 39.
42 Elizabeth Grosz, "Derrida and Feminism: A Remembrance," *Difference: A Journal of Feminist Cultural Studies* 16.3 (Fall 2005): 88–94, 89.
43 Diane Elam, *Feminism and Deconstruction* (London and New York: Routledge, 1994), 25.
44 Gayatri Chakravorty Spivak, "Feminism and Deconstruction, Again: Negotiations," *Outside in the Teaching Machine* (New York and London: Routledge, 1993), 132.
45 Luce Irigaray, *Speculum of the Other Woman* (Ithaca, NY: Cornell University Press, 1985), 18.
46 McDonald, "Choreographies," 108.
47 Judith Butler, *Undoing Gender* (New York and London: Routledge, 2004), 7.
48 Grosz, "Derrida and Feminism: A Remembrance," 92.
49 Houston A. Baker, Forum, "The Legacy of Jacques Derrida," *PMLA* 120.2 (2005): 466–468, 467.
50 Houston A. Baker, *Blues, Ideology, and Afro-American Literature: A Vernacular Theory* (Chicago: University of Chicago Press, 1987), 3.
51 Here, Gayatri Spivak is a little different. She really does belong to more than one heritage or tradition. On the one hand, it is very clear that she works within Derrida's common European heritage. But, on the other hand, she belongs to and works within a postcolonial heritage and feminist traditions.
52 Achille Mbembe, "What is Postcolonial Thinking?," *Eurozine*, Eurozine.com/pdf/ 2008-01-09-mbembe.pdf
53 Ibid.

54 Avital Ronell, *Fighting Theory: A Conversation with Anne Dufourmantelle* (Urbana, Chicago, and Springfield: University of Illinois Press, 2010), 161.

55 Cherif, *Islam and the West,* 42–43.

56 Ibid., 44.

57 Ibid.

58 As part of this democracy to come, Derrida defines ethics as hospitality and hospitality as welcoming the other (immigration, asylum). In *Of Hospitality*, he defines his new idea of hospitality against the old. "[I]t is as though the laws (plural) of hospitality, in marking limits, powers, rights, and duties, consisted in challenging and transgressing *the* law of hospitality, the one that would command that the 'new arrival' be offered an unconditional welcome." Jacques Derrida and Anne Dufourmantelle, *Of Hospitality* (Stanford, CA: Stanford University Press, 2000), 77.

59 Cherif, *Islam and the West,* 69.

60 In *Islam and the West*, Derrida defines the antiglobalization movement as an example of this international alliance. For Derrida, this is a heterogeneous movement of men and women from "all countries who unite in struggles against political, economic, and religious practices that must be fought." Cherif, *Islam and the West*, 73.

61 In "Beyond Eurocentrism," Enrique Dussel argues against what he calls a Eurocentric paradigm of modernity, which formulates the phenomenon of modernity as exclusively European and the periphery as other, for a planetary paradigm, which conceptualizes modernity as the center of an interregional world-system through the incorporation of the other. According to Dussel, in this planetary modern world, the other exists as subjects with their own heterogeneity and alterity. "Modernity, then, in this planetary paradigm is a phenomenon proper to the system 'center-periphery.'" (Enrique Dussel, "Beyond Eurocentrism: The World-System and the Limits of Modernity," *The Cultures of Globalization*, eds. Fredric Jameson and Masao Miyoshi [Durham: Duke University Press, 1998], 4). In discussing planetarity in *Death of a Discipline*, Gayatri Spivak prefers the term "planetary" to globalization because globalization "is the imposition of the same system of exchange everywhere . . . [She wants t]o talk planet-talk by way of an unexamined environmentalism, referring to an undivided 'natural' space rather than a differentiated political space" (Gayatri Chakravorty Spivak, *Death of a Discipline* [New York: Columbia University Press, 2003], 72). For Spivak, the "planet is in the species of alterity, belonging to another system, and yet we inhabit it, on loan" (Ibid.). Defining the planetary subject beyond citizenship, the nation-state, economic systems, Spivak, like Derrida in his democracy to come, states that with the "planetary subject . . . alterity remains undivided from us" (Ibid., 73).

62 W. Lawrence Hogue, *Postmodern American Literature and Its Other* (Urbana and Chicago: University of Illinois Press, 2009), 31–32. In *Postmodern American*

Literature and Its Other, Hogue reconfigures world history according to Enrique Dussel's concept of planetary modernity. In *Cosmodernism,* Christian Moraru identifies the critical narratives that support planetary modernity.

63 Jacques Derrida with R. Kearney, "Jacques Derrida: Deconstruction and the Other," *Dialogues with Contemporary Continental Thinkers: The Phenomenological Heritage* (Manchester, UK: Manchester University Press, 1984), 125.

64 Herman Rapaport, *The Theory Mess: Deconstruction in Eclipse* (New York: Columbia University Press, 2001), 67.

65 Ibid.

66 Ibid.

67 Ibid., xvii.

68 I think it is utterly disrespectful to those literatures if you teach a course or write a book that includes two African American writers, two Caribbean writers, and two Asian Indian writers without giving the different intellectual histories or genealogies of those three bodies of literature.

69 In an interview in *New Materialisms* (Rick Dolphijn and Iris van der Tuin, eds., *New Materialisms: Interviews & Cartographies* [Ann Arbor: Open Humanities Press, 2012]), Rosi Braidotti writes, "Thus 'new-materialism' emerges as a method, a conceptual frame and a political stand, which refuses the linguistic paradigm, stressing instead the concrete yet complex materiality of bodies immersed in social relations of power" (21). In an interview in the same collection, Manuel DeLanda says, "rejecting the linguisticality of experience . . . leads to a conception of a shared human experience in which the variation comes not from differences in signification . . . but of significance" (ibid., 47). First, rejecting the "linguistic paradigm" does not necessarily mean that they are escaping language or the role language plays in constructing meaning. Second, both Braidotti and DeLanda seem not to know that the world of language belongs to the world of things—objects, stuff, the "concrete and yet complex materiality" of everyday life.

70 I could be wrong, but I am only aware of one program that moved to institutionalized theory during this 1970s and 1980s period and that was The School of Criticism and Theory, a six-week summer program that began at UC Irvine in 1976 and later moved to Cornell University.

71 Joan Wallach Scott, "Against Eclecticism," *Differences: A Journal of Feminist Cultural Studies* 16.3 (Fall 2005): 114–13, 115.

72 Ibid.

73 Tom Grimes, *The Workshop,* qtd. in Mark McGurl, *The Program Era: Postwar Fiction and the Rise of Creative Writing* (Cambridge: Harvard University Press, 2009), 342.

74 Ibid.

75   At this moment, I can only think of two instances of institution building: what Jeffrey R. Di Leo is doing at the University of Houston-Victoria with the journal *symplokē* and the annual Society for Critical Exchange (SCE) Winter Theory Institute, and what Gabriele Schwab, director, is doing with The Critical Theory Institute and The Wellek Library Lectures.

76   Judith Butler, "Judith Butler and Cornel West, Honoring Edward Said," *Youtube,* October 30, 2013.

77   Derrida, *Learning To Live Finally,* 25, 26.

78   There is also the reality of a conservative movement emerging in France for the last twenty years, with the growth of the radical-right National Front and a decrease in "the diversity of intellectual milieux, of interests, schools, cliques," which "had to do with the university, but they weren't composed purely of academics" (James Creech, Peggy Kamuf, and Jane Todd, "Deconstruction in America: An Interview with Jacques Derrida," *Critical Exchange* 17 [Winter 1985]: 5).

79   Derrida and Roudinesco, *For What Tomorrow . . .,* 3.

80   Ibid., 5.

81   Philosophers and literary critics at elite universities were the first to embrace Derrida's habits of deconstruction because they belong to or work within the same "common" European tradition as he. I only wish that some of these critics would heed Derrida's lead and transgress the limitations of the Western philosophical tradition and take their deconstruction to the non-European other.

82   Derrida et al., "Women in the Beehive," 201.

Work cited

Anidjar, Gil. "Introduction." *Acts of Religion* by Jacques Derrida. New York and London: Routledge, 2002. 1–39.

Baker, Houston A. Forum. "The Legacy of Jacques Derrida." *PMLA* 120.2 (2005): 466–468.

Butler, Judith. "Judith Butler and Cornel West, Honoring Edward Said." *Youtube.* October 30, 2013. http://www.youtube.com/watch?v=jF5mYvjDp3U.

Butler, Judith. *Undoing Gender.* New York and London: Routledge, 2004.

Caputo, John D., ed. *Deconstruction in a Nutshell: A Conversation with Jacques Derrida.* New York: Fordham University Press, 1997.

Cherif, Mustapha. *Islam and the West: A Conversation with Jacques Derrida.* Trans. Teresa Lavender Fagan. Chicago and London: University of Chicago Press, 2008.

Creech, James, Peggy Kamuf, and Jane Todd. "Deconstruction in America: An Interview with Jacques Derrida." *Critical Exchange* 17 (Winter 1985): 1–32.

Cusset, Francois. *French Theory: How Foucault, Derrida, Deleuze & Co. Transformed the Intellectual Life of the United States.* Trans. Jeff Fort. Minneapolis: University of Minnesota Press, 2008.

Derrida, Jacques. "Becoming Woman." *Semiotexte* 3.1 (1978): 128–137.

Derrida, Jacques. *Learning to Live Finally: The Last Interview: An Interview with Jean Birnbaum.* Trans. Pascale-Anne Brault and Michael Naas. Hoboken, NJ: Melville House Publishing, 2007.

Derrida, Jacques, et al. "Women in the Beehive: A Seminar with Jacques Derrida." *Differences: A Journal of Feminist Cultural Studies* 16.3 (Fall 2005): 139–157.

Derrida, Jacques, and Anne Dufourmantelle. *Of Hospitality.* Trans. Rachel Bowlby. Stanford, CA: Stanford University Press, 2000.

Derrida, Jacques, with R. Kearney. "Jacques Derrida: Deconstruction and the Other." *Dialogues with Contemporary Continental Thinkers: The Phenomenological Heritage.* Manchester, UK: Manchester University Press, 1984. 105–126.

Derrida, Jacques, and Elisabeth Roudinesco. *For What Tomorrow . . .: A Dialogue.* Trans. Jeff Fort. Stanford, CA: Stanford University Press, 2004.

Derrida, Jacques, and Maurizio Ferraris. *A Taste for the Secret.* Trans. Giacomo Donis. Cambridge, UK: Polity Press, 2001.

Dolphijn, Rick, and Iris van der Tuin, eds. *New Materialisms: Interviews & Cartographies.* Ann Arbor: Open Humanities Press, 2012.

Dussel, Enrique. "Beyond Eurocentrism: The World-System and the Limits of Modernity." *The Cultures of Globalization.* Eds. Fredric Jameson and Masao Miyoshi. Durham: Duke University Press, 1998. 3–31.

Elam, Diane. *Feminism and Deconstruction.* London and New York: Routledge, 1994.

Grosz, Elizabeth. "Derrida and Feminism: A Remembrance." *Difference: A Journal of Feminist Cultural Studies* 16.3 (Fall 2005): 88–94.

Hogue, W. Lawrence. *The African American Male, Writing, and Difference: A Polycentric Approach to African American Literature, Criticism, and History.* Albany, NY: SUNY Press, 2003.

Hogue, W. Lawrence. *Postmodern American Literature and Its Other.* Urbana and Chicago: University of Illinois Press, 2009.

Irigaray, Luce. *Speculum of the Other Woman.* Trans. Gillian Gill. Ithaca, NY: Cornell University Press, 1985.

Kandell, Jonathan. "Jacques Derrida, Abstruse Theorist, Dies at 74." *New York Times* October 10, 2004. Section 1:1.

Mbembe, Achille. "What is Postcolonial Thinking"? *Eurozine.* Eurozine.com/pdf/2008–01–09-mbembe.pdf.

McDonald, Christie. "Choreographies." *Points . . . Interviews, 1974–1994.* Trans. Peggy Kamuf et al. Stanford, CA: Stanford University Press, 1995.

McDonald, Christie. "Notes on an Unfinished Question." *Differences: A Journal of Feminist Cultural Studies.* 16.3 (Fall 2005): 35–40.

McGurl, Mark. *The Program Era: Postwar Fiction and the Rise of Creative Writing.* Cambridge: Harvard University Press, 2009.

Moraru, Christian. *Cosmodernism: American Narrative, Late Capitalism, and the New Cultural Imaginary.* Ann Arbor: University of Michigan Press, 2011.

Rapaport, Herman. *Later Derrida: Reading the Recent Work.* New York and London: Routledge, 2003.

Rapaport, Herman. *The Theory Mess: Deconstruction in Eclipse.* New York: Columbia University Press, 2001.

Ronell, Avital. *Fighting Theory: A Conversation with Anne Dufourmantelle.* Trans. Catherine Porter. Urbana, Chicago, and Springfield: University of Illinois Press, 2010.

Scott, Joan Wallach. "Against Eclecticism." *Differences: A Journal of Feminist Cultural Studies* 16.3 (Fall 2005): 114–113.

Smith, James K. A. *Jacques Derrida: Live Theory.* New York: Continuum, 2005.

Spivak, Gayatri Chakravorty. *Death of a Discipline.* New York: Columbia University Press, 2003.

Spivak, Gayatri Chakravorty. "Feminism and Deconstruction, Again: Negotiations." *Outside in the Teaching Machine.* New York and London: Routledge, 1993: 121–140.

Taylor, Mark C. "What Derrida Really Meant." http://www.press.uchicago.edu/books/derrida/taylorderrida.html.

2

The Humanists Strike Back: An Episode from the Cold War on Theory

Herman Rapaport

The death of theory is a euphemism for the sharp decline of attention paid to critical theory that began occurring in the late 1990s, a period that will be of concern for my paper, since that is the time in which the languages and literatures transitioned to an increasingly conservative point of view with respect to theory, which inevitably set the stage for its winding down as a privileged object of profession-wide attention.[1] Looking at this history today, it is obvious that if theory had once threatened to become a sine qua non for researchers in the languages and literatures, that this supposedly dreadful threat has passed. The result is that much work is being published now, which just two decades ago would have been considered methodologically naïve by the theoretically savvy. This signals the advent of a renewed dedication to positivism (in today's terms: cognitive science, climate change, evolutionary biologistic explanations of storytelling, the "anthropocene," the advent of "big data"), which not that long ago would have been considered unthinkable. For those of us who imagined a much better future for the discipline of the languages and literatures, the trending of an empirical-positivist approach is especially disheartening. Indeed, it is hard to overlook that even a theory journal such as *Critical Inquiry* has been showing a positivist tendency as scholars turn theory into a field of old-fashioned historical research in which obscure and not particularly significant documents by figures such as Levinas, Derrida, and Blanchot are retrieved for no other reason than that they are not public knowledge.[2] This positivist approach to scholarship assumes that faculty are merely supposed to be prospectors mining for facts, however miniscule, and that hermeneutical thinking (interpretation, conceptual development) is to be kept to a minimum. Theory, whatever its faults, had the virtue of rejecting such a hard-boiled trivialization of academic research.

Of course, theory still takes place today on the margins of everything else that calls itself research. Indeed, there are still a sizable number of people active in the field, among them, Slavoj Žižek, Judith Butler, Chantal Mouffe, Jean Luc Nancy, Catherine Malabou, Julia Kristeva, Lauren Berlant, Sianne Ngai, Etienne Balibar, Jacques Rancière, Alain Badiou, Quentin Meillassoux, Francois Laruelle, Jacques Alain Miller, Lawrence Grossberg, Fredrick Jameson, Bruno Latour, Gayatri Spivak, Peter Sloterdijk, Mieke Ball, and Giorgio Agamben, among others. In addition, thinkers such as Martin Heidegger, Michel Foucault, Roland Barthes, Jacques Lacan, and, most recently, Jacques Derrida have been publishing as if from the grave. Even Walter Benjamin, whose collected works have recently appeared in what was thought to be an exhaustive publishing project for the ages, is being republished by Suhrkamp Verlag in a reedited mul-tivolume series entitled *Werke und Nachlass* that will include every draft of every piece Benjamin ever wrote, as well as works that weren't included in the original *Gesammelte Schriften*. Lacan's seminars are still being redacted and officially published, some forty-five years since the first volumes appeared, and are still the occasion for a vast number of books and essays by Lacanians, many of whom have been concentrating on Lacan's conceptions of the Real.

Certainly, since the turn of the millennium, general theoretical interest in the Lacanian Real has been very conspicuous. This is largely due to the efforts of Slavoj Žižek who began popularizing the concept in the 1990s, though such interest also relates to a widespread preoccupation with materialism that has sources in positivism, certainly, but also in Gilles Deleuze's appropriation and modification of Henri Bergson's work on matter and memory. In cultural stud-ies, this sort of materialism has been associated with "affect studies" in which affect is considered in terms of a bodily immersion in the world that enables thought to be translated into or identified with environmental physical pul-sations, the movement of objects, variations of intensities of light, interrup-tive static objects, and/or what the Buddhists call "suchness." Simultaneously in France, attention has turned to Michel Henry whose career as a philoso-pher was devoted to materialist phenomenology, a subject that can be related to the Birmingham School (Raymond Williams, et al.) and, of course, the sort of materialist investigations undertaken by Benjamin in *The Arcades*. Henry himself, however, was a supporter of traditional humanism, whose return in academia will be my theme later on. As Henry put it, we "cannot escape the fact that the setting aside of the sensible and affective properties of the world presupposes the setting aside of life itself, that is to say, of what makes up the humanity of the human being."[3]

A more hard core materialist orientation, endemic to high modernism, concerns the materiality of the signifier, something that was evident already in Ezra Pound's incorporation of Chinese ideograms in *The Cantos*, though it was also central to Tel Quel's concerns in the 1960s and 1970s. Lettrism, Language Poetry, and, most recently, Conceptual Poetry have staunchly emphasized the materiality of signification, something that recently got Kenneth Goldsmith in trouble when he took the autopsy report of Michael Brown, an unarmed black teenager shot dead by a policeman in Ferguson, Missouri, as the material or substance for a conceptual poem ("The Body of Michael Brown" [2015]) that, in essence, was a near literal reading of the medical examiner's remarks. Various poets and academics decried this act on social media as insensitive to the humanity of Brown and his grieving family, if not an outright racist reenactment of an authoritarian dehumanization of an African American teen. Whether one agrees with these criticisms or not, there can be no question that Goldsmith's performance caused people to make a binary distinction between materialism versus humanism, the letter versus the spirit.

There is an argument to be made that Goldsmith's conceptual work raises the question, particularly in the context of "The Body of Michael Brown," whether a materialist orientation doesn't presuppose a noncorrelation between sign and referent. Noncorrelationism, in fact, has been gaining currency in what might still be called High Theory in terms of writings advanced by figures such as Jacques-Alain Miller, Alain Badiou, Quentin Meillassoux, and Francois Laruelle. For all of them, the Lacanian Real is a point of departure, given that by definition it is noncorrelationist. Indeed, when Lacan first defines the Real in *Seminar 1 (1953–54)*, he says it is "what resists symbolization absolutely."[4] In recent years a rather fully developed noncorrelationist philosophy has been advanced by Francois Laruelle in terms of "non-philosophy," which repudiates the Husserlian conviction in the something that consciousness is conscious of, as if that something were an object correlative to consciousness. Alain Badiou's notion of the Event advances noncorrelationism as well in that the event concerns a break or rupture that in and of itself exists outside of any correlation, though in the aftermath of its having taken place, one can retroactively provide it with correlations, something that typifies the work of historians. Laruelle incorporates this idea into his thinking as follows: "Non-philosophical decision is determined-in-the-last-instance by the Undecided (of the) Real, whereas philosophy is intertwined with the Undecidable (to various degrees of irreducibility). This is what distinguishes a transcendental-axiomatic decision, break or abstraction from its philosophical [correlationist] forms."[5] The reference to

Derridean undecidability is hard to miss, and clearly Laruelle is attempting to distinguish himself as a thinker who has taken a monumental step beyond deconstruction.

Having identified some trends in what one might call latter-day theory, I want to excavate some of the complexities at the end of the twentieth century that led to the death of theory, which, I think everyone may agree, turned out to be but one of many so-called deaths: the death of the humanities (replaced by STEM), the death of affordable higher education, the death of tenure, the death of professionalization (professors demoted to "guides on the side," the hiring of MAs instead of PhDs), and also the death of *the university itself* as a noncorporate institution based on a participatory model of administration and governance. The death of theory, therefore, is but one of many transformations leading to a more brutal neoliberal style of institution that, as I will indicate, merged some of the worst tendencies in Liberal and Conservative thinking.

As to what I am calling a cold war on theory, this has been going on for a very long time and contrasts with a hot war on theory that broke out conspicuously in the middle of the 1970s. The hot war was largely a strident repudiation of French theory fought by academics with theoretical interests, among them, Meyer Abrams, Walter Jackson Bate, Gerald Graff, Frank Lentriccia, Alan Sokal, Walter Benn Michaels, Roger Shattuck, Allen Bloom, Dennis Donoghue, Richard Wolin, if not the majority of American feminists, Adrienne Rich and Barbara Christian among them, who had turned their backs on French feminist writers and "theory" in the name of political pragmatism. That hot war was abetted by practically everyone who wrote for the *New York Review of Books* (*NYRB*) on the topic of theory, which meant that traditional literary and cultural historians felt vindicated in their open contempt for theorists of all kinds. The negative press for theory put out by the *NYRB* actually exploded into a full-scale attack, circa 1993, on Derrida's having withdrawn a chapter from an anthology edited by Richard Wolin. As Derrida saw it, Wolin had misrepresented the project in order to unfairly ambush Derrida in print. In response, Derrida took legal action in which suppression of the book was at issue, something that the *NYRB* exploited as an attack on freedom of expression when, in fact, the issue was malicious slander, according to Derrida and his supporters.[6]

Public as that was, far more serious was the well-known Paul de Man affair of 1987, which for the theory movement was supposed to be a sort of Waterloo in the minds of adversaries, especially when combined with the Heidegger Affair of around the same time.[7] Both de Man and Heidegger were found, posthumously, to have lied or remained silent about their pasts under fascism. De

Man, who in the postwar period became a major theorist at Yale University, actively collaborated with Nazism as a journalist for a Belgian newspaper, and broached anti-Semitism in pieces written during the Holocaust, whereas Heidegger, whose philosophy was indispensable for developments in French theory, had involvement with Nazism that had been found to have been much more deliberate and extensive than he had admitted in his lifetime.[8] This made people wonder: if theorists are so dishonest, is theory itself to be considered dishonest? The worry about dishonesty, of course, had always been latent insofar as theory is often hard to parse and comprehend; was this obscurity purposefully conducted by shady thinkers who are trying to build reputations on double-talk? Why can't someone like Heidegger write comprehensible prose the way that Schiller and Dilthey did? Clearly, lack of writerly transparency coupled with moral indecency made sense to theory haters who found it to be a matter of Charlatanism.

In fact, even as late as 1996, Alan Sokol, a mathematician at New York University, undertook an action for the hot war on theory by intentionally publishing an essay in *Social Text* made up of egregiously bogus scientific blather for the sake of demonstrating that in the theory world one can easily get away with academic fraud by publishing obfuscating rubbish.[9] Sokol argued that theorists write about all kinds of things in the absence of actually having any factual competence or proper disciplinary training and that their work is consequently bogus. That the languages and literatures were already making a positivist turn was perhaps not coincidental to the Sokol affair, given that for at least two or three decades people unacquainted with theory were suspicious of its academic credibility.

Whereas the hot war on theory relied quite heavily upon the staging of affairs, scandals, and/or uncomfortable confrontations at symposia, the cold war on theory has been waged seemingly by way of tacit agreement less as a matter of negative reinforcement than of no reinforcement at all. In the 1980s, there were positions crafted by language and cinema departments for critical theorists; the thinking was that students should be familiar with various analytical methods of literary and cultural study and that theory bridged disciplines from a transdisciplinary perspective. It was noticed that feminism, race studies, psychoanalysis, post-colonialism, ethnic studies, cultural studies, film studies, and even literary criticism all had theory in common. That graduate and perhaps even undergraduate students should be trained in the history of literary criticism and theory was an accepted assumption, one underscored by the publisher, Norton, which produced one of its signal anthologies in the field.[10]

Today, not only are there no longer positions being offered in critical theory, the conviction that one should know something about the history of critical thought in the humanities is a view held by only a small minority of faculty, largely because the methodology issue has been resolved supposedly by means of returning to positivism as the only viable option for conducting research (forensic fact-finding, identification, and correlation). By cold war, then, I am referring to a new status quo that has been reached with respect to theory not by outright opposition, but by general neglect: a lack of recognition, interest, and support that disqualifies theory as a legitimate or worthwhile enterprise.

That we should have gotten to this point is peculiar, given that in the late 1980s cultural studies, and the theories upon which they drew, had such a precipitous rise in the aftermath of the de Man affair, whose effect was to put dominant Yale School criticism aside in order to welcome much more socially engaged types of critique. Recall that in the early 1990s the capstone on this newfound supremacy was the huge anthology called *Cultural Studies*, published by Routledge and edited by Cary Nelson et al.[11] Its publication had secured a place for cultural studies in English departments, particularly, which contributed to an ebullient intellectual mood. It appeared that the humanities had turned an important corner of progressivism that would emphasize the cross-cultural and the socially embedded. Instead of reading texts exclusively, people would be reading the material culture for the sake of examining how the order of things constructs the order of social subjectivities, if not of the social per se. Literature, consumer culture, film, television, music, individual self-fashioning, and much else were put into conversation.

Amazingly, in spite of this, already by the mid-1990s it was clear that cultural studies was not going to be the future of the languages and literatures, after all. Part of the problem was that graduate student dissertators of the late 1980s and early 1990s, whose books would be forthcoming, had played it safe in graduate school by substituting a politically correct ideological master narrative in place of the work they should have done in terms of mastering various aspects of critical theory for the sake of coming up with conceptual narratives of their own. If one compares the conformity of American cultural scholarship of that time with the nonconformity that was coming out of France (e.g., Jean Baudrillard's controversial "The Gulf War Did Not Take Place"), one can see why cultural studies in America could not hold people's attention for long.[12] Its political master narrative was based on the worn out feminist theme that marginalized subjection leads to generalized subversion. At some point, people were arguing that even the silence of the subaltern was thought capable of overturning cultural dominants. No matter how many variants of the subjection/subversion argument there were, or how counterintuitive these variants became, the fact was that everyone knew the plot in advance and began to wonder if there was any point in delving into recherché cultural histories of seemingly trivial importance, such as Barbie dolls, Mexican soap operas, women on Star Trek, rituals of American football, comic book fandom, and Zoot Suits.

Despite its drawbacks, cultural studies, with its strong emphasis on the agency of the social subject, did nevertheless manage to complement the rise of another trend that, however inconspicuous and buttoned down, would become quite prominent by the end of the 1990s, namely, the emergence of neo-humanism. Such a turn back to an academia the 1950s is something that elsewhere I have called "restoration politics," the idea being that the theory years were seen as a misguided sort of interregnum and that a moral restoration of traditional ways of scholarly research was in order.[13]

As the de Man affair brought out, American academics hadn't been comfortable with the idea that a field as opaque as theory could ever have been on the "up and up," but this legitimacy issue aside, academics had a hard time stomaching the concept of "the death of the subject." It was all well and good for Barthes and Foucault to proclaim the death of the author, for Lacan to say that the subject comes about retroactively as an effect in the defiles of language, or for Derrida to prioritize writing over speech, but none of that could convince the American academy that anyone could seriously challenge an anthropocentric understanding of humankind, even if for a brief moment that view was hard to maintain in the absence of being labeled naïve by followers of poststructuralism. This antihumanist view was challenged already in 1986 by the unsinkable Martha Nussbaum who made her case in *The Fragility of Goodness* (1986) and other books that followed for reestablishing a familiar humanist framework by recycling Aristotle's writings in order to bring the humanities back in line with a traditional moral philosophy in tandem, at times, with literary readings that could serve as a reliable guide for addressing contemporary ethical problems. Nussbaum's intellectual stomping ground was ancient Athens, which prioritized man, and not Jerusalem, which prioritized the letter. Coming to prominence in the 1990s, Nussbaum, too, was a theorist, of course, but hardly of the French persuasion. Her work regressively mothballed the Lacanian idea that a social subject is a signifier mediated by another signifier and reminded everyone that, in fact, a social subject is a free social actor with obligations, responsibilities, and choices to make. In other words, she reintroduced that familiar American concept known as the liberated self that has to adapt its behavior to the world around it. This was complemented by Seyla Benhabib and Iris Young at Harvard, if not the African American critic, Barbara Christian, who insisted that a deconstructed social subject was useless for those who wanted to deal with public policy issues, given that public policy requires a self, not some form of disarticulated Dasein.[14] In this way, humanism was being restituted to the full light of acceptance, and French theory, that supposedly dubious politically tainted enterprise, was being given the boot. Later, we will see that in the context of American politics, this was a huge mistake, because it actually mirrored and bolstered socially regressive approaches in America initiated in the 1980s by the Reaganites.

As it happens, this picture gets more complicated, because in addition to the momentary dominance of cultural studies around 1991 and the simultaneous reconstruction of humanism that was on the rise, a sort of critical theoretical settlement had been reached with respect to the debates over essentialism/anti-essentialism that had taken up the attention of feminists and others who had been participating in identity politics for some ten years at least. In other words, in the world of social theory, a sort of pause was introduced in the early 1990s into all the frenetic paper-giving on race, gender, and ethnicity in order to evaluate the take-away. Consensus emerged among participants in the identity wars that the socially constructed subject, advocated by Michel Foucault, Gayle Rubin, and Judith Butler, could be taken as the most viable working assumption upon which to construct theories of identity.

Clearly by 1992 or so everyone wanted to move on, and even figures such as Gayatri Spivak made allowances for the strategic redeployment of the self, if, in fact, it helped the cause of subalterns.[15] Thus what the critical pause of the early 1990s suggested, for many people, was that critical theory had done its job and therefore could go into remission. Whereas for a long time this kind of thinking, which Derrida had dubbed "turning the page of history," was unrealistic because of the many innovative books coming out of Paris, by around the end of the 1990s another transformative phenomenon occurred. A large number of the more influential critical theorists were being laid to rest, at times with Derrida in charge as chief mourner. In memoriam we recall: Levinas, de Certeau, Lyotard, Marin, Kofman, Guattari, Gadamer, Althusser, and Deleuze, just to name some of the more famous thinkers. In time their deaths would necessarily register on the humanities as a sort of conceptual power vacuum, which was all to the good if one was a neo-humanist, though it has to be said that Deleuze, especially, has had a posthumous influence that he might have envied in life.

Yet another simultaneous development—and there will always be something additional in my account that speaks to a certain historical overdetermination—concerns a matter of collateral damage. In the midst of all the fighting over identity in the 1980s, cultural study, however politically conformist, had come to replace literary criticism in importance. As noted, the de Man affair factored into this. However, literature itself became subsumed as a cultural discourse, a view promoted especially by the New Historians who put the study of legal documents in Queen Elizabeth I's reign on a par with passages from Shakespeare. Parallel to this transformation of literary texts into cultural texts were the debates over identity that had promoted a sociological approach to literature, which quickly devolved into content analysis, thematically focusing on social roles and stereotypes, thereby obviating matters of form and language. This meant a de facto exclusion of the avant-garde. Social studies critics believed that avant-garde literature put too much emphasis on formal innovation for form's sake, but what these critics found even less palatable was Kate Millet's observation that avant-garde literature tended to morally wander off the reservation and run amok. Also, avant-garde literature, or what Charles Bernstein has called "Attack of the Difficult Poems," couldn't be accessed by content analysis. For in order to access content, a text first has to "make sense," which is something that doesn't quite happen in the case of, say, language poetry in which ordinary and even literary "sense" is under attack. That's understandable enough. But by the 1990s the kind of literary criticism advanced by, say, a Geoffrey Hartman or Helen Vendler, or earlier by someone like Northrop Frye or Erich Auerbach, was also very much out of favor, as if these were embarrassments of a prior age.

It didn't help the cause of literary study that in addition to promoting content analysis, the identitarian movement launched attacks on canonical English and American literature. Given that identitarianism is largely utilitarian, it tends to see literature almost exclusively as an instrument through which to discourse about identity, which means that for many people anything that calls itself a novel will often do. In fact, for many such utilitarian critics the less literary a novel is, the better, because the identitarian content can be extracted with more considerable ease. So in addition to Nussbaum's challenging the deconstruction of the social subject and the sense that an accommodation or settlement of critical debates had been reached, there was at the same time a repudiation of the literary, that is to say, of the complexities of language, so fundamental to European critical theory, which emphasized *significance*. Consider, for example, how important literary language in its formal dimensions had been to Foucault in his book on Roussel, to Derrida in the essay on Sollers entitled "La dissémination," to Deleuze in *Proust and Signs*, to Lacan in his seminars on Poe, Shakespeare, Claudel, Joyce, and Sophocles, and to Badiou in his seminars on Hölderlin and Mallarmé.[16] In place of such analyses, American social literary critics merely talked about content in terms of issue-based topics—or social facts—upon which they applied a preconceived political viewpoint relative to their interests in race, gender, ethnicity, and sexual orientation. In all the instances I have mentioned, so-called high theory was being thrown under the bus, even as its major exponents were literally dying.

Of course, what critical theory had in common with cultural studies as opposed to neo-humanism was the messianic expectation that a theory of some sort could save the world from itself. Cultural studies promoted countercultural thinking, which liberals in humanities departments were hoping could change America for the better, whereas critical theory, if not always countercultural in the 1960s sense, was at least generally antiauthoritarian, pluralistic, and open to radical ideas that challenged traditional conceptions of identity and hierarchy. Yet, by the late 1990s it had become clear that neither cultural studies nor critical theory were going to profoundly affect much in the real world, which meant that the fantasy of being part of some grand transformative intellectual revolution would never materialize anywhere else than in academic books and papers with rather tiny readerships. This deflationary realization was intensified by the collapse of the Soviet Union, because it was clear by 1992 that Marxist theory—which people had thought could still transform the world for the better—was beginning to look more and more absurd in the light of how shockingly the East had lagged behind the West in terms of overall human rights, prosperity, efficiency, and innovation once the façade of military strength and propaganda had been torn down. Hence so-called Marxist theory either had to take a holiday or face the ugly reality that Marxism in practice had been an incredible historical embarrassment. Even Communist China, once a bastion of fanatical socialist insularity, had been credited with seeing the light by converting over to mercantilism as a transition to capitalism. In the American academy, humanists responded by abandoning or toning down their leftism, which brought people more in line with Nussbaum's neo-humanism. As if to take up Jean Baudrillard's battle cry, by the very end of the 1990s, one could imagine a whole profession screaming "Oublier Foucault," which is exactly what Valerie Traub did when she revised out theory in her book *The Renaissance of Lesbianism in Early Modern England* (2002).

No doubt, the restoration of humanism was less a concerted movement than a logical choice for many scholars. But rather than abandon theory altogether, people who were skeptical that capitalism had, in fact, saved the day, and who had interests in political philosophy, especially, were thinking that it might be advantageous to tone down theory somewhat. Symptomatic was the signal replacement of the more radical female role model Simone de Beauvoir with the less radical Hannah Arendt. This occurred in the last half of the 1990s and continued well into the early 2000s.[17] It was a very telling substitution because it brokered an alliance between political-philosophical theory (not literary theory) and a newly refound humanism. The promotion of Arendt was a conciliatory move that restored a 1950s orientation to social and humanist study mediated not by identitarian social studies faculty but by political philosophers who wanted to preserve a space in the humanities for discussing the work of Carl Schmitt, Walter Benjamin, Ernesto Laclau, Etienne Balibar, Jacques Rancière, Jürgen Habermas, Alain Badiou, and Jacques Derrida. Recall that by the early 2000s even Derrida was advocating for democracy, as well as the abolishment of the death penalty, liberal humanist causes, if ever there were. In fact, humanism had retaken the French intellectual scene already in the 1980s, having dismissed the thinkers of *soixante-huit* as dreamers. Alain Finkelkraut, André Glucksman, and Bernard Henri-Levi were media-savvy proselytes for accepting a middle way. What they opposed was genocide, or, less dramatically, violations of human rights, which they saw as the consequence of any sort of political extremism. Telling is that inauguration of Arendt as academic female role model in Anglo-American circles in the 1990s, meant that everyone was being asked to admire a woman who had a hatred of feminists and, in particular, lesbians, which she revealed in a letter to Heidegger as late as 1972.[18] Therefore, in choosing Arendt over de Beauvoir (who had been so lionized by feminist Toril Moi and others in the 1980s), the political philosophers and neo-humanists were signaling that feminism had run its course and that many thousands of feminist books later, everyone had "been there" and "done that." Here again a settlement or accommodation had been reached whereby people were drawing a line under feminism in order to move on. The resulting move to a sort of political middle is revealing in that even someone such as Julia Kristeva, the former radical Tel Queller and feminist who had never been on the same page with countercultural feminists in America (Kristeva promoted motherhood, not abortion; heterosexuality, not queer relationships), could converge with neo-humanism, not just by writing a book on Arendt in the late 1990s, but by addressing policy issues in French society that more or less fall under the rubric of public hygiene: that is, managing disability, mental disorder, addiction to media, and so on. Theory, in this case, took a backseat to one's being a counselor to society and to the state.[19] Of course, such a restoration of humanism (shared also rather strongly among academics in the United Kingdom) was intended to normalize theory, and bring it in line with mainstream social concerns, as if the Humpty-Dumpty of a conflicted and fragmented field of critical-theoretical theses and elaborations could be sorted out and rationalized, or, alternatively, simply disregarded and supplanted by something rather more commonsensical: emphasis on individual selfhood, which was considered important for reestablishing norms for the social good.

But was this emphasis upon the self (in contrast to the death of the subject) really as advantageous for the social good as the humanists had been imagining? In the book *Age of Fracture* (2011), Daniel T. Rogers points out that whereas under President Eisenhower everyone presumed a social contract in which the social subject was obliged to sacrifice for the common good of humanity, in the 1980s under President Ronald Reagan people were merely supposed to dream and look after themselves. As Rogers points out, reference to dreaming was frequent in Reagan's speeches. Social responsibility, the common good, and sacrifice were not part of Reagan's rhetoric, in part because focus groups listening to speeches didn't push the warm-and-fuzzy button when they heard words such as "sacrifice" and "responsibility." During the Reagan years, people on the right were talking about the rise of yuppies and gentrification, rational-choice analysis, the rise of free-market thinking, and supply-side economics (entrepreneurship). A new postwar culture of selfish corporate takeover and merger facilitated the cannibalizing of industries in places such as Flint Michigan and Gary Indiana, leaving them virtual wastelands. Increasingly, self-centered corporations were looking overseas for cheap labor as well as for tax havens. The knock-on effect was that everyone began noticing an increase in homelessness and the growth of the so-called service industry that came on the heels of vanishing well-paying jobs elsewhere in factories. Many observers got the impression that something disastrous had happened to America's job security and social safety net under the Reagan administration.

Meanwhile in American universities, academics were writing about the political unconscious, hegemony, hyphenated identity, multiculturalism, the subaltern in postcolonial societies, gender, sexual orientation, and deconstruction. Whereas, the political right focused on the preference-calculating self in light of finance-driven efficiency in the context of business,[20] humanities academics on the left were contemplating Foucault's death of the subject, capillary power, and Deleuze and Guattari's schizophrenic account of capitalism with its flows and parts without wholes. Oddly, while the dispossessed were suffering on the streets of Manhattan to Seattle, collective norms and social conformity were dismissed by middle-class professionals on *both* sides of the political divide, given that the right was stressing individuality and personal advantage—that is, greed—whereas the left had embraced "difference" and "otherness," terms that can negate commonality and foster narcissism. The right, of course, still believed in the commonality of desire insofar as everyone wants money and luxury goods, as the novel *American Psycho* underscored, whereas the left stressed the uncommonality of desire as it began to underscore differences of sexual orientation, gender identity, and variations in perceived racial belonging, as instantiated by Alice Walker's novel, *The Color Purple*.[21]

What both the left and the right shared, however, was a focus on the micro—that is to say, the sociality of the individual's desires, not that this helped people thrown out of work in the rust belt. In the writings of Jacques Derrida and Jean-Luc Nancy in the 1980s, one began to see the word "singularity" appear. Quite in line with what Rogers calls the age of fracture was Nancy's notion of the anti-community and, Giorgio Agamben's intense interest in that most grotesque of anti-communities, the death camp, whereas Derrida had turned to writing studies on what one might call micro-social relations, among them, that of the friend, the host, the witness, the mourner, and so on.[22] Apparently, identity was being aggressively disaggregated, which was one of the major currents in the postcolonial writings of Gayatri Spivak and Homi Bhabha in which the "discriminatory" mindset of those in power had the effect of overdetermining difference to such an extent that identity was said to be continually displaced and recreated in a way that subverted norms.[23] Subversion, of course, *is* fracturing, but so was the making of choices, according to folks on the right, given that choices individualize and set people apart. Here it should be apparent that both the right and the left emphasized individuality, the right in terms of rational choice, the left in terms of the identitarian freedom to be Other. Indeed, the neo-humanist emphasis upon the self encouraged by Nussbaum and Benhabib only served to further reinforce a disaggregative tendency in late-twentieth-century America. What the identitarians and neo-humanists failed to see is that determinacy, which they held in such high disregard as a matter of nihilistic, European fatalism, was, in fact, the better alternative conceptually, if what one wanted was to better understand social, economic, and political developments that would have long-term negative consequences. In other words, structuralism, despite whatever flaws it may have had in any of its incarnations, would have been the superior alternative to liberal forms of individualism committed to selfhood and/or notions of difference and alterity.

Another way of putting this would be to say that Louis Althusser would have likely provided a better theoretical foundation for understanding social and economic developments than anyone concerned essentially with identity, rights, and personhood, important as those concerns are. In fact, what we're seeing today in terms of the pauperization and contingency of labor within academic departments of the university is directly traceable to a predictable determinacy of structural economic/labor trends that began under Reagan, not to issues of identitarian self-fashioning and demanding subjectivity, which presume a stable work environment. The overthrow of theory, if that's the right word, by those who saw the self as key to making social change by simply demanding it—I am referring here to activism as well as the pleas for a return to humanism—was precisely the wrong move at a time when theories liberated from the mystifying yoke of self-assertion (*Selbstbehauptung*, Heidegger called it in a very different political context, albeit an academic one) would have been much more enlightening. Therefore what I have been identifying as neo-humanism, the theory settlement, and the turn away from language to content has to be situated in terms of what turned out to be an emphasis upon self-assertion that rejected the very theoretical possibilities that would have been useful at the end of the twentieth century. Another way of putting this would be to say that we should have paid more attention to base and less attention to superstructure. But a less reductive approach would be to reflect that all the "events" I have been discussing constitute what Althusser called "conjunctures," the intersection of *concrete circumstances* (say, the void opened up by the passing away of a generation), *class forces* (expressed in terms of the politics of gender, race, and ethnicity), *uneven development* (in the context of the theory wars: i.e., old versus new, idealist versus realist, hermeneutical versus positivist, etc.), and what Althusser speaks of as the *determinacy of negation* (proclaiming the death of theory, or simply ignoring theory, etc.).[24]

That the conjuncture of these elements or events is messy speaks not to a static state of affairs simply, but to what Althusser calls unpredictable necessity that is reflected, for example, in the unpredictable publication or reanimation of influential texts. Retroactively these can be made to appear accidental, dialectical, teleologically predestined, or revolutionary, depending on how one wants to manipulate causality, though all of these dimensions of the chance/ necessity distinction are, in fact, operative at once and speak to a temporalization of the conjunction that begins with an inventory of events, something that is essentially what I have presented. Among the temporal determinations that got buried in what unfolded in the 1990s was that, as already indicated, an approaching death of theory would be accompanied by many other deaths of greater consequence: the death of tenure, the death of affordable higher education, the death of English (and foreign language units) in terms of decreasing enrollments, if not the death of participatory governance in higher education as corporatization has increasingly imposed a dictatorial management/labor model. As noted earlier, neo-humanism, and much else besides, took our eyes off the ball. However, to bring that point home in more theoretical terms, consider what Etienne Balibar pointed out in "A Point of Heresy in Western Marxism: Althusser's and Tronti's Antithetical Readings of *Capital* in the Early 60s."

> [For Louis Althusser and Mario Tronti], the dominant form of ideology against which the Marxian critique of the wage labor form must now be reasserted is a combination of economic calculation, or, in the case of Tronti, planning. *Humanist discourses of justice—or even social justice—blurs or defers the class structure of the production process.* This is the core of the dominant bourgeois ideology that has become reiterated from within the labor movement including [what was once] Stalin's anticipations of the discourse of human capital—Stalin, forerunner of Gary Baker, *Man, the Most Valuable Capital.*[25] (emphasis added)

In other words, humanist notions of man, justice, rights, and equality, even within Marxism itself, blur a certain class structure whereby antagonism to the production process can be perceived and expressed. Identitarianism, in short, occludes orthodox Marxist understandings of class. Theory talk, in its humanist guises, has only contributed to this blur, something we could see by way of Rogers' *The Age of Fracture*, which, incidentally, isn't a Marxist book, just an observant one.

Conjunctures change, and cultural circumstances in the new millennium have radicalized trends in the late 1990s, resulting in the abandonment of idealism (hermeneutics, speculation, constructivism, if not *theory*) and the embrace of its opposite, realism (facticity, materialism, positivism, which are often *anti-theory*). Apparently, since the mid-1990s, we started living in a period of Restoration that in the new millennium has turned into an extremist mix of crude positivist-pragmatic tendencies, on the one hand, and an equally vicious sort of political correctness, on the other, both of which are hostile to independence of thought and freedom of speech. The recent flap over feminist film-critic Laura Kipnis' struggles at Northwestern University to preserve her right to theorize in print without getting dismissed speaks to the latter, whereas the death of theory obviously speaks to the former.[26] In a society where no one wants to be judged and everything is quite relativized, it's best, according to many, if we let the facts speak for themselves. Hence people don't want to hear profound interpretations from master thinkers, since these interpretations are considered merely authoritarian, opinionated, judgmental, and debatable, if not "privileged"; preferable are data-driven descriptions that come with the security of being uncontroversially tautological. In a time when the impersonal trumps the personal, and security trumps insecurity, it is not surprising that information management and data-driven research have quickly begun to assume dominance as a sort of fundamentalism. In line with dialectical materialism, the great mind has been replaced by the great machine.

Notable is that in an age of computer-assisted research, people presuppose that the sheer amount of information to be handled in any discipline precludes the assumption that one would be able to internalize that data in one's own head; hence, only a computer could be deemed capable of algorithmically "thinking" through the facts. The idea that our brains are insufficient to handle all the information we are required to know has been fundamental to the sciences for quite some time, but only recently has it become so generalized that students in the lower schools are brought up with the view that the world is so factually complex that it would be absurd to imagine one should store all this information in one's head. Since every student is given computers to work with from toddlerhood, memorization and internalization are downplayed and even considered irrelevant, as Michel Serres points out in *Petite Poucette* (*Thumbelina*). If the calculator once caused some social concern about students not having to memorize their times tables, the advent of the "smart phone" much more absolutely takes on the role of an external brain, relieving us of the labor of recollection, something that has caused no stir whatsoever. Instead of memorizing directions on a map, we just appeal to automated directions by means of GPS. Instead of memorizing how words are spelled, we just appeal to "auto-correct." If this observation is reminiscent of Socrates's critique of writing in *The Phaedrus*, one still has to ask whether the smart phone or the tablet are of the order of writing or something else entirely. Doesn't the outsourcing of even common knowledge to Google have the pernicious side-effect of intentionally sabotaging what the Germans call *Bildung*? And has it not always been to the advantage of capitalism to provide an opiate to the people that will ensure their ignorance? Here one can begin to speak of an inadequation of the subject to a computerized order whose forces of production negate one's capacity to be in possession of one's own faculties. In other words, we could think of the death of theory, however minor a phenomenon it is in the grand scheme of things, as part of an overdetermined historical moment today in which *techne* is replacing *psyche*—in which an artificial, positivist, superficial intelligence, incapable of reflection, self-awareness, synthesis, and hypothesis is fast becoming the only intelligence most people will ever know.

Notes

1   Some might argue that addressing a war on theory is invalid, given that everything one thinks is always already critical-theoretical in some sense. Such a view vitiates the term. Theory, as I am addressing it, speaks historically to the influx of revolutionary innovations in European thought transmitted to Anglo-American universities during the 1970s and after that derived from philosophy, linguistics, anthropology, psychology, and socioeconomic analysis. Such thinking invalidated Cartesianism, positivism, humanism, and ethnocentrism. Although the detractors of these innovations may be theoretically informed, they are not theorists in the sense of developing new ideas, methods, and perspectives. Rather, they are revanchist thinkers. Their aim is to reestablish old, familiar ways of thinking. Later I will speak of this as a form of restoration politics.

2   See Edward Baring, "Liberalism and the Algerian War: the Case of Derrida," *Critical Inquiry* 36.2 (Winter 2010): 239–261 and Michaël Lévinas, "Final Meeting between Emmanuel Lévinas and Maurice Blanchot, *Critical Inquiry* 36.4 (Summer 2010): 649–651. Between 2010 and the present, *Critical Inquiry* has substituted another war for the theory wars, namely a propaganda war on Israel that sides with its enemies. However one thinks about this politically, it is interesting to me that a journal so interested in theory always has to be at war with something. This speaks to *polemos* (as war).

3   Michel Henry, *Barbarism*, trans. S. Davidson (New York: Continuum, 2012), 17.

4   Jacques Lacan, *The Seminar of Jacques Lacan, Book I, Freud's Papers on Technique 1953–54*, trans. J. Forrester (New York: Norton, 1988), 66.

5   Francois Laruelle, *Dictionary of Non-Philosophy*, trans. T. Adkins (Minneapolis: Univocal, 2013), 43.

6   See "L'affaire Derrida," February 11, 1993, and responses to the "affair": March 23, 1993 in *New York Review of Books*.

7   See Werner Hamacher, Neil Hertz, and Thomas Keenan, eds., *Responses: On Paul de Man's Wartime Journalism* (Lincoln: University of Nebraska Press, 1989).

8   See Martin Heidegger, *Reden und andere Zeugnisse eines Lebenweges*, vol. 16, *Gesamtausgabe* (Frankfurt am Main, Vittorio Klostermann, 2000). *Reden* contains addresses and correspondence to and from National Socialists and other writings written during the National Socialist period that reveal Heidegger's prolonged interlocution with and adoption of fascist ideology. Because this text hasn't been translated into English, puritanical Americans, in particular, can't seem to get over being scandalized every time they hear a new bit of information about Heidegger's involvement with National Socialism. *Reden* obviates the need for self-righteous academics to opportunistically make a fuss over this issue, because the volume flat-out presents a substantial amount of the documents, and one can judge for oneself whether those documents disqualify Heidegger from further consideration or not. There's no need for hypocritical show trials of the dead.

9   Alan Sokal, "Transgressing the Boundaries: Toward a Transformative Hermeneutics of Quantum Gravity," *Social Text* 14.1–2 (1996): 217–252.

10 Vincent Leitch, ed., *Norton Anthology of Theory and Criticism* (New York: Norton, 2010).

11 Lawrence Grossberg, Cary Nelson, and Paula Treichler, eds. *Cultural Studies* (New York: Routledge, 1991).

12 Jean Baudrillard, *The Gulf War Did Not Take Place* (Bloomington: Indiana University Press, 1995). Baudrillard originally published installments of this in the newspaper *Libération* in 1991.

13 Herman Rapaport, "Restoration Politics," *Oxford Literary Review* 28 (July 2006): 133–147.

14 Barbara Christian, "The Race for Theory," *Cultural Critique* 6 (Spring, 1987): 51–63.

15 Gayatri Chakravorty Spivak, *The Postcolonialist Critic* (New York: Routledge, 1990).

16 Alain Badiou, *Lacan: l'antiphilosophie 3* (Paris: Fayard, 2013).

17 See Seyla Benhabib, *Reluctant Modernism of Hannah Arendt* (Thousand Oaks: Sage, 1996) and Julia Kristeva, *Hannah Arendt* (Paris: Fayard, 1999), which are among a spate of books on Arendt that were written in the 1990s.

18 Martin Heidegger, *Briefe* (Frankfurt am Main: Vittorio Klostermann, 1999), 231–232.

19 Julia Kristeva, *La haine et le pardon* (Paris: Fayard, 2005).

20 Daniel T. Rogers, *The Age of Fracture* (Cambridge: Belknap, 2002), 89.

21 One can see this confluence today in 2015 in terms of Bruce Jenner's transsexual identity, which ticks the boxes of leftist approval in terms of

otherness, difference, and its challenge to heteronormativity (the commonality of sexual and gendered norms), while it also ticks the boxes of Jenner's own Republican ideology, which favors freedom of choice, individuality, and economic self-promotion (Jenner is a reality TV star for whom the publicity matters).

22 See Jacques Derrida, *The Politics of Friendship* (Chicago: University of Chicago Press, 1994). Giorgio Agamben, *Remnants of Auschwitz* (New York: Zone Books, 2002).

23 Homi Bhabha, *Location of Culture* (New York: Routledge, 1994), 159.

24 Louis Althusser, *Machiavelli and Us* (London: Verso, 1999).

25 Etienne Balibar, "A Point of Heresy in Western Marxism: Althusser's and Tronti's Antithetical Readings of Capital in the Early 60s." www.princeton.edu/~benj/ReadingCapital.

26 Among many newspaper articles on what happened to Kipnis, see Michelle Goldberg, "The Laura Kipnis Melodrama," *The Nation*, March 16, 2015.

Works cited

Agamben, Giorgio. *Remnants of Auschwitz*. New York: Zone Books, 2002.

Althusser, Louis. *Machiavelli and Us*. London: Verso, 1999.

Badiou, Alain. *Lacan: l'antiphilosophie 3*. Paris: Fayard, 2013.

Balibar, Etienne. "A Point of Heresy in Western Marxism: Althusser's and Tronti's Antithetical Readings of Capital in the Early 60s." www.princeton.edu/~benj/Reading Capital/.

Baring, Edward. "Liberalism and the Algerian War: The Case of Derrida." *Critical Inquiry* 36.2 (Winter 2010): 239–261.

Barthes, Roland. Oeuvres Complètes, 5 vols. Paris: Seuil, 2002–03.

Baudrillard, Jean. *The Gulf War Did Not Take Place*. Bloomington: Indiana University Press, 1995.

Benhabib, Seyla. *Reluctant Modernism of Hannah Arendt*. Thousand Oaks: Sage, 1996.

Benjamin, Walter. *Werke und Nachlass*. 21 vols. Frankfurt am Main: Suhrkamp Verlag, 2010.

Bernstein, Charles. *Attack of the Difficult Poems*. Chicago: University of Chicago Press, 2011.

Bhabha, Homi. *The Location of Culture*. New York: Routledge, 1994.

Christian, Barbara. "The Race for Theory." *Cultural Critique* 6 (Spring 1987): 51–63.

Deleuze, Gilles. *Proust and Signs*. New York: Braziller, 1972.

Derrida, Jacques. *Dissemination*. Trans. B. Johnson. Chicago: Chicago University Press, 1980.

Derrida, Jacques. *The Politics of Friendship*. Chicago: University of Chicago Press, 1994.

Foucault, Michel. *Cours au Collège de France, 1970–83*. 13 vols. Paris: Seuil, 1997–2014.

Goldberg, Michelle. "The Laura Kipnis Melodrama," *The Nation*, March 16, 2015.

Gregg, Melissa, and Gregory J. Seigworth, eds. *The Affect Theory Reader*. Durham: Duke University Press, 2010.

Grossberg, Lawrence, Cary Nelson, and Paula Treichler, eds. *Cultural Studies*. New York: Routledge, 1991.

Hamacher, Werner, Neil Hertz, and Thomas Keenan, eds. *Responses: On Paul de Man's Wartime Journalism*. Lincoln: University of Nebraska Press, 1989.

Heidegger, Martin. *Briefe (1925–1975), #144*. Frankfurt am Main: Vittorio Klostermann, 1999.

Heidegger, Martin. *Reden und andere Zeugnisse eines Lebenweges*, vol. 16. *Gesamtausgabe*. Frankfurt am Main: Vittorio Klostermann, 2000.

Heidegger, Martin. *Überlegungen II-XV (Schwarze Hefte)*, vols. 94–96. Frankfurt am Main: Vittorio Klostermann, 2014.

Henry, Michel. *Barbarism*. New York: Continuum, 2012.

Kristeva, Julia. *Hannah Arendt*. Paris: Fayard, 1999.

Kristeva, Julia. *La haine et le pardon*. Paris: Fayard, 2005.

Lacan, Jacques. *Les séminaries*. 21 vols. Paris: Seuil, 1974.

"L'affaire Derrida." *New York Review of Books*. February 11, 1993 and March 23, 1993.

Laruelle, Francois. *Dictionary of Non-Philosophy*. Minneapolis: Univocal, 2013.

Leitch, Vincent, et al., eds. *Norton Anthology of Theory and Criticism*. New York: Norton, 2010.

Lévinas, Michaël. "Final Meeting between Emmanuel Lévinas and Maurice Blanchot." *Critical Inquiry* 36.4 (Summer 2010): 649–651.

Millet, Kate. *Sexual Politics*. New York: Avon, 1971.

Nussbaum, Martha. *The Fragility of Goodness*. Cambridge: Cambridge University Press, 1986.

Rapaport, Herman. "Restoration Politics." *Oxford Literary Review* 28 (July 2006): 133–147.

Rogers, Daniel T. *The Age of Fracture*. Cambridge: Belknap, 2011.

Serres, Michel. *Petite Poucette*. Paris: Pommier, 2012.

Sokal, Alan. "Transgressing the Boundaries: Toward a Transformative Hermeneutics of Quantum Gravity." *Social Text* 14.1–2 (1996): 217–252.

Spivak, Gayatri Chakravorty. *The Postcolonialist Critic*. New York: Routledge, 1990.

Traub, Valerie. *The Renaissance of Lesbianism in Early Modern England*. Cambridge: Cambridge University Press, 2002.

Young, Iris Marion. *Throwing Like a Girl*. Bloomington: Indiana University Press. 1990.

3

The Afterlife of Critics

Henry Sussman

When someone dies, they leave a growing corona behind them, an afterglow in the souls of those who were close to them. Inevitably, as time passes, the afterglow fades and finally goes out, but it takes many years for that to happen. When eventually, all of those close ones will have died as well, then all the embers will have gone cool, and at that point, it's "ashes to ashes and dust to dust."[1]

A person is a point of view—*not only a* physical *point of view (looking out of certain eyes in a certain place in the universe), but more importantly a psyche's point of view: a set of hair-trigger associations rooted in a huge book of memories. The latter can be absorbed, more and more over time, by someone else. Thus it's like acquiring a foreign language step by step . . . One gradually becomes a fluent speaker in and speaker of the other's language, and it is no longer "fake," even if one has an accent in it. So it is with coming to see the world with someone else's soul.*[2]

If you seriously believe, as I do . . . that concepts are active symbols in a brain, *and if furthermore you believe that* people, no less than objects, are represented by symbols in the brain *(in other words, that each person that one knows is mirrored internally by a concept, albeit a very complex one, in one's brain), and if lastly you seriously believe that* a self is also a concept, just an even more complicated one *(an "I," a personal "gemma" . . .), then it is a necessary and unavoidable consequence of these beliefs that* your brain is inhabited to varying extents by other I's, other souls, *the extent of each one depending on the degree to which you faithfully represent, and resonate with, the person in question. In include the proviso "and resonate with" because one can't slip into any old soul, no more than one can slip into any old piece of clothing; some souls and some suits simply "fit" better than others do.*[3]

Afterlives and symbolic networks

My objective in the remainder of this chapter is to introduce a cybernetic perspective within the inquiry into the persistence of critics beyond their active practices of inscription and their biological lives, which is perforce an inquiry into what makes critics vivid, memorable, worth taking and keeping in account. The tangential inquiry as to whether there are considerations involved in the persistence of critics that do not quite pertain to the recording, archiving, and cultural memory of artists or art-producers, or that do pertain, but in a slightly different way, is every bit as indispensable as the overall interrogation framing the current volume, in which I'm absolutely delighted to be participating.

If I have already assaulted my readers with an unseemly barrage of citations from Douglas Hofstadter's 2007 *I Am a Strange Loop*, it is because they, with exemplary compression, combine and articulate my operating assumptions and perspectives in joining the fray. Before this essay is over, I will be testing some of the obvious inferences available from the statements by Hofstadter cited at the beginning of the chapter: that critics, like other people and forces in our lives, are translated into entries within our collective and individual symbolic repositories and networks where, until forgotten, they fluctuate in strength, relative prominence, and staying power. The work of a critic may be "deactivated" through lack of current interest, or "reactivated," as was Erich Auerbach's *Mimesis* in an article in *The New Yorker* on September 12, 2013 and the recent reissue by New York Review Press of his *Dante: Poet of the Secular World*.

Now elucidating the mind or consciousness as a network or circuitry of images or symbols may be a fruitful metaphor or trope, but it is by no means exclusive or necessary. I recall that Plato performed a perfectly credible job in this sphere with the image of an aviary in *Theaetetus*. I insist on the network-image, though, for a number of reasons: First and foremost, to the degree that the structure of a symbolic network is built into a plethora of features characterizing cybernetic operations, among them the configuration of certain programs and operating systems and the storage and retrieval of information and data, it is a highly *convenient* metaphor. The network-figure may in fact be described as an *interface* between the interpretation and inscription that critics perform and the prevailing technological operating system of our age. Whatever easy or uneasy peace we have made with the technology, thinking of our calling as critics in cybernetic terms affords us a common cause with our colleagues and students, who, like us, spend countless hours under cybernetic regimes and protocols, where we *transcribe* our thinking and feeling into binary codes and other digital notations. Like us, our colleagues and students are to a certain extent clueless regarding the broader and long-term social, cognitive, and even phenomenological implications of this stampede, or lemmings' run into a cybernetic ontology, but there is an indelible cybernetic imprint upon the way we gather information and arrange our lives, the way we think and write, also upon the way we interact. In a 2011 publication, *Around the Book: Systems and Literacy*, I characterized this backlog of computer-implemented conditions and relations as a "cybernetic unconscious," and I suggested that we were all saddled, willingly or not, implicitly or explicitly, with working our ways through its subliminal, or offshore operations. It is only in this sense that Hofstadter's image of a symbolic network is more compelling to us today as a platform for tracing the vicissitudes of critics and their commentary, than the Platonic birdcage. One of Hofstadter's ways of *performing* the partial liftoff to a meta-critical oversight common to musical, graphic, poetic, and cybernetic notations summoning themselves into what he calls a "strange loop"—whose trajectory emulates the swing of Derrida's *brisure* or hinge in *De la Grammatology*, briefly but not definitively *outside* the system of Western metaphysics—is through out-and-out humor. *Nota bene*: in his playful *re-mark* of his notion of the brain as an arrangement of multiple symbolic networks, each with relatively weighted and unweighted elements, Hofstadter terms these atomic units "simmballs," atoms of simulation, "dancing" around not a cranium but a "careenium." He thus highlights the *physical* contingency of symbols bouncing around our highest-level processor, effecting a very active homology—or again—isomorphism—between particle-physics and *meta*physics in the brain: "Consciousness is the dance of symbols inside the cranium . . . Most of the time, any given symbol in our brain is dormant, like a book sitting inertly in the remote stacks of a library. Every so often, some event will trigger the recall of this book from the stacks."[4]

(Also to be duly noted: the struggle of an individual reader, drawing upon the archive of prior readings and personal experience in order to render a compelling and to some degree innovative read-out of a cultural artifact whose exigency is embedded within the process of cultural encounter, itself approximates the model of an "open system," as characterized by Anthony Wilden and others. This is the mythological toil of the solitary reader. Blanchot traces the reader to her hideout in literary space that he invests with the dimensions of an Orphic underworld, and he persists in adumbrating the multiple compulsions driving

her there. This endeavor is to be sharply distinguished from institutional selec-
tions [the term is Luhmann's, with respect to social systems], whether within
the framework of a discipline, a department, or a sub-specialization, to establish a ranking or weighting for an artifact or cultural figure. The result of this
latter sort of deliberation, I would surmise, is in the name of personal or group
self-interest advanced by deals and compromises conducted on the stock market of intellectual prestige and properties.)

One additional initial aside: Freud's background in neurology lent a palpa-
ble proto-cybernetic dimension to his schemata for memory in such sites as
the end of his coauthored (with Breuer) *Studies on Hysteria* and in the "dream-
work" chapter of the *Traumdeutung*. Like so many other human fabrications,
Hofstadter's imagery and the challenge that it poses to humanists would not
have raised a Freudian eyebrow. Not only did Lacan go to town with such figuration: it is the Freudian mystical notepad that also gives rise to Derrida's
earliest and still-consequential musings on media and artificial memory. It is
in a Blanchotian "space of literature" that Derrida will situate the Freudian
dream-work as a "scene of writing." In preparation for my final turn, which
will be in the direction of Derrida's appeal to sub-semantic elements in con-
figuring an interface linking Hegel and Genet in ongoing modal feedback,
I want to underscore the topographical dimension with which Derrida, from
the very start, fits out Freudian interpretation. At one end of this pitched scene
of reading and exegesis may well be situated Blanchot's gravitation to mythology and Deleuze/Guattari's appropriation of vacant systematic premises with
a unique mythological (read: virtual)[5] twist of their own. But in keeping with
Derrida's prescient insight, the space of textual encounter that he renders coe-
qual to psychoanalytical interpretation has at its far flank nothing other than
cyberspace itself: "Topographical, temporal, and formal regression in dreams
must be interpreted, henceforth, as a path back to a landscape of writing. Not
a writing that only transcribes, a stony echo of muted words, but a lithography
before words: metaphonetic, non linguistic, alogical. (Logic obeys consciousness, or preconsciousness, the site of verbal images, as well as the principle of
identity)."[6] Consciousness, as first teased out by Freud in its multidimensional
complexity, programs itself as a scene of writing. "But we must think of [it] in
other terms than individual or collective psychology, or even anthropology. It
must be thought in the horizon of the scene/stage of the world, as the history of
that scene/stage. Freud's language is *caught up* in it."[7]

Calibrating the afterlives, or in Hofstadter's language, "afterglow" of critics on a cybernetic platform impacts directly on the scope of our inquiry and

the questions that we can most productively pose. For example, it doesn't matter an iota whether the critic happens to be alive or deceased in order for her to figure within the personal network of a critic rendering a reading or within the collective memory of an interpersonal network or community of fellow-readers. Indeed, *I Am a Strange Loop* is Hofstadter's far more "everyday" and "human" sequel to his magisterial 1980 *Gödel, Escher, Bach*, which may be regarded as an introductory computer science textbook, which he grounded in graphics, music, games, and religious experience as well as in math and science. He issued it to the populations of "advanced societies" who were party to the initial widespread dissemination of cybernetic technology. The sequel, on which I'm concentrating, was largely and explicitly motivated (as in the first citation above) by the undiminished poignancy attached to his wife Carol, who had died much too early, in 1993. In characterizing the weighting that a loved one, even deceased, can operate within a personal archive of images, Hofstadter writes: "The name 'Carol' denotes for me far more than just a body, which is now gone, but rather a very vast pattern, a *style*, a set of things including memories, hopes, beliefs, loves, reactions to music, sense of humor, self-doubt, generosity, compassion, and so on."[8] The fact that Hofstadter includes *style* among the parameters determining a person's status as a symbol within the rhizome or network of memory indicates just how important literary manifestations are to him. Not only is *Gödel, Escher, Bach* chock-full of literary allusions, to wit the figures of Achilles, the Tortoise, and the Anteater with which he populates the fanciful dialogic interchapters between the doses of number theory and computer design that he delivers. As it is written, *Gödel, Escher, Bach* is a masterful literary as well as scientific work. It is at once playful, poetically innovative and rich, generically diverse and inventive, and nonlinear by design (indeed, as illustrative of "strange loopings").

The fact that Hofstadter juxtaposes Carol's style with the *pattern* that she imports to his memory is an instance of an isomorphism. A *pattern* is what scientists struggle to discern at the empirical level, whether in numbers, chemical interactions, or biological traits. Patterns are ultimately quantifiable: they can be schematized and compressed into shorthand. The script of patterns becomes the operative part of computer programs, what enables them to arrange, sort, recall, merge, and even analyze phenomena of a far more enigmatic nature, whether moods or colors or smells. Like rhetorical tropes and performatives before them, computer programs, as Hofstadter brilliantly demonstrates in *Gödel, Escher, Bach*, are themselves isomorphic in structure. They interface or coordinate the calculable with the incalculable, the quantifiable with the nonquantifiable. They encompass a "hard" flank, a numerical one, and a much "softer" one, whose traits and qualities are often aesthetic. And they even denote a transitional zone, as in D. W. Winnicott's "transitional objects," where the calculable and the incalculable merge into the supplement or the remainder, the irreducible quanta of the yet unthinkable and the yet inexpressible. It is in these senses that computer programs become the insignias as well as the lingua franca of our times.

Carol's compelling persistence to Hofstadter, as a motivation for his extrapolating "the cybernetics of everyday life" is of material assistance to us in our tracing the afterlives of critics. It does not matter for one, as suggested above, whether they are alive or dead. A Jacques Derrida, who we lost much too early in 2004, can be very much more alive, in terms of the network of critical exchange and thinking, than a very much extant Henry Sussman. I want you all to know that I am, according to Amazon, the 1578th most important living US critic. I was able to purchase recently on Amazon a used copy, in very good condition, of a book into which I had poured my *qi* or life force in the mid-1990s, for $.48. This was the hardbound edition, in excellent condition. I was amused that the postage for sending the book home was over five times the price, and I was happy to clear shelf space for the independent dealer, who, by the way, had received positive reviews from 98 percent of his customers. Needless to say, such analytics have played a decisive role in determining the course of my own investigations.

Not only do contemporary cybernetics and systems theory stretch the notions of life, afterlife, and shelf life when applied to cultural artifacts and their producers, but they also help us specify the terms and parameters according to which criticism remains vibrant and *au courant*. In effect, art works and critics can remain "lit up" within memory banks or symbolic networks in multiple ways and along a full spectrum of parameters. I want to suggest in the remainder of my comments precisely how it is, in cybernetic terms, that Maurice Blanchot, Deleuze/Guattari, and Jacques Derrida could still pack such a wallop on my personal critical practice, however notable or not it may be—and no doubt upon the practices of others. This will relieve us, I hope, of anxieties we may be nursing with regard to our writings' status as it is impacted by our personal life events, and it may suggest qualities of captivation and virtual intensification that we would do well to harness in our upcoming critical investigations if we have not yet done so in our standing bibliographies.

Writing and virtuality

First and foremost, we remember thinkers and cultural critics of the stature of Maurice Blanchot, Gilles Deleuze, Félix Guattari, and Jacques Derrida because of the vividness of their points of view and because of the paradigm-stretching impact of the highly innovative modes and media of expression that they set into play. In these senses, they are very much alive, or if they are dead it is because they inhabit the virtual crypt of reading and writing that has been homesteaded by the entire community of cultural criticism. The present discussion will look at their very different achievements within the frameworks of one of the prevalent logics driving Hofstadter's 1980 rallying cry, the proto-cybernetic organization and processing within artifacts and other cultural achievements before there is any computer hardware to instantiate these formations. It is in this sense that Hofstadter reads above all Bach's canons but also his fugues as folding back on themselves and reversing their organizing formats to the degree that they *perform* (not only articulate) their own musical phrasings, most famously in the "Crab Canon," *and* they render an account of the musicality of music. In parallel fashion, Hofstadter reads the engravings of M. C. Escher as a medium in which two-dimensional representation expands outward against its inherent limitations and toward the expansiveness of three-dimensionality, only to retreat again within its systematic limits. Even where such famous drawings as "Convex and Concave," "Drawing Hands," and "Dragon," have *not* morphed themselves into three-dimensional objects, they have graphically embellished the drama of contingent experience reaching toward critical synthesis and oversight, even if only to fall back within the visual medium that allowed their schematic expression. Escher's engraving "Dragon" affords Hofstadter a vivid occasion for couching this struggle, which pursues the trajectory of the "strange loop," the uneasy alliance between different levels of critical apprehension, both at the heart of memorable criticism and driving computer software. Hofstadter has cited Escher's own comment on this graphic:

> However much this dragon tries to be spatial, he remains completely flat. Two incisions are made in the paper on which he is printed. Then it is folded in such a way as to leave two square openings, and in spite of his two dimensions he persists in assuming that he has three, so he sticks his head through one of the holes and his tail through the other.

Seeing that Escher, in his theoretical as well as graphic rendering of the "Dragon" has lobbed him the ideal précis to a slam dunk, Hofstadter comments as follows:

> The message is that no matter how cleverly you try to simulate three dimensions in two, you are always missing some "essence of three-dimensionality. The dragon tries very hard to fight his two-dimensionality. He defies the two-dimensionality of the paper on which he thinks he is drawn, by sticking his head through it, yet all the while we outside the drawing can see his pathetic futility of it all, the dragon and the holes and the folds are all merely two-dimensional simulations of those concepts, and not a one of them is real. But the dragon cannot step out of this two-dimensional space, and cannot know it as we do."[9]

In radically different ways, Blanchot, Deleuze/Guattari, and Derrida entice us with "dragons" of their own configuration: Blanchot through his exigent philosophical rearticulation of his invasion and critical nesting within what are first and foremost virtual *literary* spaces, whether epic (Homer), poetic (Hölderlin), or fictive (Kafka); Deleuze/Guattari both by building out, at the cost of the most extreme formulations ventured by postwar theory, the implicit spaces intrinsic to the systems of capital and psychoanalysis *and* by devolving philosophical oversight, as "high" a "high-level" processing" as exists (hence also digital) to the absolutely immanent level of apprehension on the part of the Body without Organs and the pack; and Derrida, as suggested above, by crystallizing rhetorico-conceptual figures of such radicality that they graft or suture "high-level" thinking and "low-level" articulation (e.g., of the "gl" intonation on which he bases his contrapuntal reading of Genet with Hegel in *Glas*) into an endlessly resonant feedback loop. This not only explains, in the case of each of these authors, why their telling readings survive, vividly and sustainably, in the critical community's collective "careenium." It demonstrates an uncanny predilection, on the part of all four critics and cultural programmers, for the digital and virtual operating conditions under which we currently labor to extend their marvelous inquiries.

Blanchot, Deleuze/Guattari, and Derrida thus remain players in a virtual universe in which through masterful and innovative critical performances, they remain dazzlingly *au courant* in at least a double sense: more than other writers, their discourse gravitates toward the virtual space of representation that had in fact been theorized by the uncannily intuitive visionaries of Early Romanticism, in their speculations on the image, reflection, and reciprocity, better and more comprehensively than anyone else (but that is the subject of a disquisition far broader than the present one); *and*, in very different ways, their writerly performance definitively establishes their proto-cybernetic apprehensions, in the mode of Hofstadter's Bach and Escher, of a world whose operating languages would become digital, whose reality would become virtual, and whose time would become "real." It is in this sense, however inadequately, I would hope to reintroduce the above masters: the approximation of genius, in each instance, couples conceptual virtuosity with writerly performance, forming the parallel, mutually indexical scales of isomorphism. A crucial intermediary step making this rereading or reappropriation possible is Hofstadter's approach to Kurt Gödel. Hofstadter meticulously demonstrates, in a manner with which I strongly doubt the founder of deconstruction would take issue, how Gödel decisively destabilized the perfect intercalation between logic and number theory that Whitehead and Russell had putatively canonized in their edifice to set theory, the *Principia Mathematica*. Very much in the vein and drift of the release of such Derridean bombshells to systematic complacency extending from the Platonic *pharmakon*, or from *différance* and the *supplément* themselves, to the wheel, both of global capital and torture in *Rogues*, Hofstadter's Gödel synthesizes numerical strings, rather than meta-tropes, of such magnitude and suppleness as to henceforth disqualify the possibility of closed mathematical systems sufficient to themselves. As Bach did in his canons and fugues and Escher achieved in his graphics, Hofstadter's Gödel launched mathematical theories and the sets and systems they predicated on the inherently endless quest for their own elusive "points of incompletion." I cannot imagine any of my subjects, Blanchot, Deleuze/Guattari, or Derrida, railing too vehemently against the charge that they opened up, by means of their ingenious devices and phrases, "points of incompletion" in systems otherwise too stratified, frozen, blind, or complacent to recognize these lapses, that always comprise, I would add, opportunities.

Blanchot: Virtual spaces of literature

Helping to reboot Europe from its postwar cultural ruins, Blanchot does not shy away from a reprise of the most fundamental questions regarding literature: What makes it compelling? What are its exigencies? What are the multiple parameters of the alternate world that it entices us to enter? What is so striking, when he takes up the enigma posed by the Homeric Sirens, is his ability to *inhabit* their mythical space, to occupy an alien environment with vehemence:

> Remember that this song was sung to sailors, men prepared to take risks and fearless in their impulses, and it was a form of navigation too; it was a distance, and what it revealed was the possibility of travelling that distance, of making this movement into the expression of the greatest desire, of making the song into a movement towards the song and of making this movement into the expression of the greatest desire. Strange navigation, and what was its goal? . . . Others have claimed that the goal . . . had been overshot; the enchantment held out an enigmatic promise and through this promise exposed men to the danger of being unfaithful to themselves, unfaithful to their human song and even to the essence of song, by awakening in them hope and the desire for a marvelous beyond, and that beyond was only a desert . . . Does this mean that there was something evil in the invitation which issued from the depths? Were the Sirens nothing more than unreal voices, as custom would have us believe, unreal voices which were not supposed to be heard, a deception intended to seduce, and which could be resisted only by disloyal or cunning people?[10]

It is of course well-known that Blanchot, in jump-starting a postwar literary-critical practice and indeed in attempting a high philosophical platform for the understanding of literature's exigency, its distinctive space, its relation to death, and other substantial issues, is working at the limits of the most sophisticated Cultural Operating System available to him. Like Kojève and Lacan, he is deeply engaged with the postwar apprehension of the uncanny degree to which Hegelian dialectics continued to undergird every conceptual program of significance, from Marxist thought to classical psychoanalysis to surrealism. In an appropriately *engagé* way, he embraces the inquiries and stances that have been taken up by existentialism, relating, for example, to purpose, fatality, and death. Full-service critic and writer that he is, whose practice may be described as a general writing, one encompassing fiction and poetics as well as discourse, an all-out commitment to wired inscription that is also relevant today, he is drawn to Heidegger's retrofitting of philosophical speculation as a poetic excavation (this comes out particularly in his commentary on Hölderlin of this moment, the 1950s). In keeping with the above, he has read his Kafka. He knows that Kafka ventured, in his "Das Schweigen der Sirenen," "Now the Sirens have a still more fatal weapon than their song, namely their silence. And although admittedly such a thing has never happened, still it is conceivable that someone might possibly have escaped from their singing; but from their silence certainly never."[11] Blanchot's entry onto the stage of the Siren's venerable cultural site, and the rehab to which he submits it, sets out in an appreciation of the radical dimensional expansion that the Kafkan fracturing of the myth has already accomplished. This dimension-shattering updating of the myth was of course the very bread and butter of modernist practice, whether by Joyce, Eliot, Pound, Woolf, Picasso, Miro, de Chirico, Mahler, Stravinsky, or so many others.

Yet this is also the moment when I want to make the plea for a notable cybernetic premonition and motive on Blanchot's part as well. Blanchot's rendition of the Sirens's place, as of the Orphic myth, the latter crucial to his reception of Rilke, is as a virtual site that he, like any other *engagé* reader, is free to enter and update according to his compelling critical constructs or motives. Of more recent readers, no one has "nailed" the virtual nature of the literary locations that poets and fiction writers invent more compellingly than J. Hillis Miller. How he describes this state of affairs, although in relation to Henry James's *The Wings of the Dove*, is relevant to Blanchot's treatment of the Sirens, and more importantly, to his overarching topos of literary and imaginary space:

> The world seems to be created by the words of the novel and therefore to be James's invention. After we have entered it, however, this virtual reality seems to refer or correspond at a distance to a realm that has always been there already, waiting to be revealed, dis-covered, uncovered, by the novelist's words. Within that virtual world, the reader, after the first sentence, can now dwell through all the time it takes to the novel's last page and last sentence, Kate Croy's "We shall never again be as we were."[12]

Miller, in the above citation, is intent on establishing the reader's "squatting rights" within the virtual fictive spaces that s/he is inclined to enter. This is in keeping with the radical democracy pervasive throughout his writing style, his teaching, as well as his long-standing *conduct* of one of the most productive critical *dojos* or ateliers. This articulation of the *virtual* conditions of a compelling literary scene is also characteristic of his fascination with literary media, going back to his rendition of a "Fractal Proust," in the *Black Holes* volume that he coauthored with Manuel Asensi, and extending to his most recent work, in which, both in depicted fictive communities and in actual ones, characters' minds communicate through a telepathic hookup or wiring.[13]

To a certain extent, the Blanchot who penetrates to the Sirens episode of the *Odyssey* or to the mythical underworld of Orpheus's feverish quest for Eurydice is yet another Millerian close reader claiming his squatter's rights over these virtual spaces that literature has not only invented but managed to transmit, orally and in writing, over the millennia. When Blanchot celebrates the access to death that Kafka's musings on the topic afford him—in certain dimensions more resonant than the wartime close scrapes with death he recounts in his fiction—he plunks himself squarely *in* the space of Kafka's writing: "Just as the poet only exists once when the poem faces him, only after the poem, as it were—although it is necessary that first there be a poet in order for there to be a poem—so one senses that if Kafka goes toward the power of dying through the work which he writes, the work is itself by implication an experience of death which he apparently has to have been through already in order to reach the work, and through the work, death."[14] It is the virtuality of the work as a scene of intense cultural programming, in philosophical as well as poetic terms, that establishes some continuity with death and the real, what Beckett terms the unnameable.

Blanchot is the advance party to Miller's apprehension of the virtual features of those imaginary spaces that particularly haunt us. Blanchot's insistence on the spatial parameters of literature's fascination, on precisely formulating the calibration of these parameters as they pertain to the inventions of a range of favored writers among whom Hölderlin, Rilke, Dostoyesvky, and Kafka loom prominently, is proto-cybernetic in its own right. Blanchot is stunningly free-wheeling in skewing the critical input and the critical output of his forays into virtual literary space. Blanchot insists just as firmly as Miller, upon entering one of his desired literary destinations, upon his ownership and his rights, whether to death or to art, or to the happenings of the work. Criticism, as embodied by Blanchot, is the radical transcription of literary device into philosophical dia-lect. The space of literature, a phrasing that Blanchot applied to one of his pivotal essay collections, is the foyer where literature, as an open-ended battery of figu-rative devices and improvisations, seamlessly segues into a philosophical zone, no less virtual, whose drift is the updating and re-storage of a historical lexicon of conceptual prompts and protocols rather than the "careening" of irreducibly poetic "simmballs" within diverse representational media. Here is situated the interface where literary invention and conceptual programming cross-reference one another, forming the "correspondence" of an isomorphism. In this instance, philosophical initiatives, whether Blanchot takes them from Hegel or Heidegger, occupy the relative position of codification and record-keeping while literature pushes toward the limit of that which eludes schematization and quantification.

It is no accident that when Blanchot, adrift in this literary space where two decisive text-media, literature and philosophy, interface, contemplates the artwork, its configuration and performance coincide with any number of the features that Hofstadter attributes to self-referential cybernetic processing:

> Art has a goal: it is this very goal. It is not simply a way of exercising the mind; it *is* mind—which is nothing if it is not a work. And what is the work? The exceptional moment when possibility becomes power, when the mind—law or empty form rich only in undetermined potentiality—becomes the certainty of a realized form, becomes the body which is this form, and this beautiful form which is a body. The work is mind, and the mind is the passage, within the work, between the supreme indeterminacy to the determination of that extreme. The unique passage is real only in the work—in the work which is never real, never finished, since it is only the realization of the mind's infiniteness. The mind, then, sees once again in the work only an opportunity to recognize and exercise itself ad infinitum. Thus we return to our part of departure.[15]

Blanchot's vocabulary in the passage still derives from the radical updating to mind-body relationships, with the mind as an image within the body every bit as much as the inverse, offered by Bergson in the first round of modern phenomenology, only to be raised to even higher powers of finitude and specificity by Husserl in the next bout. In this citation, Blanchot is measuring the play of mind and body against the work of aesthetics, performed in the artwork. He labors to make beauty, the artwork's consummate value and truth of its own exigency, immanent to this fundamental human predicament in its phenomenological articulation, to make beauty emerge from the phenomenon of corporeality itself, a body-work transpiring on multiple planes. The vocabulary in this passage remains very nineteenth century, with a nod to twentieth-century aesthetics, but the trajectory described by mind in spending itself on and testing itself in the artwork is, to those familiar with Hofstadter, nothing other than a strange loop. A certain power accrues to mind in the exercise of aesthetic playfulness that ups the ante in the artwork: it confers a specific form upon an indeterminate flow of possibility. Mind configures artwork; artwork expands mind. The aesthetico-cognitive transaction, akin to the Heideggerian hermeneutic circle, leads us back to a thinker, the maker, and to a cultural artifact, but having pursued a "unique loop" through a work event "never real, never finished . . . We thus return to our point of departure." The trappings may be of a postwar existential update to aesthetics under the aura of twentieth-century phenomenology, but the process is unmistakably cybernetic.

Deleuze/Guattari: The philosophy of "lower-level processing"

Now if Blanchot is able to discern the work of the Lacanian Real or evidence of Heideggerien opening or *Lichtung* where he occupies the literary spaces of Greek mythology, Hölderlin's odes, or Kafka's meditations and parables, what happens when we veer into the phantasmatic philosophical environments configured by Deleuze/Guattari is somewhat different. In their performance as the nomadic hermit crabs of the cybernetic age, these two thinkers reprogram the historical operating system of philosophy from a site in the virtual "bare ruined choirs" that the unrealized architectures of Marxism and psychoanalysis have left vacant. Deleuze/Guattari occupy incomplete systematic architectures, not literary scenes, as they are embellished and communicated down a long tradition. Their modus operandi may well be more consistent than Blanchot's (indeed they are fascinated by striking instances of symbiotic codependency). Yet in both cases, Blanchot and Deleuze/Guattari, penetration to a preexistent site of cultural production, usurpation of this space, facilitates the articulation of pronouncements otherwise unsayable. The term that Derrida established for such locations when, quite early on, he turned to Freud, was "scenes of writing." Blanchot and Deleuze/Guattari cannibalize different materials in establishing their respective scenes of writing. But their results are parallel: articulations so outrageous as to teach us something new—even from within the epistemological and ontological systems comprising our standpoint.

Not only do Deleuze/Guattari furnish us with the blueprints of the invariably mobile and plastic architectures out of which they write, but they also struggle to bring philosophy back into a confrontation with the ground-level processing, akin to the Hegelian zero-point of "sensible certitude," from which it invariably departs on an odyssey of higher and higher abstraction, meaning further and further abandonment of the analog in favor of the digital. The "new, improved" version of philosophy is invariably more digital, in the sense of more concerned with boundaries, relations, and relativities than qualities, than the prior update, which it dismisses precisely on the basis of its analog limitation. Wasn't this Derrida's early brief against Lévi-Strauss, of "post-structuralism" against structuralism? That there was an analog subtext to the play of structures, as illustrated in *Tristes Tropiques*, for example, by the "game of proper names," that could not, in the end, stand up to an all-out, completely open-ended semiotic, more digital variety of philosophy that Derrida insisted on mobilizing? Isn't this, in a nutshell, the case that Lacanian psychoanalysis, with its recalibration of the "interpsychic agencies" into cognitive faculties, has against "classical," that is, Freudian psychoanalysis? The new, updated theoretical paradigm on the marketplace is invariably the digital model. It is in the name of breaking this momentum to abstraction, occultation, sublimation, or becoming-digital that Deleuze/Guattari redirect philosophy into a phenomenology of the zero-points of abstraction, signification, and ontological hierarchy: the experiences of the "Body without Organs," the rush of heroin intoxication, the masochist's utter submission to intensity. As we shall see before this is all over, the mutual trumping of analog by digital and vice versa is a basic dynamic making the contemporary world, whose Prevailing Operating System is resolutely cybernetic, what it is. Even the practice of criticism is impacted by this configuration. When I display a citation, even if to "read it out" in an unexpected or contrapuntal direction, my display is at that moment irreducibly analog. What could be more analog than grounding the discussion of a text in samples of itself? The memorable transformations of close exegesis occur when these text-based printouts veer into a dimension not at all encompassed by the initial, disciplinarily sanctioned, context of review or processing. In this sense, the very customary vacillation between close exegesis and theoretical homily that is the bread and butter of so many contemporary literary and cultural studies, follows the trajectory that the Derridean *brisure* or hinge has in common with Hofstadter's enigmatic "strange loop." It is a dimensional journey fated to inevitable recursion back to the source—but under whose sway thinking and programming "stack" to an unanticipated level of theoretical power.

There is, then, something irreducibly picturesque if not literal about the successive scenes of organization and articulation that Deleuze/Guattari excavate from the Marxian and Freudian imaginaries. *A Thousand Plateaus* is structured by a nonsequential string of decisive thresholds of articulation in the history of civilization. The constants, for Deleuze/Guattari, are rhizomatic networks of expansion and transfer, the tension between molar and molecular organizations, between restricted and what they call "smooth" movements. The constants are *not* core concepts in the "history of ideas." Deleuze/Guattari remember 1227 AD as the highpoint of nomadic terror, enabling the Mongolians, in keeping with the loosest, most portable, and most improvisational administrative apparatus imaginable, to overrun the sturdiest and most stable infrastructure and opposition that Western feudalism could marshal in its defense. Out of Deleuze/Guattari's recapitulation of unmotivated, raw nomadic aggression emerge the parameters of what they term the War Machine, the dissolution of a social order into a state they would, drawing on

Spinoza and Bergson, term "becoming-war," an all out devolution into raw collective force. To Deleuze/Guattari, 586 BC, the date of the destruction of the first Hebrew temple, itself a "barbarian" takeover, coincides with the emergence of full-fledged semiosis, an embedded cultural language system with fully operative symbolic networks and grammar. What is primary to Deleuze/ Guattari is the accumulation of desire, the distribution of intensities, the disintegrative torque on organizations issuing simultaneously from the center and the periphery. In 586 BC, these volatile force fields configure themselves into hitherto unattained strata of grammatical complexity; as of 1227 AD, these seismic conflicts become iterated within those "smooth spaces" identified since as the planet's decisive battlefields, from the Central Asia of the Great Game to the Russia of the Napoleonic wars and World War II, to cyberspace today. In a notable passage, Deleuze/Guattari find a playful analogon to the War Machine in the function of the stones in the game of Go, particularly over and against the precise, hierarchical, proto-industrial division of labor between the pieces on the chessboard.

> Chess is a game of the State, or of the court; the emperor of China played it. Chess pieces are coded; they have an internal nature and intrinsic properties from which their movements, situations, and confrontations evolve. They have qualities . . . Each is like a subject of the statement endowed with a relative power, and these relative powers combine in a subject of enunciation . . . Go pieces, in contrast, are pellets, disks, simple arithmetic units, and have only an anonymous, collective, or third-person function: "It" makes a move. "It" could be a man, a woman, a louse, or an elephant. Go pieces are elements of a nonsubjectified machine assembly with no intrinsic properties, only situational ones . . . All by itself a Go piece can destroy a constellation synchronically. A chess piece cannot.[16]

It cannot be entirely coincidental that Hofstadter, who drew the contemporary fashions of the 1970s as illustrative examples into his first Computer Science primer whenever possible, the game of chess furnished a concrete example both of "working inside a system and simultaneously thinking about what [one] is doing."[17] He recounts his admiration for the weakest chess-playing program he tried out in an early computer chess tournament, because as opposed to more competitive models, it knew early on when to resign from the game. Deleuze/ Guattari's instruction manual to Go, on the other hand, is indicative of why Hofstadter devoted minute attention to Zen kōans in *Gödel, Escher, Bach*. The kōans, for Hofstadter as in actual meditative practice, are miniature machines, arranged by order of complexity, of double-bind logic. When a computer program, grounded in elaborate strings of numbers and encompassing a complex menu of prompts and commands, runs into a double bind, it ups its processing power. It has managed to "step out of itself." As suggested in the above citation, the addition of a single Go stone, through its nonidentity and indifference, can upset an elaborate dialectical balance of power. In Derrida-talk, Zen kōans are precise tropings or figurations of aporia; to Deleuze/Guattari, they set into play the schizzes that are a far more apt byproduct of capitalism than Freudian neuroses. They write, in *Anti-Oedipus*, "Our society produces schizos the same way it produces Prell shampoo or Ford cars, the only difference being that the schizos are not saleable."[18] Indeed, Deleuze/Guattari, in their project of ramping down Western speculative philosophy so that it might once again accommodate its immanent, corporeal, and nonabstract underpinnings, advance the supplanting of psychoanalysis by a schizoanalytic purview setting out from the double messages systematically issued by capitalism and Oedipal family politics.

Let the pitched contrast between classical psychoanalysis and what Deleuze/Guattari introduce as "schizoanalysis" serve as our introduction to their pivotal role within a corpus of contemporary critical theory in many respects *avant la machine* if not exactly *avant la lettre*.

Take psychoanalysis as an example again: it subjects the unconscious to arborescent structures, hierarchical graphs, recapitulatory memories, central organs, the phallus, the phallus tree—not only in its theory but also in its practice of calculation and treatment. Psychoanalysis cannot change its method in this regard: it bases its own dictatorial power upon a dictatorial occupation of the unconscious. Psychoanalysis's margin of maneuverability is therefore very limited. In both psychoanalysis and its object, there is always a general, always a leader (General Freud). Schizoanalysis, on the other hand, treats the unconscious as an acentered system, in other words, as a machinic network of finite automata (a rhizome), and this arrives at an entirely different state of the unconscious. These same remarks apply to linguistics.[19]

The task of schizoanalysis is that of a tirelessly taking apart of egos and their presuppositions: liberating the interpersonal singularities they enclose and repress; mobilizing the flows they would be capable of transmitting, receiving, or intercepting; establishing always further and more sharply the schizzes and the breaks well below conditions of identity; and assembling the desiring machines that countersect groups and group everyone with others. For

everyone is a little group (*un groupuscule*) and must live as such—or rather the
Zen tea box broken in a hundred places, whose every crack is repaired with
cement made of gold, or like the church tile whose every fissure is accentuated
by the layers of paint or lime covering it (the contrary of castration, which is
unified, molarized, hidden, scarred, unproductive). Schizoanalysis is so named
because throughout its entire process of treatment, it schizophrenizes, instead
of neuroticizing like psychoanalysis.[20]

What is perhaps most striking about Deleuze/Guattari's accomplishment—
and when we remember critics and theorists it is always by dint of their *impossible* feats of articulation—is that the pivotal scenes of writing that they configure
have a tangible feel to them, the feel of abstract systems rendered in virtual
space. One of Deleuze/Guarrari's favorite terms for these stage trappings is
assemblages, a term they derive from the French translation of Marx, and the
one I am about to cite derives from that crystallizing moment of linguistic
hierarchy that Deleuze/Guattari attribute to the Hebrews' first transformation
into an exilic culture, one whose relations of power and ownership had to be
schematized:

> We are not suggesting an evolutionism, we are not even doing history. Semiotic
> systems depend on assemblages, and it is assemblages that determine that a
> given people, period, or language, and even a given style, fashion, pathology,
> or miniscule event in a limited situation, can assure the predominance of one
> semiotic or another. We are trying to make maps of regimes of signs: we can
> turn them around or retain selected coordinates or dimensions, or depending
> on the case we will be dealing with a social formation, a pathological delusion
> (*délire*), a historical event, etc. We will see this on another occasion, when we
> deal with a dated social system, "courtly love," and then switch to a private
> enterprise, masochism.[21]

The year 586 BC ushers in a civilization under "regimes of signs." The notion
of a political hegemony wrought by schemas of syntax and semantics is not only
nonintuitive but also highly abstract, yet in the citation immediately above,
Deleuze/Guattari graphically represent the *assemblages* on which semiotic systems, as later will systems of capital, depend. This insistence on the *graphic
intensity* of a space of systematic coherence and dispersion is even at play in
10,000 BC, a date before the emergence of any "full-service civilization," when
all there is the circulation of people, energies, and intensities themselves, the
occupation and subsequent defense of "territorialities." "10,000 BC," then, is a
condition of force, movement, and schematics *an Sich*, as it were, for their own

sakes. Its depiction is no less graphic than that of the formation of "regimes of signs":

> Territorialities, then, are shot through with lines of flight testifying to the presence within them of movements of deterritorialization and reterritorialization. In a certain sense, *they* [my emphasis] are secondary. They would be nothing without these movements that deposit them. In short, the epistrata and parastrata are continually moving, sliding, shifting, and changing on the Ecumenon or unity of composition of a stratum; some are swept away by lines of flight and movements of deterritorialization, others by processes of decoding or drift, but they all communicate at the intersection of the milieus.[22]

The fact that few of us are likely to have a clear picture of what Deleuze/Guattari mean by such terms as "lines of flight," "parastrata," or "Ecumenon" in no way disqualifies this passage from demarcating the virtual environment of certain of the shifts and flows that philosophy and social science tend to exclude when keyed to such "higher-level" values as "pure reason" or "the phenomenology of mind." The uneasy feeling that such a passage may give readers, as if they have been just been party to a long tirade in schizophrenic "word salad," is not entirely divorced from Deleuze/Guattari's design. The performative dimension of the discourse of the "Capitalism and Schizophrenia" diptych (*A Thousand Plateaus* with *The Anti-Oedipus*) is precisely hijacking the reader into the midst of a defamiliarized philosophical war zone, where s/he is free to radically reconsider everything s/he holds near and dear about philosophy. The parallel Lacanian performance, especially in the *Seminars*, is to supplant psychoanalysis' traditionally stilted rhetoric and analytical imperative with the spontaneously offhanded indirection of the therapeutic session.

Just as Deleuze/Guattari's exemplary heroin-takers want it "cool . . . and cooler," the overall drift of their philosophical investigations is, following Alice, "down, down." Devolving philosophy back to its foundations in inarticulation, transporting the reader to the virtual scenes of civilization's organization and dissolution, is not merely in the name of perversity. It involves discourse perforce in the play between upper-level and lower-level processing, between digital and analog organizations, which is the sine qua non of cybernetic operations. Frankly, nothing could be more mystifying and off-putting than some of the terms that Deleuze/Guattari deploy within this project. But when the same interactions are elaborated by one of the visionary avatars of Computer Science, unidirectional philosophy's need to bring itself around makes much more sense. What follows is Hofstadter's scenario for a humanity landlocked within the intrinsic compulsions of its abstraction

> A dog does not imagine or understand that certain large arrays of colored dots can be so structured that they are no longer just huge sets of colored dots but become pictures of people, houses, dogs, and many other things. The higher level takes perceptual precedence over the lower level, and in the process becomes the "more real" of the two. The lower level gets forgotten, lost in the shuffle.

> Such an upwards-level shift is a profound perceptual change, and when it takes place in an unfamiliar, abstract setting, such as the world of strings of *Principia Mathematica*, it can sound very improbable, even though when it takes place in a familiar setting (such as a TV screen), it is trivially obvious . . .

> Your typical human brain, being blissfully ignorant of its minute physical components and their arcanely mathematizable mode of microscopic functioning, and thriving instead at the infinitely remote level of soap operas, spring sales, super skivaganzas, SUV's, SAT's, SOB's, Santa Claus, splashtacular specials, snorkels, snowballs, sex scandals (and let's not forget sleazeballs), makes up as plausible a story as it can about its own nature, in which the starring role, rather than being played, by the cerebral cortex, the hippocampus, the amygdala, the cerebellum, or any other weirdly named and gooey physical structure, is played instead by an anatomically invisible, murky thing called "I," aided and abetted by other shadowy players knows as "ideas," "thoughts," "memories," "beliefs," "hopes," "fears," "intentions," "desires," "love," "hate," "rivalry," "jealousy," "empathy," "honesty," and on and on—and in the soft, ethereal, neurology-free world of *these* players, your typical human brain perceives its very own "I" as a pusher and a mover, never entertaining for a moment the idea that its star player might merely be a useful shorthand standing for an myriad of infinitesimal entities . . . every single second.[23]

In this passage Hofstadter negotiates the seam between brains and selves. Subjectivity, for him, is an unavoidable illusion akin to the "marble" he discovers in a stack of envelopes[24] because of multiple levels of interpretation attending the sense of touch. The brain is the physiochemical platform for processes endowed with subjectivity and agency when it is a matter of the social interactions negotiated by selves. Hofstadter *performs* the primarily physical or material underpinnings to thinking furnished by the brain through a homonymic concatenation of the kinds of signifiers that the brain stores and processes: "SUV's, SAT's, SOB's, Santa Claus, splashtacular specials, snorkels, snowballs, sex scandals (and let's not forget sleazeballs)." On the lower level of processing, such as the colored dots that dogs see instead of images, these words are defined by the "s-sounds" that is the basis for their affinity. On a much higher level of cognitive function, it is a joke that such a series of arbitrary terms is possessed of any common denominator whatsoever, even the sonorous one furnished by the "esses."

In a way very much conditioned by Hofstadter's distinction between the brain and the "self-symbol," Deleuze/Guattari send their own running tab on desire, the fetish, and flow under capitalism into a precipitous "downward-level shift." This takes place in the very *drift* of their critical allegory.

The BwO is what remains when you take everything else away. What you take away is precisely the phantasy, and significances and subjectifications as a whole. Psychoanalysis does the opposite: it translates everything into phantasies, it converts everything into phantasy, it retains the phantasy. It royally botches the real, because it botches the BwO.[25]

A BwO is made in such a way that it can be occupied, populated only by intensities. Only intensities pass and circulate . . . The BwO causes intensities to pass; it produces and distributes them in a *spatium* that that is itself intensive, lacking extension. It is not space, nor is it in space; it is matter that occupies space to a given degree . . . Matter equals energy. Production of the real as a relative magnitude beginning at zero . . .

After all, is not Spinoza's Ethics the great book of the BwO? . . . The masochist body as an attribute or genus of substance, with its production of intensities and pain modes based on its degree 0 of being sewn up. The drugged body is a different attribute, with its production of specific intensities based on Absolute cold = 0 . . . A junky does not want to be warm, he wants to be cool-cooler-COLD . . . Drug users, masochists, schizophrenics, lovers—all BwO's pay homage to Spinoza. The BwO is the field of immanence of desire, the plane of consistency specific to desire (with desire defined as a process of production without reference to any exterior agency, whether it be a lack that hollows it out or a pleasure that fills it).[26]

In such passages as the above, Deleuze/Guattari drive philosophy toward an early contemporary acknowledgment that in spite of what might be called its "intrinsic will toward digital syntax and open-ended rhizomes of signification," it remains rooted in a substratum of analog relations as well. The human, such as it exists for Anthony Wilden, is precisely an interdependent marshalling and coordination *between* analog and digital organizations. At the dawn of the digital age, Deleuze/Guattari issue a *stark* reminder regarding the indispensability of *threshold* sensation, perception, and articulation.

Sub-syllabic deconstructive "dots"

Sperm, saliva, glair, curdled drool, tears of milk, gel of vomit—all these heavy and white substances are going to glide into each other, be agglutinated, agglomerated, stretched out *(on)to the edge* of all the fixtures and pass through all the canals.

The word *"glaviaux"* ["globs"] will not be uttered until later, after invisible assimilation and deglutition, after elaboration, agglutinated to *"glaïeul"* ["gladiolus"].

But even before being presented in the text and blooming there right next to the flower, the word animates with its energetic and encircled absence the description of spit.[27]

gl tears the "body," "sex," "voice" and "writing from the logic of consciousness and representation that guided these debates. While ever remaining a bit-effect (a death-effect) [*effet de mors*] among others, gl remarks in itself as well—whence the transcendental effect, always, of taking part—the angular slash [*coupure*] of the opposition, the differential schiz *and* the flowing [*coulant*] continuum of the couple, the distinction *and* the copulating unity (one example, of the arbitrary and the motivated). It is one of, only one but as a party to, the de-terminant sluices, open closed to a rereading of the *Cratylus* . . .

It is not a word—gl hoists the tongue but does not hold it and always lets the tongue fall back, does not belong to it—even less a name, and hardly a *pro-prénom*, a proper (before the first) name.[28]

Now invoking Derrida at the place where the *gl*-glottal performs a mix of sexual, aggressive, and corporeal, and even poetic violence may not be the most seemly place for making this appeal to his thinking and his work. In these citations, we witness *gl*, in French, as it runs the gamut from ejaculation, cum, and oral sex to nausea and vomit, to glove and sword. Yet Derrida's holding to this sub-semantic letter combo, which by its very nature cannot *mean* very much, as the pivot of his double reading in *Glas*, both undermining the sanctity of Hegel's mainstream morality and restoring a nobility to Genet's vision initially eluding the reader's glance is very much in the drift of Deleuze/Guattari's gravitation to cognitive processing as performed by the masochist, the drug addict, and the BwO. And this communications loop between the very highest confections of idealist philosophy (to Derrida, Cratylism is perfectly amenable to his bottom-up approach to Genet) and putatively *pure* reason is cybernetic, or at least proto-cybernetic, to the core.

Glas is in many senses a special case, even in the radically improvisational corpus of Derrida's work. In no other of his productions is the very *design* of a book (placing Hegel and Genet in bi-columnar supplementary opposition), the pivotal position of a speech element that doesn't even turn out to be a trope or a figure. There are other instances where a single signifier, such as the concatenation of *coups* or hits in perhaps the pivotal passage explaining/performing the *pharmakon* in "Plato's Pharmacy," manages all by itself to bring down a sacrosanct edifice of entrenched Western values. And a second telling counterinstance to *gl*, in the Mallarmé gloss of "The Double Session," would be the *hymen* as a kind of extreme in the resonation that the weaving of textual fabric attains. Derrida's hymen adventure marks the rather abrupt limit of a certain sexual politics in his work. (He, like all of us was a time-travelling *bricoleur*, working with the materials that drifted in and out of hand.) Yet at stake in neither of the virtuoso performances of "Plato's Pharmacy" or "The Double Session" was the architectural configuration of a double message structuring an entire metaphysical regime. In no other critico-philosophical performance did the architecture of a book—Hegel column facing Genet column with strategic crumbling and reversals of this infrastructure at telling points in the feedback—simulate what was at stake on the profoundest level of ideological, moral, and sexual politics—and in emergent cybernetic technology.

Derrida's glottal (or glassal) performance in *Glas* was at all times disciplined and measured. He surely took issue with the drugged-out bravado of Deleuze/Guattari's alternate-culture posturing, as with the *literality* seeming to overrun their discourse—whether pertaining to philosophical positions and places or to the body itself. And yet it is in *Glas*, where gl "would band erect the transcendental accomplice of skzz,"[29] where Derrida makes one of his most direct allusions to their project. Derrida is very much by Deleuze/Guattari's side in effecting a cybernetic mutual processing of philosophy at the high end by philosophy, semiotics, and literary criticism at the low end. The double columns of *Glas* are the literal imprint of the interface between unprocessed sub-molecular particles and tachyons and the most sophisticated concepts that theory can synthesize. As computers, in their inner workings, have been explicated by Hofstadter and other savvy readers, the interplay between both processors, the high-end and the low-end, is absolutely critical to opening of systematic escape routes and to keeping intellectual fabrication honest. Hence the considerable insistence that Derrida places, for example, in "Limited Inc . . . abc," on conceptual specificity in the conceptual recalibration of cultural artifacts.

This is all in the interest of dissecting and counteracting the double binds to which all systematic organizations give rise. Double messages are the very idiom of systems: corporate ones, academic ones, familial ones, political ones. Systems speak only in double messages. Gregory Bateson, in his *Steps to an Ecology of Mind*, was the modern-day prophet of the insanity that results when the exit routes, the "lines of flight" delivering us from the extractive double-bind logic of systems, get closed off. It is on this "plane of consistency" where an intricate deconstructive reading by Derrida, a Zen kōan invoked by Hofstadter in explanation of computers, a terrific conversation with a counselor or friend abiding by the conduct of personal conversation, an excursion of discovery to an art museum, and a sonnet or a comedy-routine composed by a brilliant fifteen-year old in Houston, Texas, show common cause. This is a political as well as conceptual statement. Such events simultaneously occupy a shared positionality both within and outside the Prevailing Operating System. Each one of these random cultural epiphenomena configures an irreducibly *critical* readout: building up, on the analog side, toward meaning and on the digital flank toward signification. The cumulative impact of such ambient "culture events" in profusion upon the prevailing subsystems of governance, administration, education, and cultural preservation is the opening of a salutary "point of incompletion." The upgrading and rebooting of software defining the public sphere begins precisely at this point. It is in the very lacunae surfacing without anticipation in established protocols of critico-aesthetic conduct where new generations of sociocultural programming take off.

Inextinguishable "simmballs" and virtual performers—these parameters determine the afterlife of critics in our own vertiginous but also limited age. Each one of us configures the lifetime rhizome of our own most luminous critics; each one of us the librarian to her private "Library of Babel."

Notes

1   Douglas Hofstadter, *I Am a Strange Loop* (New York: Basic Books, 2007), 258.
2   Ibid., 234.
3   Ibid., 248.

4 Ibid., 276.

5 To access a virtual notion of mythology, one in full keeping with twentieth-century literary and cultural updating of classical myths, all one need do is to glean the sense that Roland Barthes imparts to "Mythologies," the concluding segment to the early collection of the same title. The moratorium on linguistic free play that Barthes pursues within his contemporary mythological examples is by no means dissonant with the hyperreality and absorptive fixation prevailing within virtual environments. See Roland Barthes, *Mythologies,* trans. Annette Lavers (London: Vintage Classics, 2009).

6 Jacques Derrida, *Writing and Difference,* trans. Alan Bass (Chicago: University of Chicago Press, 1978), 207.

7 Ibid., 229.

8 Hofstadter, *I Am a Strange Loop,* 230.

9 Douglas R. Hofstadter, *Gödel, Escher, Bach: An Eternal Golden Braid* (New York: Vintage Books, 1980), 473–74.

10 Maurice Blanchot, *The Gaze of Orpheus: And Other Literary Essays* (Barrytown: Station Hill Press, 1981), 106.

11 Franz Kafka, *The Complete Short Stories of Franz Kafka,* ed. Nahum N. Glatzer (New York: Schocken Books, 1995), 431.

12 J. Hillis Miller, *Literature as Conduct Speech Acts in Henry James* (New York: Fordham University Press, 2005), 169.

13 See J. Hillis Miller and Manuel Asensi, *Black Holes: J. Hillis Miller; or Boustrophedonic Reading* (Stanford: Stanford University Press, 1999); also see J. Hillis Miller, *Communities in Fiction* (New York: Fordham University Press, 2015).

14 Maurice Blanchot, *The Space of Literature: A Translation of "L'Espace litteraire,"* trans. Ann Smock (Lincoln: University of Nebraska Press, 1989), 93.

15 Ibid., 88.

16 Gilles Deleuze and Félix Guattari, *A Thousand Plateaus: Capitalism and Schizophrenia,* trans. Brian Massumi (Minneapolis: University of Minnesota Press, 1987), 352–353.

17 Hofstadter, *Gödel, Escher, Bach,* 38.

18 Gilles Deleuze and Félix Guattari, *Anti-Oedipus: Capitalism and Schizophrenia,* trans. Robert Hurley, Mark Seem, and Helen R. Lane (Minneapolis: University of Minnesota Press, 1983), 245.

19 Deleuze and Guattari, *A Thousand Plateaus,* 17–18.

20 Deleuze and Guattari, *Anti-Oedipus,* 362.

21 Deleuze and Guattari, *A Thousand Plateaus,* 119.

22 Ibid., 55.

23 Hofstadter, *I Am a Strange Loop,* 202–203.

24	Hofstadter, *I Am a Strange Loop*, 92–95.
25	Deleuze and Guattari, *A Thousand Plateaus*, 151.
26	Ibid., 153–154.
27	Jacques Derrida, *Glas*, trans. John P. Leavey Jr. and Richard Rand (Lincoln: University of Nebraska Press, 1986), 139b–140b.
28	Ibid., 235–236b.
29	Ibid., 234b.

Works cited

Barthes, Roland. *Mythologies*. Trans. Annette Lavers. London: Vintage Classics, 2009.
Blanchot, Maurice. *The Gaze of Orpheus: And Other Literary Essays*. Barrytown: Station Hill Press, 1981.
Blanchot, Maurice. *The Space of Literature: A Translation of "L'Espace litteraire."* Trans. Ann Smock. Lincoln: University of Nebraska Press, 1989.
Deleuze, Gilles, and Félix Guattari. *Anti-Oedipus: Capitalism and Schizophrenia*. Trans. Robert Hurley, Mark Seem, and Helen R. Lane. Minneapolis: University of Minnesota Press, 1983.
Deleuze, Gilles, and Félix Guattari. *A Thousand Plateaus: Capitalism and Schizophrenia*. Trans. Brian Massumi. Minneapolis: University of Minnesota Press, 1987.
Derrida, Jacques. *Glas*. Trans. John P. Leavey Jr. and Richard Rand. Lincoln: University of Nebraska Press, 1986.
Derrida, Jacques. *Writing and Difference*. Trans. Alan Bass. Chicago: University of Chicago Press, 1978.
Hofstadter, Douglas R. *Gödel, Escher, Bach: An Eternal Golden Braid*. New York: Vintage Books, 1980.
Hofstadter, Douglas R. *I Am a Strange Loop*. New York: Basic Books, 2007.
Kafka, Franz. *The Complete Short Stories of Franz Kafka*. Ed. Nahum N. Glatzer. New York: Schocken Books, 1995.
Miller, J. Hillis. *Communities in Fiction*. New York: Fordham University Press, 2015.
Miller, J. Hillis. *Literature as Conduct: Speech Acts in Henry James*. New York: Fordham University Press, 2005.
Miller, J. Hillis, and Manuel Asensi. *Black Holes: J. Hillis Miller; or Boustrophedonic Reading*. Stanford: Stanford University Press, 1999.

Part Two

Derrida, Death, Theory

4

Thanatographies of the Future:
Freud, Derrida, Kant

Jean-Michel Rabaté

Freud's systematic confrontation with death took place after the great War, in 1920, when he wrote *Beyond the Pleasure Principle,* a book in which he begins by exploring notions of repetition, of pleasure, and of reality taken as three fundamental principles. In chapter five only do we see Freud generalizing and moving from the compulsion to repeat to the "natural" tendency he finds everywhere, a tendency to return to a previous state of things, in other words, to a principle of entropy. Life would just be a detour, a "circuitous path" along a return to inorganic matter from which it has come. This could then be rephrased via the old motto: "The aim of all life is death."[1] A whole page develops this idea, with the striking image of the "guardians of life" who helped the organism strive for survival then, transformed into the "myrmidons of death."[2]

When Derrida comments on Freud's text in the *Postcard,* he makes at this point a detour via Heidegger, arguing that *Beyond the Pleasure Principle* and *Sein und Zeit* have a similar program: "When Freud speaks of *Todestrieb, Todesziel, Umwege zum Tode,* and even of an *"eigenen Todesweg des Organismus,"* he is indeed pronouncing the law of life-death as the law of the proper. Life *and* death are opposed only in order to serve it. Beyond all oppositions, without any possible identification or synthesis, it is indeed a question of an *economy* of death, of a law of the proper (*oikos, oikonomia*), which governs the detour and indefatigably seeks the proper event, its own, proper propriation (*Ereignis)* rather than life *and* death."[3] Derrida has perceived something crucial here, although I believe that this conflation of Heidegger and Freud is misleading. Moreover, he is not paying attention to the text's rhetorical progression. Above all, he bypasses the fact that those pages state a thesis that Freud will then reject.

However, once Freud has reached this point in his argument, he turns around and exclaims: "It cannot be so."[4] This is the complex movement fraught with detours and contradictions that takes us from the end of chapter V to chapter VI, in which Freud multiplies aporias and counterexamples. And this is the moment when he introduces the death drive, although it is at first almost surreptitiously. We find the phrase in a parenthesis in the original text: "The opposition between the ego or death instincts and the sexual or life instincts would then cease to hold."[5] The previous collapsing of the two sides is not allowed any longer. Hence this surprising assertion, "Let us turn back, then, to one of the assumptions that we have already made, with the exception that we shall be able to give it a categorical denial."[6] The assumption that he is attacking from now on is the theme of life and nature moving inexorably to death. We tend to think that we are all destined to die from internal causes and that there is nothing to do about it. Here we find the trope of *"c'est la vie"* proffered when we hear of someone's sad but anticipated death. Such a thought is debunked by Freud who reasons by saying that this idea, illustrated by countless poets, is in fact a simple comfort: "Perhaps we have adopted the belief because there is some comfort in it. If we are to die ourselves, and first to lose in death those who are dearest to us, it is easier to submit to a remorseless law of nature."[7] In short, Freud is telling us in no uncertain terms that if universal entropy can be construed as a "law of Nature," there is no reason to believe that we have voted it, to paraphrase Joyce's quip in *Exiles*.[8]

In an effort to test the validity of this widespread belief about the inescapability of death, Freud comes to a surprising conclusion. Following Weissmann, Freud reopens the biological debate and contrasts the dying cells of any organism with an undying germ-plasm. Death has therefore become less "natural" since it is a late acquisition of organisms; Freud quotes the findings of Woodruff who had shown that infusorians can, if placed in a refreshed environment that nourishes them, reproduce themselves by fission for more than 30,000 generations.[9] The focus of the discussion then becomes that of "senescence" versus "rejuvenation." Besides, in cases when the solution has not been renewed and a certain degeneration can be observed, this process can be reversed when two animalculae blend together; then they achieve an instant regeneration and avoid the degeneration that leads to death. It is in the context of such speculations that Freud asserts forcibly that he believes in a dualism of the drives, a principle that is constructive (*aufbauend*) and a principle that is "de-structive" or "deconstructive" (*abbauend*).[10]

In an earlier passage, Derrida objected to such a translation; he criticizes the eagerness of those who retroactively import "deconstructive" themes in translations of Marx and Nietzsche. Nevertheless, he grudgingly accepts that one engages in such a project, albeit with some ambivalence: "If one were to translate *abbauen* as 'to deconstruct' in *Beyond* . . . perhaps one would get a glimpse of a necessary place of articulation between what is involved in the form of an athetic writing and what has interested me up to now under the heading of deconstruction."[11]

In these introductory pages to a long and detailed reading of Freud's *Beyond the Pleasure Principle* (Freud's text is less than 80 pages whereas Derrida's commentary is more than 150 pages long), Derrida discusses Freud's debts to philosophy, insisting rather on his denial of any debt. Derrida lists Schopenhauer and Nietzsche above all, noting indeed the curious fact that as soon as Freud seems to agree with Schopenhauer, he takes his "bold step forward." Derrida even quotes the text in German[12] before describing Freud's strategy in startling terms: it does not come back to itself in a Hegelian manner, it does not follow a hermeneutic circle but it progresses according to a series of detours: "It constructs-deconstructs itself according to an interminable detour (*Umweg*): that it describes 'itself,' writes and unwrites."[13] This entails that theses such as "death is the result or end of life" cannot be ascribed to Freud just like that. Neither can the Nietzschean tag of the "eternal recurrence of the same" apply to Freudian metapsychology. Freud even turns into the devil, or at least he is the "devil's advocate," and this devilish turn explains his constant shifting between theory and autobiographical writing.[14]

However, a hundred pages later, Derrida seems to have forgotten the methodological prudence displayed at the beginning. When he reaches the same passage at the end of his commentary, Derrida all too quickly identifies Freud both with Schopenhauer and with Heidegger, perhaps because he was afraid that the equation between a Freudian deconstruction (*Abbau*) and the death drive would carry negative connotations, perhaps because he is simply too eager to superpose Freud and Heidegger. However, as we may guess, an equation between "deconstruction" and death would not bother Freud in the least.

Indeed, at this point of his "speculation," Freud realizes that he has come too close to the dualistic theory of Schopenhauer, whose philosophy, before that of Heidegger, presents death as the purpose of human life. Schopenhauer's concept of the "will" embodies an unconscious sexual instinct that is on the side of life.[15] We have to read Freud with great care: "We have unwittingly (*unversehens*, which means both 'unexpectedly' and 'without being fully aware') steered our course into the harbour of Schopenhauer's philosophy."[16] This suggests that one should not want to remain in this safe but dead end: "Let us make a bold attempt at another step forward."[17] This "bolder" step is to assume that libido or love can "rejuvenate" certain cells, while noting that too much narcissism (seen here as the opposite of love for another being) will lead to death in some cases, as witnessed by the uncontrolled reduplication of cells we find in cancer: cancer offers the paradox of a disease brought about by a refusal to die, which thus destroys the organism. We now understand better why the ego-drive can be equated with death, while the sexual drive can be equated with a life-giving force. This is clearer in the original: "*Wir sind ja vielmehr von einer scharfen Scheidung zwischen Ichtrieben = Todestrieben und Sexualtrieben = Lebenstrieben ausgegangen.*"[18] In the analysis that follows, Freud is not saying that more love could cure cancer, but he is not that far from such a thought. The couple of ego-drive and death-drive is opposed to the second couple of sexual drive and life. If we can identify here the seeds of the dualism of Eros versus Thanatos, we may note—a point that will not be lost on Lacan—that it is the Ego that is placed on the side of Thanatos.

Following Lacan's central intuitions about the death drive, Slavoj Žižek has expressed clearly the paradoxical nature of Freud's thought. He returns to Lacan's main thesis that the death drive provides the general form for all drives. Here, Žižek uses the example of Wagner's Flying Dutchman to make a point that rings very close to the position taken by Adorno on the death drive: "Where is the death drive here? It precisely does not lie in their longing to die, to find peace in death: the death drive, on the contrary, is *the very opposite of dying*, it is a name for the 'undead' eternal life itself, for the horrible fate of being caught in the endless repetitive cycle of wandering around in guilt and pain."[19] A Wagnerian hero like Tristan is presented as being caught up in the same structure: in act III, Tristan does not despair because of his fear of dying but because of his fear of losing Isolde: "what makes him so desperate is the fact that, without Isolde, he *cannot die* and is condemned to eternal longing—he anxiously awaits her arrival so that he can die. The prospect he dreads is not that of dying without Isolde (the standard complaint of a lover) but, rather, that of endless life without her."[20] Is this exactly what Freud has in mind in his speculations on death in *Beyond the Pleasure Principle?* His thinking has become so tentative and paradoxical at the end of the essay that it is hard to assume a linear development of a thesis, but while agreeing with Žižek's forceful reading, I would add here that Freud posit on top of his metapsychology geared to enhance the power of love another level in the dialectics by opposing "obsolescence" and "juvenescence." He trusts "juvenescence" fully, even though he may still look to Derrida as a "granddaddy," and in this sense agrees with Adorno's refusal to admit that the fate of individuals is bounded by an absolute Death that has replaced an absolute God.

The word "juvenescence" was creatively renewed when abbreviated as "juvescence" by T. S. Eliot in his famous poem "Gerontion": "In the juvescence of the year / Came Christ the tiger."[21] Freud might not have allowed himself to be devoured whole by such a tiger. Undoubtedly, he would have preferred the ending of another poem: "I should be glad of another death" ("The Magi"), but he would have formulated it as: "I would be glad of another theory of death." This is what Freud attempted to do in *Beyond the Pleasure Principle*. A good illustration of the lasting impact of his speculative forays of the 1920s is given by a letter that Freud wrote in December 1938 to the novelist Rachel Berdach, who had just sent him a novel. Freud thanked her and wrote, "Your mysterious and beautiful book [*The Emperor, the Sages and Death*] has pleased me to an extent that makes me unsure of my judgment. I wonder whether it is the transformation of Jewish suffering or surprise that so much psychoanalytical insight should have existed at the court of the brilliant and despotic Staufer which makes me say that I haven't read anything so substantial and poetically accomplished for a long time . . . Who are you? Where did you acquire all the knowledge expressed in your book? Judging by the priority you grant to death, one is led to conclude that you are very young."[22] How could Freud deduce that Rachel Berdach was young just because she saw death everywhere? We tend to see young people totally oblivious of death and mortality. Not Freud. This baffles Max Schur when he mentions this letter.[23] In fact, we know that Berdach was not so young at the time, but she confessed that she had written this historical novel when she was quite young and had just lost a dear friend. However, the answer to the question is given by the conclusions of *Beyond the Pleasure Principle*. According to Freud, very early on, we need to give ourselves the comforting thought that death is due to a sad but common fate, an *anangke* against which nothing can be done. A young person will emphasize death as the ultimate truth of life, preferring to steel her heart in advance against future losses. An older man who has less to lose and everything to gain by betting on science and sexuality held firmly together will be less tempted to take death as an absolute end.

It is in this context that one can understand Freud's decision to be treated for a Steinach operation that would "rejuvenate" him. In November 1924, Freud had a vasectomy performed that would leave him "rejuvenated," which was the term used by Steinach who promoted this as a male-enhancement surgery. What would make older people younger was an infusion of homegrown male hormones. This same simple vasoligation was performed on Yeats in 1936, after which he reported an increased vitality in his sexual life and poetic creativity. Freud was less enthusiastic, although he felt that the operation had brought about a respite from his cancer. Harry Benjamin, a disciple of Steinach, asserted that he had heard from Freud that the operation had achieved its aim.[24] This would tend to show, first, that Freud trusted the then budding science of endocrinology, and also that he saw in the new interventionist medicine tools for a possible reversal of the ageing process. It is quite likely that this belief had informed his attitude facing the "future" when discussing religion in 1927.

There would be a future to be thought of as a categorical imperative, but curiously such a transcendental can only be reached via death. Death is a *via negativa* leading to this a priori of the future. By saying "No Future," we can be truly ready for the future. We cannot give any content to the future: it should remain a pure form. Here we see a curious alliance between Freud and Kant. Freud had mentioned Kant in his 1913 introduction to *Totem and Taboo*: "taboo still exists in our midst. To be sure, it is negatively conceived and directed to different contents, but according to its psychological nature, it is still nothing else than Kant's 'Categorical Imperative' which tends to act compulsively and rejects all conscious motivation."[25] In 1920, Freud adds a decisive complement to Kant's theory that time and space are "necessary forms of thought" when he includes the timelessness of the Unconscious into the process.[26] And we know that the latest notes that Freud took contained an attempt at distinguishing his metapsychology from Kant's system: "Space may be the projection of the extension of the psychical apparatus. No other derivation is probable. Instead of Kant's a priori determinants of our psychical apparatus. Psyche is extended; knows nothing of it."[27] In the same way that it does not know that it exists in space, our psychical apparatus knows nothing about death, since it steadily but mistakenly believes in its own immortality. A consideration of death is thus a good spot to try and think both a priori conditions of human psyches and the general question of the future.

I use this bridge toward Kantian philosophy to move on to Kant's considerations of the future. I start from a text written not by Kant, but by a disciple who spoke in Kant's name as he was responding to an attack on his system, Kraus's review of Ulrich's *Eleutheriology*.[28] Johann August Heinrich Ulrich's *Eleutheriology, or On Freedom and Necessity* (Jena, 1788) was a total refutation of Kant's main tenets. Ulrich, a professor of philosophy at Jena, a disciple of Leibniz, was a proponent of a determinist, rationalist, and scientific philosophy. He denounced what he took to be Kant's contradictions. Kant, he argued, believed in determinism facing an intellectual reason but postulated an absolute freedom facing practical reason, for which freedom is an absolute principle. Ulrich refused the idea that morality should require an absolute freedom for its deployment. What he attacked in Kant were timeless and abstract categories like the "categorical imperative." If freedom remained an ideal, the question should be: how to mediate between absolute categories and the banal demands of experience, in which chance plays a certain role. Kant took some notes and gave them to Kraus, an old friend from Königsberg. Kraus discussed this *Eleuthériologie* and showed that Kant had not bypassed the link between the practical and the theoretical. The question was to reconcile an insight into natural necessity, by nature determined, with the "unconditional spontaneity" of understanding that alone can lead us to the world of morality. Both Kant and Kraus assert that nothing can be known of freedom: it is not an object in the world, but a principle. This enhances the need for principles that are valid for all time. A principle will by definition include the future. Thus freedom and its future have to be defined as absolutely constitutive, exactly as time and space are constitutive of our perception of the empirical world. They reject scientific determinism that finds an ultimate foundation in a vague providence. A future of the future will be Kant's fine line drawn between the unpredictable and the unconditional.

One finds a similar transcendental move in Kant's famous essay on "Perpetual Peace," an essay whose title sounds more like "Eternal peace" than "Perpetual peace," the phrase used by the philosophers who discussed it from Bernardin de Saint Pierre to Rousseau. As Kant reminds us, if we take the expression literally, "perpetual peace" refers to death, which is why the sign appeared, as a joke, in front of a cemetery.[29] The joke soon generates a paradox: while peace is close to entropy and death, any real theory about peace needs to opt for perpetuity or "perennity." The very concept of peace entails a certain idea of sustainability.

We all dream of seeing the world being one day, at last, in peace. Kant's philosophy tries to think the conditions for a lasting peace, a peace not for the next generations, but for all the foreseeable future. He proves that "peace" equals "perpetual peace" by establishing a maxim: "No Treaty of Peace Shall Be Held Valid in Which There Is Tacitly Reserved Matter for a Future War."[30] True peace is not a truce; a peace treaty that would be a truce, the temporary suspension of hostilities while each side is busy rearming, is the opposite of peace. If therefore peace and perpetual peace are synonymous, a transcendental futurity has to be built in the handling of all peace negotiations, in any effort at creating international tribunals, guidelines for adequate treaty-signing, and so on. Kant believed that a representative democracy would establish a state of law among the nations, while entertaining no illusions about man's true nature: human nature is "depraved." Only a rule of law can mitigate the original sin of human propensity to murder. Thus, one should promote hospitality and cosmopolitanism.

The recurrent objection is that all this remains pure theory that can never be applied. The divorce between theory and practice may be the consequence of his attribution to any system of international relations the imperative to assert perpetual peace. Kant has foreseen the objection and deals with it in the essay that attacks the "common saying": "This May be True in Theory, but it does not Apply in Practice." If doctors and lawyers fail because they are good in theory but ignorant of their theories' applications, any amelioration will come from more theory, not less.[31] Kant is here replying to Moses Mendelssohn who denied the idea that humanity could be seen as progressing toward a greater good. Anticipating Walter Benjamin's skepticism facing the myth of progress, Mendelssohn multiplied reasons why humanity seems to be constantly lapsing into barbarism. Kant refuses this thesis, arguing that without a minimal belief in progress, all we have is a world reduced to a bad play. History turns into an old farce, not even a tragedy: "To watch this tragedy for a while might be moving and instructive, but the curtain must eventually fall. For in the long run, it turns into a farce; and even if actors do not tire of it, because they are fools, the spectator does, when one or another act gives him sufficient grounds for gathering that the never-ending play is forever the same."[32] Not blind to the endless succession of wars that have marked the march of humanity, Kant decides to hope for better times. His optimism is not devoid of stoicism or skepticism, yet it ushers in an anthropology that furthers the program of the Enlightenment. It offers hope in spite of all: we have to hope even if is without any ground for hope. If our present can be thought absolutely, it has to be thought from the point of view of the law, and the law inherently contains a future—perhaps not a historical future, but at least the conditions for a future. The law's "Nos," its very prohibitions, its very "death threats" are factors that keep open a future for the future. If the law's main function is to say "No," saying "No" even as in "No Future," this is to provide a transcendental structure that can give access to a future. I more than one sense, then, we are condemned to the future.[33]

Notes

1   Sigmund Freud, *Beyond the Pleasure Principle*, trans. James Strachey (New York, Norton, 1989), 46.

2   Sigmund Freud, *Jenseits des Lustprinzips, Studienausgabe III, Psychologie des Unbewussten* (Frankfurt: Fischer, 1982), 249; and Freud, *Beyond the Pleasure Principle*, 47.

3   Jacques Derrida, *The Postcard: From Socrates to Freud and Beyond*, trans. Alan Bass, (Chicago: University of Chicago Press, 1987), 359.

4   Freud, *Beyond the Pleasure Principle*, 47.

5   Ibid., 53. "*Der Gegensatz von Ich(Todes-)trieben und Sexual(Lebens)trieben würde dann entfalle*n" (Freud, *Jenseits des Lustprinzips*, 253).

6   Freud, *Beyond the Pleasure Principle*, 53; Freud, *Jenseits des Lustprinzips*, 253.

7   Freud, *Beyond the Pleasure Principle*, 53.

8   "Robert (*impatiently*): No man ever lived on this earth who did not long to possess— I mean to possess in the flesh—the woman whom he loves. It is nature's law. Richard (*contemptuously*): What is that to me? Did I vote it?"
     James Joyce, "Exiles," *Poem and Exiles* (London, Penguin, 1992), 190.

9   Freud, *Beyond the Pleasure Principle*, 57.

10 Freud, *Beyond the Pleasure Principle*, 59; Freud, *Jenseits des Lustprinzips*, 258.

11 Derrida, *The Postcard*, 268.

12 Ibid.

13 Ibid., 269.

14 Ibid., 271.

15 Freud, *Beyond the Pleasure Principle*, 59-60.

16 Freud, *Beyond the Pleasure Principle*, 59, Freud, *Jenseits des Lustprinzips*, 259.

17 Freud, *Beyond the Pleasure Principle*, 60.

18 Freud, *Jenseits des Lustprinzips*, 261. "Our argument had as its point of departure a sharp distinction between ego-instincts, which we equated with death-instincts, and sexual instincts, which we equated with life-instincts" (Freud, *Beyond the Pleasure Principle*, 63).

19 Slavoj Žižek, *The Ticklish Subject: The Absent Centre of Political Ontology* (London, Verso, 1999), 352.

20 Ibid.

21 T. S. Eliot, "Gerontion," *The Waste Land and Other Poems* (London, Faber, 1988), 18.

22 Sigmund Freud, *The Letters of Sigmund Freud*, ed. Ernst L. Freud (London, Dover, 1992), 1192.

23 Max Schur, *Freud: Living and Dying* (Boston: International Universities Press, 1972), 516.

24 See "Freud got Steinached" in Patricia Gherovici, *Please Select Your Gender* (New York, Routledge, 2010), 79–80.

25 Sigmund Freud, *Totem and Taboo* (New York: Random House, 1946), x.

26 Freud, *Beyond the Pleasure Principle*, 31.

27   Sigmund Freud, "Findings, Ideas, Problems," *The Standard Edition of the Complete Psychological Works of Sigmund Freud, Volume XXIII (1937– 1939): Moses and Monotheism, An Outline of Psycho-Analysis and Other Works,* ed. and trans. James Strachey (London: Hogarth Press, 1964), 299.
28   Immanuel Kant, *Practical Philosophy,* trans. Mary J. Gregor (Cambridge: Cambridge University Press, 1996), 125–131.
29   Immanuel Kant, "Toward Perpetual Peace" (1795) in Mary J. Gregor, *Practical Philosophy,* 317.
30   Gregor, *Practical Philosophy,* 317.
31   Ibid., 279.
32   Ibid., 305–306.
33   This is an excerpt from chapter 7 of Jean-Michel Rabate, *Crimes of the Future* (New York: Bloomsbury, 2014).

Works cited

Derrida, Jacques. *The Postcard: From Socrates to Freud and Beyond.* Trans. Alan Bass. Chicago: University of Chicago Press, 1987.
Eliot, T. S. "Gerontion." *The Waste Land and Other Poems.* London, Faber, 1988.
Freud, Sigmund. *Beyond the Pleasure Principle.* Trans. James Strachey. New York, Norton, 1989.
Freud, Sigmund. "Findings, Ideas, Problems." *The Standard Edition of the Complete Psychological Works of Sigmund Freud, Volume XXIII (1937–1939): Moses and Monotheism, An Outline of Psycho-Analysis and Other Works.* Ed. and Trans. James Strachey. London: Hogarth Press, 1964.
Freud, Sigmund. *Jenseits des Lustprinzips, Studienausgabe III, Psychologie des Unbewussten.* Frankfurt: Fischer, 1982.
Freud, Sigmund. *The Letters of Sigmund Freud.* Ed. Ernst L. Freud. London, Dover, 1992.
Freud, Sigmund. *Totem and Taboo.* New York: Random House, 1946.
Gherovici, Patricia. *Please Select Your Gender.* New York: Routledge, 2010.
Joyce, James. "Exiles." *Poem and Exiles.* London: Penguin, 1992.
Kant, Immanuel. *Practical Philosophy.* Trans. Mary J. Gregor. Cambridge: Cambridge University Press, 1996.
Rabate, Jean-Michel. *Crimes of the Future: Theory and its Global Reproduction.* New York: Bloomsbury, 2014.
Schur, Max. *Freud: Living and Dying.* Boston: International Universities Press, 1972
Žižek, Slavoj. *The Ticklish Subject: The Absent Centre of Political Ontology.* London: Verso, 1999.

5

Ghosts in the *Politics of Friendship*

Paul Allen Miller

Ghosts always pass quickly, with the infinite speed of a furtive apparition, in an instant without duration, presence without present of a present which, coming back, only haunts. The ghost, le re-venant, the survivor, appears only by means of figure or fiction, but its appearance is not nothing, nor is it a mere semblance.[1]

In testifying for a work that needs to be studied (read without prejudice) more than praised, I think I am remaining faithful, however clumsily, to the intellectual friendship that [Foucault's] death, which was very painful for me, allows me to declare to him today, even as I remember the phrase attributed by Diogenes Laertius to Aristotle: "Oh my friends, there is no friend."[2]

Derrida begins the *Politics of Friendship* with a quotation from Cicero's *De Amicitia*, "wherefore both the absent are present . . . and, what is more difficult to say, the dead live." There is, unsurprisingly, nothing accidental about this quotation or the extensive reading of Cicero with which the text begins.[3] The *Politics of Friendship*, which was published immediately after *Specters of Marx*, is a text haunted by the ghosts of friends past, both those who have died and those who are no longer friends, a text whose wager on a democracy to come is predicated on the force of those friendships and the loss they necessarily entail. *Specters of Marx* in turn, as Derrida acknowledges in a footnote to *Khora*,[4] published the same year, represents a return to the topic of his seminar at the Ecole Normale Supérieure twenty years prior, a period when political conflicts concerning the interpretation of Marx were tearing apart the editorial collective surrounding *Tel Quel*, conflicts that would eventually lead to a permanent breach in his friendship with Julia Kristeva and Philippe Sollers.[5] While the *Politics of Friendship* begins with Cicero and an explicit invocation of a type of haunting—the return of the dead, the spectral—through friendship, it ends with an evocation of Derrida's own complex, critical, and sometimes silent friendship with Foucault. In between, there are readings of Nietzsche on solitary and silent friendships, Schmitt on politics as constituted by the figure of the enemy (as the corollary of the friend), and Montaigne, whose meditation on his loss of the rare friendship he experienced with La Boétie leads him, like Blanchot, to quote Diogenes Laertius, citing a possibly apocryphal saying of Aristotle, "Oh my friends, there is no friend." This phrase in turn becomes a refrain throughout Derrida's own text, from its first chapter to its last. Finally, haunting this text in the footnotes, obliquely but insistently, is the figure of Paul de Man, the memory (*Mémoires*) of whom, as we see above, is the first place within the Derridian corpus that we find the concepts of the ghost, the haunting, the *re-venant*, as well as the *à-venir* articulated. The death of de Man was both a deep personal loss to Derrida and a political blow as well, as de Man's prewar collaborationist, anti-Semitic writings were discovered.

In this paper, I concentrate on three structurally significant moments within the text: the reading of Cicero at its beginning, which establishes many of the most important themes; the turn to Foucault and Blanchot at its end; and the evocation of Paul de Man in between, who haunts the margins of the text, existing only as a ghostly trace, and yet who, I would argue, is central to its project. The *Politics of Friendship*, then, as we shall see, is a haunted text, in which "both the absent are present . . . and, what is more difficult to say, the dead live." This invasion of the present by a now absent past, both on the personal and the historico-political level, is, as first articulated in *Mémoires for Paul de Man* and then resumed in *Specters of Marx* and the *Politics of Friendship*, what produces the possibility of a future, of a difference to come ("*à-venir*"). The spectral is at the heart of the *Politics of Friendship's* project, which in turn offers a rethinking of both democracy and friendship, and the relationship they necessarily imply, as observed since at least Aristotle.[6]

At the same time, the *Politics of Friendship* is in surprising ways a profoundly personal text, at times even an autobiographical text. It is perhaps no accident that one of the texts by de Man to which Derrida refers in the footnotes is "Autobiography as De-Facement."[7] He makes particular reference to its reading of Wordsworth's *Essay upon Epitaphs*, a text on the verbal evocation of the dead. "Autobiography as De-Facement" is also an essay to which Derrida pays particular attention in *Memoires for Paul de Man*, a series of lectures first given shortly after de Man's death at Yale in 1984 (the year Foucault died as well). In it, de Man observes, "Autobiography . . . is not a genre or a mode, but a figure of reading or of understanding that occurs, to some degree in all texts . . . any book with a readable title page is, to some extent, autobiographical."[8] The *Politics of Friendship* indeed has a readable title page and through this citation acknowledges itself as such. Moreover, as Derrida observes of his own text, "Epilogue. Everything here has the form of an epilogue or an epitaph."[9] The genre of the funeral oration, as we shall see, is central to the *Politics of Friendship*, and it always is in the last analysis at least as much about the speaker as it is about the dead.[10] *Il n'y a pas de hors-texte.*

The Ciceronian dialogue, with which Derrida begins, is in many ways exemplary. The main speaker, Laelius, whose name often serves as an alternative title for the dialogue, is long dead by the time Cicero wrote in 44 BCE. In the immediate aftermath of the assassination of Julius Caesar, with civil war and the end of the Roman republic looming on the horizon, the ghosts of the past spoke with particular power. (There are many ways in which we are haunted.) The text begins with a brief introduction in which Cicero explains that he is writing the dialogue in response to a request from his closest friend, Atticus, to write something on friendship. In doing so, he acknowledges that his text is simultaneously an autobiographical allegory and a treatise on friendship.[11] It is also, as we have indicated, a political text as well. After this introduction, the now ghostly Laelius is asked by his two sons-in-law to speak to them about his friendship with the recently deceased Scipio Africanus Aemilianus, a Roman political figure and general of the first rank, who had been the main speaker of Cicero's *De Republica*, a treatise on the Roman constitution written ten years prior but dramatically set just days before, a text that famously ends with Scipio's vision of the afterlife in the *Somnium Scipionis*.

Laelius's relationship with Scipio is presented within the dialogue as exemplary in two senses. First, it is the example that we are supposed to accept as "embodying the ideal" of friendship, with all the ontological conundra that inhere in that phrase. Second, the friend is also an exemplar of the self, and insofar as this other (Scipio) is both the model and the representation of the self (Laelius), he then lives on within the self as the ghost of that self's past affections and the promise of its future identity. My friend is my likeness, and I am his reflection. We are both the same and necessarily different. For Derrida, Ciceronian friendships confound the ontological categories that normally govern our thought and hence our world, and Cicero is more than aware of the paradoxes thus created.[12] To quote Derrida's exemplary passage from the dialogue in full:

For he who perceives a true friend, it is as though he perceives an *exemplar* of himself. Wherefore the absent are present, the poor are rich, the weak are strong, and what is more difficult to say, the dead live: so great is the respect, the memory, and the desire that follows after our friends. Hence, for the ones, death seems happy and, for the others, life is worthy of praise.[13]

Derrida returns to this Ciceronian reading of the friend as exemplar of the self throughout the *Politics of Friendship*, but it would be a mistake to see this positive reading as the only lesson taught by the *De Amicitia* or by the *Politics of Friendship*. Friendship only occurs between mortals. There is no friendship without death.[14]

In both texts, not only do our friends haunt us, but so does political struggle and the necessity of enmity, a necessity that realizes itself most completely in the absolute hostility of civil war, when my brother and my friend become my existential foe, as Derrida shows in his reading of the unrepentant Nazi, Carl Schmitt.[15] The whole of *De Amicitia* plays out not only against the background of Caesar's assassination and the imminent threat of civil war but also against a reading of two exemplary friendships gone awry. The first is that of Publius Sulpicius and Quintus Pompeius Rufus. They are from the generation after Laelius and were two fast friends who wound up on opposite sides in the internecine conflicts surrounding the Roman Social Wars. Pompeius became consul and colleague of the aristocratic Sulla, Sulpicius tribune of the people and ally of the plebian Marius. The conflict put an end to their friendship. Each died in the war that ensued, killed by the friends of their friend. ("Oh my friends, there is no friend.") The whole of this story of friendship, politics, and death is invoked, almost in a passing manner at the beginning of the dialogue to describe how Cicero came to know of the story of Laelius's discourse on his friendship with the recently deceased Scipio. It is a bit of marginalia, and yet Cicero's decision to begin with it haunts the reader as the text unfolds.

The second is the story of Blossius and Gracchus. It is recounted within the discourse of Laelius. Gracchus was a revolutionary tribune of the people from the previous generation whose radical proposals for land reform led to his being beaten to death by a senatorial gang. Blossius was his friend and, when Laelius led a senatorial inquiry into the events leading to his death, Blossius was asked whether if Gracchus had told him to burn down the Capitoline, the administrative and religious center of the Roman republic, would he have complied? After initially denying that Gracchus would have ever asked such a thing, when he was pressed, Blossius eventually answered in the affirmative. Laelius condemns this answer: true friendship, he contends, is founded on virtue not treason, on universal values not the whims of private affection.

Nonetheless, the example is telling. Laelius himself admits that Blossius remained faithful when all others abandoned Gracchus. In such momentous events and at the risk of death, who, in fact, could say that Blossius was not a true friend of Gracchus? Montaigne who recounts this same tale, praises Blossius's response, because the perfect friend both knows and so ultimately controls the will of the other—who is after all a second self, or as Cicero argues, an *exemplar* of the self.[16] Blossius, Montaigne contends, would never allow Gracchus to demand such a thing. And yet Blossius, as Laelius acknowledges, did in the end commit treason, fleeing to Asia and joining the rebellion of Aristonicus, after whose defeat he committed suicide. *De Amicitia* too is a haunted text: haunted by the exemplary ghosts of the Roman statesmen who speak within its bounds, haunted by the recently deceased Scipio, haunted by Caesar, haunted by the treasons and betrayals that constitutes the margins of its discourse on the exemplary friend.

The *Politics of Friendship* too opens with ghosts, with the living dead. In *De Amicitia*, as Derrida underlines, the dead live (*mortui vivunt*). Death itself lives. It threatens Cicero and the republic, but it also promises that they might live on, not quite immortal, like a god, but haunting our thoughts and our discourse, even our unconscious assumptions, as exemplars. Only their death makes this afterlife possible. Exemplarity depends on finitude. And the figure for that exemplarity as de Man observes in "Autobiography as De-Facement," the text to which Derrida refers in both the *Politics of Friendship* and *Memoires for Paul de Man* is prosopoiea, literally the "making of a face," often referring to the personification and address of an abstraction. At its most basic, it denotes the use of words to produce the illusion of an authentic person: the fictive moment in which the universality of the signified is given a face and in which it is at the same time shown to be an effect of the signifier, a fiction, a personification. This tropic turning between the creation of a face and its defacement is what constitutes prosopoiea. And this is precisely what happens in the autobiographical moment: the text is revealed as participating in both the intelligible, and hence the universal, and at the same time it is shown to be a product of a contingent set of conditions, a deliberate manipulation of language for specific ends, and hence "merely" rhetorical. The face of prosopoiea is both present and absent, living and dead, an exemplar to be copied ("I model myself on my friend") and a copy derived from a preexisting model ("I carry my friend's image in my heart"). The dead friend "in himself, by himself, he is no more, nothing more. He lives only in us. But *we* are never *ourselves*, and between us, identical to us, a 'self' is never in itself or identical to itself."[17]

It is, moreover, this moment of conjuring whereby the dead come to exist in the living, *epitaphically*, even as the living see their existence reflected in the dead, that is one of the central meanings of the concept of "hauntology," which, Derrida contends, lies at the base of friendship, philosophy, and democracy: the promise of a future that is at once radically particular (rooted in the affections of the past) and open to all and hence universal—a politics of friendship. "Oh my friends, there is no friend." And this possibility of a future is what Cicero's dialogue and its initial framing promise as well, even as it mourns the lost promises of the past. "A spectre is haunting Europe."

> To be just: beyond the living present in general—and its simple negative inverse. Spectral moment, a moment that no longer pertains to time, if one understands by this noun the linkage of modalized presents (past present, actual present: "now," future present) . . . Furtive and tempestuous, the apparition of the specter does not pertain to this time, it does not give the time, "*Enter the Ghost, exit the Ghost, re-enter the Ghost*" (Hamlet).[18]

The search for justice—to be just—is the search for this friendship to come, which is also the search for a democracy to come. This logic of a future possibility, which inheres in the past, and which is never quite present, is what Derrida develops in *Specters of Marx* as *hauntology*, "neither living nor dead, neither present nor absent, but . . . a specter. It is not a matter of ontology."[19]

Moreover, as it is in no way random or accidental that we open with Cicero's evocation of Laelius and Scipio, in responding to his friend Atticus, and with the specter of civil war that haunts every word he writes in 44 BCE, it is likewise no accident that Derrida in 1994, the year after publishing *Specters of Marx* and *Khôra*, his final rejoinder to Kristeva, Sollers, and the political conflicts that tore apart the theoretical scene in Paris in the early 1970s, ends the *Politics of Friendship* with Blanchot's haunting evocation of his friendship with Foucault, written the day after he died and whom Blanchot never met: *Michel Foucault tel que je l'imagine*. Blanchot begins by saying he thinks he saw Foucault from a distance in Mai 68 at the Sorbonne but then acknowledges that during this time he often asked "why isn't Foucault here" and people would reply "he is rather reserved" or "he is out of the country."[20] He was in fact in Tunisia: a merely spectral presence, a face in the crowd created by Blanchot's text. Blanchot's conjuring of Foucault in the days after his death is cited extensively at the end of the last chapter of the *Politics of Friendship* as is Blanchot's short essay "Amitié," which was written after the death of Bataille. In both texts, it is precisely the distance between the friends, their mutual regard and profound discretion, a form of silence, which made their friendship possible, which made them exemplary.

The final chapter of the *Politics of Friendship*, "For the First Time in the History of Humanity" begins, however, by examining a passage from Kant's *Anthropology from a Pragmatic Point of View*.[21] It is not insignificant, however, that Derrida chooses to quote from Foucault's translation and notes it as such: for this final chapter is very much about where friendship in all its singularity meets democracy in its claim to universality, or in Kantian terms, where the empirical approaches the universal in the moment of the transcendental. The transcendental, as Žižek and others have taught us, is to be understood not as a place or a thing, but as a parallactic or aporetic moment articulating a necessary relation between two mutually exclusive alternatives, between presence and absence, the living and the dead.[22] Or as Derrida wrote ten years prior, in *Mémoires for Paul de Man*,[23] "this 'synthesis as a phantom' enables us to recognize in *the figure of the phantom* the working of what Kant and Heidegger assign to the transcendental imagination."

The reason for Derrida's reference to Foucault in such a context may not be obvious to the casual reader or even to the well-informed student of theory. But, Foucault's ghost looms large over these texts.[24] In 1961, Foucault, Derrida's tutor at the Ecole Normale Superieure, had defended both his major and minor theses in philosophy. The major thesis, which was subsequently published as *Histoire de la folie*, sought in its original preface to give a voice to madness in its absolute singularity, to allow those to speak whom the universality of reason as constituted by the particularities of power at the beginning of the modern era had confined, silenced, removed to the workhouse, the prison, the asylum. It was this preface that Derrida would later attack and Foucault remove before making his own bitter response to what seemed a friendship betrayed.[25] At the same time as he defended his major thesis, Foucault also defended a minor or complementary thesis, which was a translation and commentary on Kant's philosophical anthropology. A portion of this thesis was later published as the translation Derrida cites at the beginning of his final chapter of the *Politics of Friendship*, a chapter that ends with an evocation of Foucault's death and Blanchot's avowal of his friendship for this man whom he has never met, never spoken to: "Oh my friends, there is no friend."

It would, of course, be ridiculous to reduce this final chapter to a naïve allegory of Derrida's complex and troubled friendship with Foucault. The argument takes place at the level of philosophical universality, after all. We are discussing Kant, after all. But it would be equally naïve to believe that Derrida was unaware of the resonances of his choices or to believe that we are somehow precluded from tracing those resonances in precisely that transcendental space defined by the conjunction of the empirical and the universal, in which the madness of our absolute particularity for a brief flickering moment seems to speak in intelligible tones.

In 1984, shortly before Foucault's death, the two reconciled, after Derrida's arrest on trumped up marijuana charges in Czechoslovakia. *Il n'y a pas de hors-texte.* In 1992, Derrida published a final text on *Histoire de la Folie* in a volume dedicated to Foucault, the year before *Specters of Marx*, two years before the *Politics of Friendship.*[26] Though much has been made of their disagreements and public polemics, Derrida would later say in an interview with Elizabeth Roudienesco that he saw himself as "in solidarity with" and as part of the same "general movement" of "thought" as Foucault, despite his reticences in regard to this or that particular point.[27] He would declare a friendship that could only be declared after death, only declared through a critical reading of the texts of a friend held in such regard.

Ghosts haunt the *Politics of Friendship*. Indeed, they are fundamental to friendship itself, or at least death and its survival—*le re-venant*—are. It is no accident, as Derrida writes, that "the great canonical meditations on friendship (Cicero's *De Amicitia*, Montaigne's 'De L'amitié,' Blanchot's *L'Amitié*, for example) pertain to the experience of grief, at the moment of loss."[28] Friendship at its most profound level is the presence of the other in the self as constitutive of the self, but also as forever other. Friendship is only fully realized in the moment of survival,[29] in the presence of absence: the living dead, the exemplary ghost. Friendship is only fully realized when we surrender to the absolute otherness of the friend in the moment of death. As Derrida quotes Blanchot as saying in the passage cited at the beginning of this essay, death alone permits him to declare his friendship.[30] This declaration, of course, is made immediately before citing Aristotle's famous and contradictory saying, "Oh my friends, there is no friend," the saying with which Derrida begins his own inquiry. The recursive quality of this refrain is difficult to miss, tying together the beginning and end of the *Politics of Friendship*: Blanchot, Foucault, and Cicero.

Blanchot, ultimately, does not talk about Foucault, but to him, addressing to him the performative contradiction that this apothegm enacts as a sign of fidelity.[31] Or as Derrida paraphrases, "Thanks be to death! It is thanks to death that friendship can be declared. Never before. Never otherwise."[32] To declare friendship before death, or before the acknowledgment of an absolute separation (which is the same thing), is to render it not an act of discretion, not a moment of esteem, nor even a moment of love, but another appropriation, another movement in the infinite process of exchange, to which death alone puts an end. I declare you to be my friend. I make my claim. I demand a return. But if I do not, then I acknowledge our absolute separation—the moment of exemplarity—and hence I acknowledge death, which is also the basis of any rapport.[33]

Immediately before the passage quoted from Blanchot's text at the beginning of our text, Blanchot refers to Foucault's final interview with Dreyfus and Rabinow in which Foucault, when asked about his future projects, exclaims, "Oh, I'm going to take care of myself first of all." As Blanchot notes, the phrase is gnomic at best, but it seems almost certainly to refer to Nietzsche's return to the Greeks in search of an ethics and to their valorization of *philia* or friendship "as the model of excellence in human relations. Friendship was promised to Foucault as a posthumous gift."[34] Yet as Derrida observes, while Foucault certainly was aware of the Greek problematic of friendship,[35] and while Derrida himself spends no small amount of time within the *Politics of Friendship* not only reading Cicero but also Plato and Aristotle, what Blanchot retains from Foucault's and Nietzsche's discussions of the "Greek model" is not an exemplar of reciprocity or even of mutual specular realization, but precisely a moment of aporia, a moment in which friendship only exists in the declaration of its negation, in the faithful and critical reading of Foucault in death, not his praise in life.[36] Friendship exists not in the moment of equal exchange, but in the absolute respect of asymmetry, in the silence that makes the moment of address possible.

Foucault, then, will take care of himself, and in that care of the self he will seek a model of self-relation made possible by an *askesis*. This ascetic moment, as Blanchot observes, is Nietzschean, both in its tone and in its relation to the shades of antiquity. Yet, as Derrida notes, with clear Foucauldian resonances, that *askesis*, as a moment of silence, is what makes the place for friendship possible, "Nietzsche affects a mystical tone when he advances certain precepts or aphoristic sentences (*Sprüche*) on the subject of a silence he names then in Latin, *Silentium*. Askesis, kenosis, knowing how to make a void from words in order to let friendship breathe."[37] But that Foucauldian care of the self to which Blanchot and Derrida both allude, while certainly Nietzschean and ultimately profoundly Socratic, is also Kantian—as Foucault at the end of the Dreyfus and Rabinow interview acknowledges—in its profound concern with the self's relation to itself as mediated between the empirical experience of its formation through ascetic exercises and the demands of practical reason.[38] Or to put it in the terms of a more famous text published that same year by Foucault, and surely not escaping Derrida's notice, "What is Enlightenment," Foucault's commentary on Kant's text of the same name, the essential task of modernity corresponds to what Baudelaire lays down for the painter of modern life, the embrace of all the present has to offer in all its particularity, but as a moment of universality, that is to say, as a moment of the heroic.[39] This conjunction of the particular and the universal, without either being subsumed into the other, is in turn the constitutive moment of democracy on the level of community, of friendship on the level of the individual, of the transcendental on the level of critique, and this was Foucault's project from beginning to end,[40] a project for which Derrida can only articulate his profound love and respect, after Foucault's death. Or as he says on the page immediately following his lengthy quotation from Blanchot on Foucault:

> Without trying to hide it, one will have understood, I would like to speak here of those men and women who are linked to me by a rare friendship, that is to say I also want to speak to them, albeit through the rare friendships I name and that never come to me without admiration and gratitude.[41]

There are ghosts in the *Politics of Friendship* and one of them is Foucault.

Foucault died within a year of Paul de Man (December 21, 1983). Derrida perhaps inadvertently draws a parallel between these two compelling figures. The same year Foucault is citing Baudelaire's *Painter of Modern Life* to illustrate Kant's concept of enlightenment and modernity, the year after they appear in his lectures on ancient philosophy at the College de France,[42] Derrida cites this same text by Baudelaire in reference to the death of Paul de Man in what also appears to be his initial development of his concept of the ghost, the phantom, the specter, and the *re-venant*.

> At the very beginning of *Le Peintre de la vie moderne*, the work to which "Mnemonic Art," belongs, the phantom makes its first appearance—as the very attraction or provocativeness of the past . . . "Without losing anything of its ghostly piquancy, the past will recover the light and movement of life and will become present."[43]

There is a sense in which Kant and Baudelaire, Foucault and de Man, the epitaphic and the autobiographical become intimately associated with one another, on the level of abstract generality, even as they remain irremediably particular in terms of the multiple pasts and past affections that tie them to the

present. At the same time, it is this concept of the return of the past as the opening of the present to the possibility of the other, to the *à-venir*, that will go on to
found both Derrida's reading of Marx in *Specters of Marx* and his search for a
new politics and a new more expansive friendship in the *Politics of Friendship*.[44]
There is indeed a "specter haunting Europe," and "what is more difficult to say,
the dead live."

Derrida had, of course, developed a very close friendship with de Man,
exchanging numerous letters and visits from the late 1960s till de Man's death
in 1983. He was both a friend who had been lost and a friend whose politics
ultimately posed great difficulties for Derrida. When Derrida was first invited
to give a series of lectures on de Man, first at Yale and then as the Wellek lecture
at UC Irvine, he tells us that he was barely able to begin.[45] Yet, at first glance,
de Man does not figure prominently in the *Politics of Friendship*, nonetheless
I want to finish by claiming this text is haunted—in the full Derridian sense of
the word, by his shade.

There are three explicit evocations of de Man in the *Politics of Friendship*,
and as we shall see, there is at least one more covert conjuring, in addition
to the various conceptual and textual anticipations we have already observed.
Derrida was clearly haunted by these issues and returned to them in later years.
I take the references from the least problematic to the most.

In chapter 4 of the *Politics of Friendship*, poignantly titled "*L'ami revenant
(au nom de la <<démocratie>>)*" ("The Returning Friend" but also "The Friend
as Revenant," i.e., "The Friend as Returning from the Dead [in the name of
democracy]"), Derrida is reading a passage from Plato's *Menexenus* on the necessary relation between the concept of Athenian autochthony and Athenian
democracy. The context of this reading is a contestation of Carl Schmitt's
understanding of Plato's distinction between warfare proper and civil war. The
Menexenus, it will be remembered, features Socrates performing what purports
to be an exemplary funeral oration for the Athenian war dead. While claiming to recite a speech he learned from Pericles's mistress, Aspasia, he celebrates
the dead as exemplars of both the Athenian constitution and of their originary
ethnic unity and purity, at once repeating the traditional nostrums that we find
"in all the racisms, in all the ethnocentrisms, more precisely in all the national-
isms," and ironically bracketing them. The friend at Athens, the *philos*, a word
used frequently of the fellow citizen, is then a friend both because he has a relation of constitutional equality with his fellow citizen and because they share
a common *phusis* or nature.[46] And these friends are conjured from the dead
and stand before us to reaffirm our political identity and the continuity of our

future with our past. There is no difference. At the end of this passage, Derrida cites Nicole Loraux's study of the *Menexenus* on the themes of autochthony and the *epitaphios* (funeral oration). He then observes that it would be interesting to compare her work with de Man's, referring the reader to "'Autobiography as De-Facement' (concerning Wordsworth's *Essays upon Epitaphs*)" and his own funeral orations for de Man in *Mémoires for Paul de Man*, where he also reads this same essay.[47] It is of course this essay that gives the concept of autobiography as prosopoiea cited earlier, and prosopoiea is precisely the figure invoked by the *epitaphios*, as a face is given and created for the dead so that they may return and through their haunting create the possibility of a future. At the same time, through this brief evocation of de Man and of Derrida's funereal orations, de Man is also given a textual face, much like the Athenian war dead, even as the possibility of an autobiographical reading of Derrida's own text is at once conjured and then recedes. The fact that this conjuring occurs in the course of a discussion of the racist and nationalist origins of Athenian democratic discourse is of course both deeply ironic and deeply resonant. Moreover, this passage comes in the course of a broader examination of Carl Schmitt, and while de Man's wartime writings in the collaborationist *Le soir* were deeply problematic and in certain cases openly anti-Semitic,[48] Schmitt directly refused denazification after the war and continued to be involved with far right politics, including in Franco's Spain.

The next passage also comes in the context of a discussion of Schmitt and his theory of the decision in a state of exception. Derrida makes the case that the decision is often understood to be a corollary of the sovereignty of the subject (and hence of the leader in the case of the state). Yet, in so far as the decision creates the event, and hence the state of exception, it always represents the intrusion of a moment of absolute otherness that is fundamentally foreign to any theory of a self-consistent and hence self-determining subject. At this point, however, Derrida adds that this intrusion of the other within the inner sanctum of the same—the sovereign deciding subject—"does not in any way exonerate [the subject] from responsibility": "I am responsible first of all *for the other before the other.*"[49]

The heterogeneous nature of the deciding subject in its relation to the other, and its relation to the self as other, to the otherness of the self, is also the ground of its autonomy, insofar as autonomy must of necessity presume the possibility of otherness and hence of the event, of a difference to come. Antigone is deemed *autonomos* by Creon because she lives by her own law. A decision, Derrida contends, is like a gift. It is always done in/to *"the name of the other."*[50]

At this point in his reading of Schmitt, Derrida appends a footnote referring us to the very end of his three lectures on de Man, the three funeral orations given at Yale, to a page that in the French appears right before the one-hundred-page addendum in which he reads de Man's wartime journalism, "La guerre de Paul de Man." He refers us, that is, to the hinge point, the decision point, the spacing between the epitaphic and the question of responsibility. The cited passage concerns the equivocity of a promise, a gift, and a decision made for/to/in the name of the other. The irruption of otherness within the impossible dream of the same, of autochthony, is both the subversion of the self-sufficient subject and the ground of its responsibility, the possibility of both the friend and the enemy as exemplars, the possibility of a democracy to come, one that would no longer be founded on the equality of the same.[51] There is no escaping the responsibility of the decisions we make in the name of the other, neither for de Man, nor for Schmitt, nor for us. The past, which is other than the present, but not fully absent—our past—is the possibility of a future difference, to which we must respond.

The final citation of *Mémoires for Paul de Man* in the *Politics of Friendship* comes in the course of a scholarly examination of the provenance of the Aristotelian saying reported by Diogenes Laertius, "Oh my friends, there is no friend." Derrida notes that the phrase itself constitutes what Habermas in his indictment of deconstruction termed "a performative contradiction." But as he argues, and as I think any serious reading of the *Politics of Friendship* in relation to the complexities presented by *Specters of Marx*, Cicero's *De Amicitia*, Foucault, Blanchot, de Man, and Schmitt, demonstrates, "with all the reversals, with all the revolutions that [this phrase] engenders to infinity, [this] so-called 'performative contradiction' . . . has the merit of sharpening, truly of dramatizing, a desire for friendship that, while never renouncing what it says must be renounced, at least opens thought to friendship."[52] Indeed, it is precisely this contradiction that is in the end the condition of friendship from Cicero to the present, the recognition of the other within the self as both other and also as the condition of the self's existence *qua* self, as an exemplar of the self. "For he who perceives a true friend, it is as though he perceives an *exemplar* of himself. Wherefore the absent are present, the poor are rich, the weak are strong, and what is more difficult to say, the dead live."

At this point in his text, Derrida appends his third reference to *Mémoires for Paul de Man*, directing us to a very long footnote found in the appendix on his wartime journalism. I do not have space to do justice to this appendix or even to the note. Derrida is in the process of expressing his exasperation before the fact that many of the scholars and journalists who claimed to make equivalencies or "links" between de Man's wartime journalism and deconstruction had not read (let alone read carefully) either the journalism itself or many of the works that go under the name of deconstruction. At the same time, he observed, many of these same scholars condemned deconstruction's moral "irresponsibility," often in the name of democratic tolerance and the norms of scholarly discussion.[53] Nonetheless, these critics do not read the texts they indict, do not engage them in their particularity, do not treat them as true exemplars, who are simultaneously irreducible in their particularity and represent moments in which the claims of the universal, the normative, and intelligible are most acutely felt. He addresses what he sees as various examples of this phenomenon, culminating in his explication of Habermas.[54] He focuses on the irony of the performative contradiction of those charges themselves, since many of the people making them openly admit to not having read the material or very little of it, and yet, as Derrida is at pains to emphasize in the *Politics of Friendship*, this fact in no way exonerates either them or de Man from responsibility for the decisions they have made or from what they have done in the name of the other. By the same token, this performative contradiction, like Aristotle's own, does express, indeed, does sharpen a desire, which in its own turn must be read with due attention, with responsibility before the other.

This theme of responsibility to and before the other and of the necessity of attentive reading, of paying attention to heterogeneity as the ground of responsibility and of a democracy that does not become a tyranny of the same, were in fact already themes in Derrida's initial lectures on the death of de Man. There he tells us both of his reluctance to accept the invitation to give the Wellek lectures in the wake of Wellek's own attack against deconstruction in the *New Criterion*, and of his decision ultimately to accept that invitation "in order to demonstrate on which side . . . is situated . . . tolerance, the taste for reading and well argued discussion."[55] Here again there is appended a lengthy footnote, giving numerous examples of other such attacks as well as subsequent acknowledgments, sometimes by the attackers themselves, that they had not read the materials in question.[56]

This same gesture is repeated a third time in the *Politics of Friendship*. This time the figure under attack is not de Man but Carl Schmitt, and yet the echoes could not be more haunting. Again the question is not one of moral equivalence. Neither should Habermas's intolerance and inattention be deemed "the same" as de Man's implicit or explicit acceptance of anti-Semitism in his wartime journalism, nor should that journalism be deemed the same as Schmitt's open, continuing, and unrepentant fascism.[57] It is a question of responsibility—in all its meanings—before the other, and that responsibility demands a careful and attentive reading of these texts, especially of those that are at once powerful and repugnant.

> And how are we to explain the interest a certain ultra left, in more than one country, has shown for Schmitt? How to explain this still lively interest, in spite of so great a judgment? There is more to be learned from these ambiguities than many of the well-intentioned denunciations that take shelter behind a vague chronicle of contagions and objective alliances. The lazy denunciations often take as a pretext this trouble and the empirical observation of "bad influences," without having anything more to say about it, in order to turn aside and try to turn others aside from the reading, the work, the question.[58]

Schmitt becomes a specter of Paul de Man in the *Politics of Friendship*, at once his reflection and his other, the haunting of a past, to which if sufficient attention were paid, it could be made to yield a decision, a new event, a difference to come. It *could* happen, *peut-être*.

And finally it is in light of this specular/spectral identification that Derrida's observation on de Man's "amnesia," very near the end of his third funeral oration must be read. He notes that de Man in the second "Foreword" to *Blindness and Insight"* writes, "I am not given to retrospective self-examination and mercifully forget what I have written with the same alacrity I forget bad movies—although, as with bad movies, certain scenes or phrases return at times to embarrass and haunt me like a guilty conscience."[59] Derrida continues in his own voice, "Again the return of the ghost as text, or text as ghost." We can only imagine what those scenes were for de Man, but in the haunting of the present begins our responsibility to the other. Truly, *il n'y a pas de hors texte*, and what is more difficult to say, the dead *do* live.

Let us end then where we began with Blanchot on Foucault as an exemplar of the politics of friendship in all its varied forms, textual and otherwise.

> In testifying for a work that needs to be studied (read without prejudice) more than praised, I think I am remaining faithful, however clumsily, to the intellectual friendship that his death, which was very painful for me, allows me to declare to him today, even as I remember the phrase attributed by Diogenes Laertius to Aristotle: "oh my friends, there is no friend."[60]

In this passage, cited by Derrida at the end of the *Politics of Friendship*, we become aware most acutely of the performative contradiction that is the condition of possibility of friendship, of a democracy to come, and of the transcendental itself in its eternally ghostlike character. It is only by reading de Man rather than praising him that we can do justice to him, not exonerate him, but recognize in him the possibility of a friend who is no friend. It is neither by ignoring all that is haunting and repugnant in his or in Schmitt's wartime writings, nor by refusing to acknowledge the power of their work, its virtue in the most traditional sense, that we take responsibility for the other and for ourselves. Rather, it is only through a moment of love and aggression, only through taking these texts—our friends—absolutely seriously, rigorously holding them to the letter, that we can testify to a friendship that can only be fully realized in death, in the moment of our absolute separation, when all has been said and yet we continue to haunt one another in our living, loving absence. Only then can Derrida through the words of Blanchot tell Foucault that he is truly and unconditionally, unreservedly, his friend, in the moment of his death. "And when friendship declares itself among friends who are still alive, it confesses at bottom the same thing: it acknowledges the death thanks to which the chance to declare itself has finally come, which is never lacking."[61]

Cicero in 44 BCE after the death of Caesar—his enemy, his friend—sits in Rome reflecting on his next move, knowing his life hangs in the balance, knowing the lives of thousands hang in the balance, knowing that the future of the republic balances on the edge of a knife. He receives a letter from his friend Atticus who lives in Athens, safely removed from the turmoil that is Rome. "You should write something on friendship." He produces the dialogue known as *De Amicitia* or the *Laelius*. Why such indirection? Why does he not speak in his own voice? Why can he not directly, openly address his dearest friend? Why must he reanimate the voices of the dead to speak of the losses they have suffered, of the friendship that survives death itself, of friends who die at the hands of their friends' friends? Would such a direct address not do violence to Atticus? Would it kill him, freeze him in amber? If I were to turn to you and say "you are my friend and let me tell you exactly why," how would you react? Must you still be that same person tomorrow? If not, will you cease to be my friend? Have I not killed you every bit as much as Brutus killed Caesar, whom he loved?

It is only in that moment of extreme discretion, then, when we acknowledge our friendship and let it go, and when we do not say what can only be said after death, that we allow friendship to be and that we allow a life irreducible to abstract norms, irreducible to the law, to flourish. This is a life worthy of democracy, a life that calls out for us to seek the transcendental as a moment of enabling aporia, a life we recognize fully only in death. Oh my friends, there are no friends and yet the dead *do* live.

Notes

1   Jacques Derrida, *Memoires for Paul de Man*, The Wellek Library Lectures at the University of California Irvine, trans. Eduardo Cadava, Jonathan Culler, Cecile Lindsay, and Avital Ronnell (New York: Columbia University Press, 1986), 64; Jacques Derrida, *Mémoires pour Paul de Man* (Paris: Galilée, 1988), 76; emphasis in original.

2   Maurice Blanchot, *Michel Foucault: Tel que je l'imagine* (Paris: Fata Morgana, 1986), 64. All translations are my own unless otherwise specified.

3   For a fuller reading of the importance of *De Amicitia* for Derrida's text, see Paul Allen Miller, "Cicero Reads Derrida Reading Cicero: A Politics and a Friendship to Come," in *Brill's Companion to the Reception of Cicero*, ed. William Altman (Leiden: Brill, 2015), 175–97.

4   Jacques Derrida, *Khôra* (Paris: Galilée, 1993), 102–103n7.

5   Benoît Peeters, *Derrida* (Paris: Flammarion, 2010), 285–289.

6   cf. Jacques Derrida, *Mémoires pour Paul de Man*, 27, 70, 77–78, 99; Jacques Derrida, *Spectres de Marx* (Paris: Galilée, 1993), 17, 89; Jacques Derrida, *Politiques de l'amitié, suivi de L'oreille de Heidegger* (Paris: Galilée, 1994), 126–127n1, 246, 339–340.

7   Jacques Derrida, *Politiques de l'amitié*, 117–118n1.

8   Paul de Man, "Autobiography as De-Facement," *The Rhetoric of Romanticism* (New York: Columbia University Press, 1984), 70.

9   Derrida, *Politiques de l'amitié*, 191.

10   "A friendship, of the Ciceronian kind, would be the possibility of citing myself in an exemplary manner, by signing in advance my own funeral oration, the best, perhaps, but it is never certain that the friend will pronounce it standing on his own feet when I will no longer be" (Derrida, *Politiques de l'amitié*, 21).

11   Compare Jacques Derrida (*Memoires for Paul de Man*, 80–81), "Is it by chance that, in the very first steps by which he reopened the problem of allegory, Paul de Man convoked the ghost of Coleridge, and the phantom of which Coleridge speaks, precisely in relation to allegory? Allegory speaks (through) the voice of the other, whence the ghost-effect, whence also the a-symbolic disjunction."

12   Derrida, *Politiques de l'amitié*, 19–20.

13   Ibid., 23; emphasis added.

14   Ibid., 322, 327–328, 335.

15   Ibid., 103, 157, 170–171.

16 Michel de Montaigne, *Oeuvres complètes,* eds. Albert Thibaudet and Maurice Rat (Paris: Gallimard, 1962), 188.

17 Derrida *Mémoires pour Paul de Man,* 49; emphasis in original.

18 Derrida, *Spectres de Marx,* 17; emphasis in original.

19 Ibid., 89.

20 Blanchot *Michel Foucault,* 9–10.

21 Derrida, *Politiques de l'amitié,* 304.

22 Immanuel Kant, *Critique of Pure Reason,* trans. Norman Kemp Smith (New York: Modern Library, 1958), 41–42, 211–225, 244–246; Slavoj Žižek, *The Parallax View* (Cambridge, MA: MIT Press, 2006), 20–21; Paul Allen Miller, "The Repeatable and the Unrepeatable: Žižek and the Future of the Humanities, or Assessing Socrates," *symplokē* 17 (2009): 191–208.

23 Derrida, *Memoires for Paul de Man,* 64; Derrida, *Mémoires pour Paul de Man,* 76; emphasis in original.

24 Is it insignificant that Derrida in response to Schmitt calls for a "déconstruction généalogique" (Derrida, *Politiques de l'amitié,* 128)?

25 Michel Foucault, *Folie et déraison, Histoire de la folie à l'âge classique* (Paris: Plon, 1961); Michel Foucault, "Mon corps, ce papier, ce feu," *Histoire de la folie à l'âge classique suivi de Mon corps, ce papier, ce feu et La folie, l'absence de l'oeuvre* (Paris: Gallimard, 1972), 583–603; Jacques Derrida, "Cogito et histoire de la folie," *L'Écriture et la différence* (Paris: Seuil, 1967), 51–97; David H. J. Larmour, Paul Allen Miller, and Charles Platter, "Introduction: Situating the *History of Sexuality,*" *Rethinking Sexuality: Foucault and Classical Antiquity,* eds. David H. J. Larmour, Paul Allen Miller, and Charles Platter (Princeton: Princeton University Press, 1998), 6–9.

26 Jacques Derrida, "Être juste avec Freud," *Penser la folie: Essais pour Michel Foucault* (Paris: Galilée, 1992).

27 Jacques Derrida and Elizabeth Roudinesco, *De quoi demain . . . Dialogue* (Paris: Fayard/Galilée, 2001), 17–18, 21, 27.

28 Derrida, *Politiques de l'amitié,* 322.

29 Ibid., 324.

30 Ibid., 332–334. But again compare Derrida on de Man (de Man, "Autobiography as De-Facement," 149). The *Politics of Friendship,* time and again, is haunted by the ghost of Paul de Man.

31 Blanchot, *Michel Foucault,* 64; Derrida *Politiques de l'amitié,* 334–335.

32 Derrida *Politiques de l'amitié,* 335.

33 Maurice Blanchot, *L'Amitié* (Paris: Gallimard, 1971), 326–329; Derrida *Politiques de l'amitié,* 73, 84, 327.

34 Blanchot, *Michel Foucault,* 63–64; Michel Foucault, "A propose de la généalogie de l'éthique: Un aperçu du travail en cours," *Dits et écrits: 1954–1988,* vol. 4, eds. Daniel Defert and François Ewalt (Paris: Gallimard, 1994), 609–631, 611.

35 See Michel Foucault, "De l'amitié comme mode de vie," *Dits et écrits: 1954–1988*, vol. 4, eds. Daniel Defert and François Ewalt (Paris: Gallimard, 1994), 163–167.

36 Derrida *Politiques de l'amitié*, 333–334.

37 Ibid., 72.

38 Foucault, "A propose de la généalogie de l'éthique," 631.

39 Michel Foucault, "Qu'est-ce que les Lumières?," *Dits et écrits: 1954–1988*, vol. 4, eds. Daniel Defert and François Ewalt (Paris: Gallimard, 1994), 562–578.

40 cf. Blanchot, *Michel Foucault*, 17, 44.

41 Derrida, *Politiques de l'amitié*, 335.

42 Michel Foucault, *Le gouvernement de soi et des autres: Cours au Collège de France 1982–83*, ed. Frédéric Gros (Paris: Gallimard/Seuil, 2008), 9–21.

43 Derrida, *Memoires for Paul de Man*, 64; Derrida, *Mémoires pour Paul de Man*, 76.

44 Pierre Macherey, "Le Marx intempestif de Derrida," *Derrida, la tradition de la philosophie*, eds. Marc Crépon and Frédéric Worms (Paris: Galilée, 2008), 135–154.

45 Derrida, *Memoires for Paul de Man*, xiv.

46 Derrida *Politiques de l'amitié*, 112–113.

47 Ibid., 117–118n1.

48 cf. Derrida, *Mémoires pour Paul de Man*, 160–161, 169–170.

49 Derrida, *Politiques de l'amitié*, 87–88; emphasis in original.

50 Ibid., 88; emphasis in original.

51 Ibid., 340.

52 Ibid., 240.

53 Derrida, *Mémoires pour Paul de Man*, 219–221.

54 See, in particular, Derrida, *Mémoires pour Paul de Man*, 225–226n1.

55 Derrida, *Memoires for Paul de Man*, 12; Derrida, *Mémoires pour Paul de Man*, 34–35.

56 Derrida, *Memoires for Paul de Man*, 41–43n5; Derrida, *Mémoires pour Paul de Man*, 34–35n2.

57 Derrida, in fact, directly says that Schmitt's commitments are in many ways even more repugnant than those of Heidegger, and *a fortiori* de Man (Derrida *Politiques de l'amitié*, 102n1).

58 Derrida, *Politiques de l'amitié*, 102–103n1.

59 Derrida, *Memoires for Paul de Man*, 122; citing Paul de Man, "Foreword to Revised, Second Edition," *Blindness and Insight: Essays in the Rhetoric of Contemporary Criticism*, 2nd ed., rev. (Minneapolis: University of Minnesota Press, 1983), xi–xii, xii; Derrida, *Mémoires pour Paul de Man*, 121–122.

60 Blanchot, *Michel Foucault*, 64.

61 Derrida, *Politiques de l'amitié*, 335.

Works cited

Blanchot, Maurice. *L'Amitié*. Paris: Gallimard, 1971.

Blanchot, Maurice. *Michel Foucault: Tel que je l'imagine*. Paris: Fata Morgana, 1986.

de Man, Paul. "Autobiography as De-Facement." *The Rhetoric of Romanticism*.
New York: Columbia University Press, 1984. 67–81.

de Man, Paul. "Foreword to Revised, Second Edition." *Blindness and Insight: Essays
in the Rhetoric of Contemporary Criticism*. 2nd ed., rev. Minneapolis: University of
Minnesota Press, 1983. xi–xii.

Derrida, Jacques. "Cogito et histoire de la folie." *L'Écriture et la différence*. Paris: Seuil,
1967. 51–97.

Derrida, Jacques. "Être juste avec Freud." *Penser la folie: Essais pour Michel Foucault*.
Paris: Galilée, 1992.

Derrida, Jacques. *Khôra*. Paris: Galilée, 1993.

Derrida, Jacques. *Memoires for Paul de Man*. The Wellek Library Lectures at the
University of California Irvine. Trans. Eduardo Cadava, Jonathan Culler, Cecile
Lindsay, and Avital Ronnell. New York: Columbia University Press, 1986.

Derrida, Jacques. *Mémoires pour Paul de Man*. Paris: Galilée, 1988.

Derrida, Jacques. *Politiques de l'amitié, suivi de L'oreille de Heidegger*.
Paris: Galilée, 1994.

Derrida, Jacques. *Spectres de Marx*. Paris: Galilée, 1993.

Derrida, Jacques, and Elizabeth Roudinesco. *De quoi demain . . . Dialogue*.
Paris: Fayard/Galilée, 2001.

Foucault, Michel. "De l'amitié comme mode de vie." *Dits et écrits: 1954–1988*, vol.
4. Eds. Daniel Defert and François Ewalt. Paris: Gallimard, 1994. 163–167.

Foucault, Michel. *Folie et déraison, Histoire de la folie à l'âge classique*.
Paris: Plon, 1961.

Foucault, Michel. *Le gouvernement de soi et des autres: Cours au Collège de France.
1982–83*. Ed. Frédéric Gros. Paris: Gallimard/Seuil, 2008.

Foucault, Michel. "Mon corps, ce papier, ce feu." *Histoire de la folie à l'âge
classique suivi de Mon corps, ce papier, ce feu et La folie, l'absence de l'oeuvre*.
Paris: Gallimard, 1972. 583–603.

Foucault, Michel. "A propose de la généalogie de l'éthique: Un aperçu du travail en
cours." *Dits et écrits: 1954–1988*, vol. 4. Eds. Daniel Defert and François Ewalt.
Paris: Gallimard, 1994. 609–631.

Foucault, Michel. "Qu'est-ce que les Lumières?" *Dits et écrits: 1954–1988*, vol. 4. Eds.
Daniel Defert and François Ewalt. Paris: Gallimard, 1994. 562–578.

Kant, Immanuel. *Critique of Pure Reason*. Trans. Norman Kemp Smith.
New York: Modern Library, 1958.

Larmour, David H. J., Paul Allen Miller, and Charles Platter. "Introduction: Situating
the *History of Sexuality*." In *Rethinking Sexuality: Foucault and Classical*

Antiquity. Eds. David H. J., Larmour, Paul Allen Miller, and Charles Platter. Princeton: Princeton University Press, 1998. 3–41.

Macherey, Pierre. "Le Marx intempestif de Derrida." *Derrida, la tradition de la philosophie.* Eds. Marc Crépon and Frédéric Worms. Paris: Galilée, 2008. 135–154.

Miller, Paul Allen. "Cicero Reads Derrida Reading Cicero: A Politics and a Friendship to Come." *Brill's Companion to the Reception of Cicero.* Ed. William Altman. Leiden: Brill, 2015. 175–97.

Miller, Paul Allen. "The Repeatable and the Unrepeatable: Žižek and the Future of the Humanities, or Assessing Socrates." *symplokē* 17 (2009): 191–208.

Montaigne, Michel de. *Oeuvres complètes.* Eds. Albert Thibaudet and Maurice Rat. Paris: Gallimard, 1962.

Peeters, Benoît. *Derrida.* Paris: Flammarion, 2010.

Žižek, Slavoj. *The Parallax View.* Cambridge, MA: MIT Press, 2006.

6

Death, Survival, and Translation

Brian O'Keeffe

In a poem by Seamus Heaney entitled "Route 110," and published in *Human Chain*, the last collection of poems to appear before his death, Heaney reminisces about his youth. He and his friends stand before a riverbank. There is a "surface-ruck"[1] in the water. An otter: "The gleam, a turnover warp in the black / Quick water." They contemplate the riverbank field: "twilit and a-hover with midge-drifts, as if we had commingled / Among shades and shadows stirring on the brink." Heaney and his friends stand waiting and watching, "Needy and ever needier for translation."

The heart-wrench I feel, when reading these lines, is provoked by the thought of an older Heaney, anticipating his own death, and feeling ever needier for translation—feeling a need to come back to the shores of the living, back over the Acheron that divides the living and the dead. Heaney must have known that his time was limited; limited his time to tarry offshore, in the vicinities of that deathly coastline or riverbank. In view of that last *translatio* (no ferryman who can be convinced to reverse that crossing), Heaney's need is great, human, and deeply, beautifully felt.

As the shades of death gather, the need for translation is a poignant need. This need is the topic of this essay, but if, in a moment, I shall turn to a very different writer, I begin with Heaney because he expresses that need better than I can. And it has to be well-stated: humbly, but powerfully. Consider that forlorn struggle with mortality, the riverbanks of life and death as they blur in the summer's twilight, that hope for translation as a rescue, as a chance for survival, the last ferry to the field of daylight and life.

The very different writer is Derrida. He has his discursive beauties too, I think, and indeed, one way to address the matter of his survival beyond death might well be to note—and celebrate—the elegance with which Derrida expressed himself. In any case, Derrida, like Heaney, speaks of the need for translation and of the chances for a certain kind of survival beyond death, thanks to translation. This is what gives Derrida, when he thinks on such things, a poignancy and power akin (but so different) to Heaney's—a lyrical melancholy and an existential *point* that accompanies, and outlasts the convolutions, torsions, and obliquities to which Derrida submits philosophy (when it speaks of life and death) and literature (when it addresses the matter of its putative survival).

The purpose of this essay is to say something about the way Derrida thinks about translation, and also to let the idea of translation resonate with certain thoughts of death, life, and living-on. Two of the Derrida dossiers I wish to retrieve from the Derrida-base concern his thinking on survival, and on the work of mourning. On the former topic, there is, as he acknowledges, no living on beyond one's death, but a living-on is possible, Derrida maintains, as long as there are carriers of that lost life, bearers of memories sufficient to keep that lost person alive in a memorial afterlife. In that case, then, living-on must be thought of as a progression that belongs without belonging, as he says in "Living On/Border Lines," to the progression of life and death. And this means that such living-on is not the opposite of living, just as it is not identical with living. Living-on introduces the precious enigma of a supplementary living, and in doing so, begs to differ, one might say—resists the opposition between life and death. It refuses, to some extent, the finality of a death that has no possibility of a life afterward. As for mourning, I retain only one strand of Derrida's thoughts on that memorial practice. It concerns the idealized scenario of mourning that he tends to associate with a certain psychoanalytic discourse in which the body of the dead other is taken into the self. It is pictured as an introjection, an incorporation of the other. Indeed, a certain consumption of the dead other: in "By Force of Mourning," his text written in response to the death of Louis Marin, Derrida speaks of a certain Eucharistic logic—the Eucharistic body or host here is given as the great mourning object *par excellence*. "Take this and eat it, do this in memory of me."[2]

The third dossier, as I have already indicated, is the dossier entitled (though perhaps in more than one language) "translation." My central concern is a text by Derrida that is very much about mourning and survival in, and by way of translation, but let me defer Derrida by referring first to Walter Benjamin, and quote briefly from "The Task of the Translator." Benjamin says this about the life of artworks: "[A] translation issues from the original—not so much from its life, as from its afterlife . . . The idea of life and afterlife in works of art should be regarded with an entirely unmetaphorical objectivity."[3] We can appreciate why a translation "issues" from its afterlife, since we seem to be speaking of the second life that translation ensures, away from the life of the text in its original guise, when it is written in its original language. But the question here, of course, is what Benjamin might mean by "unmetaphorical objectivity." How would we regard the lives and afterlives of literary texts in this way? Does "unmetaphorical" entail refusing to say that a text lives only *as if* it enjoys the organic life enjoyed by human beings or animals? If we do that, we may have to risk a kind of literal-mindedness, and say, on the contrary, that texts live *as* we do, and survive *as* we do (by "we" I mean we who are human beings, but we who are also human animals). And if we risk that violation of commonsense (commonsense that "metaphor" safeguards), we may also have to speak—and surely we do—of the death of a text.

Here, then, are the questions I want to raise in respect of literary texts: can literary texts die? Can they anticipate their impending demise and do something about it? Is doing something about it a matter of asking us to respond to the text that senses its imminent death, and that appeals for rescue, or for translation? Are texts not "needy, and ever needier for translation?" The text that helps answer such questions is one Derrida wrote for the Italian journal *Poesia* in November 1988, and which was entitled *Che cos'è la poesia?* It was an interview, and Derrida replied in French. After it was published in the Italian journal (translated by Maurizio Ferraris, also the interviewer in question), it was published in France, and in the English of Peggy Kamuf's translation. It appears in various volumes, including the Stanford University Press collection of interviews with Derrida entitled *Points*. In that publication, the French text is on one page, and on the other, the English translation. I am going to be quoting from the English translation.

Parables of the poem

What, then, is poetry? It is an unfair and impudent question, in many ways. "In order to respond to such a question—*in two words, right?*—you are asked to know how to renounce knowledge," writes Derrida, a little tartly. "And to know it well, without ever forgetting it: demobilize culture, but never forget in your learned ignorance what you sacrifice on the road, in crossing the road."[4] The chance that Derrida might answer on his own terms, unexpectedly, or otherwise, depends on the slim possibility he might be capable of forgetting the characterizations of poetry he already knows—*poesia, poésie, poiesis*.

But Derrida is practiced in the art of *docta ignorantia*, although the stakes are too high for one to regard his eventual response as merely glib, or playfully unserious. For there is something serious registered from the outset of his reply—the hint of a dangerous scenario of a road being crossed, a busy road, one imagines, a highway of literary culture, where the grand discourses that define poetry—Greek *poiesis*, perhaps also Germanic *Dichtung*—act in concert to fix all singular poems into the crosshairs, or crossroads, of generic characterization. What is at stake is the chance for a singular poem to remain sufficiently singular to escape the generic. Imagine a poor, singular little poem, out there in the middle of the road, exposed and vulnerable before the onrush of genericity—*Poiesis* or *Dichtung*—bearing down upon it, like Mack trucks, swatting the poem in their wake.

Eventually, Derrida will call "poematic" this little bit of a poem that cannot quite be assimilated to Poem. And it is the chances of the poematic to survive long enough to cross the road that concerns Derrida—the concern is ethical, when all is said and done, and that ethics concerns the chances for a poem to survive what one might call death by definition. But Derrida, at the beginning of his text, also calls the poem something else. The poem, he declares, is a hedgehog. A little creature of a poem, cringing at the rumble of traffic, curling up into a forlorn and defenseless ball: "[T]he animal thrown onto the road, absolute, solitary, rolled up in a ball, *next to (it)self.* And for that very reason, it may get itself run over, *just so,* the *hérisson, istrice* in Italian, in English, hedgehog."[5]

This is unexpected. A poem-hedgehog—what could that be? *Che cos'è la poesia?* tells the tale of that unlikely creature as a sort of fable, like in Aesop or La Fontaine. Or perhaps better, like in Kafka, he who also imagines creaturely life—the degraded animality of human beings, but also the strange life possessed by things like that Odradek—another ball, like the balled-up hedgehog. In any case, it would seem that the fear of imminent death is what prompts Derrida to consider how a poem, like a hedgehog, might possess a kind of life. For it seems that the hedgehog-poem has life enough to fear what might happen to it, out there on the road. It understands that death is solitary—we all die our own deaths, die absolutely and alone, and this *hérisson* will have to do likewise. Already a philosopher, this poem does not need Heidegger to explain what it is to be thrown into the world, what it is to be a subject, about to be cast under the wheels of the vehicles bearing down upon it, what being-toward-death really means.

For Derrida, mortal fear provokes the hedgehog-poem into a discovery of its own self-hood. It is about sensing the vulnerability of an imperiled self, sensing one's own body as a mortal body. When it curls into its protective stance, fearing imminent death on the road, a truth about what it is to *feel* oneself is revealed. The body of the hedgehog-poem discovers its own self-proximity—it touches itself as its spiny exterior produces an interior side that protects, and reveals, an inner recess. This is a self, discovered as the sensation of an exterior and an interior touching *just so*, and this touching is the interface where a self senses its own self—this would be a sense, so to speak, of *nextness*.

Derrida will have to move quickly to pick this creaturely poem off the road, and carry (we may already say translate) it to safety. At some considerable peril to himself—perhaps he too will have to venture out into the middle of the road, and share the same fate as the poem, or else sacrifice himself for the sake of the hedgehog-poem's survival.

But why does Derrida choose a hedgehog to characterize the poem? Perhaps it is a secret, and we should let Derrida have his secrets. But he trails a set of clues, nonetheless, so there are reasons we might offer, some more revealing than others. For Peggy Kamuf, the translator of *Che cos'è la poesia?*, the Italian *istrice* places a stress on "striction," and she notes that "Throughout the text, the *str*-sound is stressed. One may hear in it the distress of the beast caught in the strictures of this translation."[6] Lest we think that translation will be a positive force in this life or death situation, translation may yet turn out to be a throttling clamp that forces one language to lose something of its own idiomatic expression as it is transported into other languages.

Then there are the hedgehogs that find a discreet place in philosophy. Nietzsche often portrayed himself as such a beast, and indeed, in *Ecce Homo*, he was moved to imagine himself as an *Igel*. Nietzsche, writing in Turin, imagines finding himself suddenly in a German city, and faced with that ghastly prospect, cringes into spiky self-protection: "Wouldn't this turn me into a *hedgehog*?"[7] His remark follows hard on the heels of a discussion of the instinct of self-defense, where the sheer effort of warding off sundry menaces becomes exhausting. The effort to say "no," as opposed to "yes," is fatiguing, and if "no" turns out to be a rebarbative, quills-outward disposition, how much better it would be, Nietzsche declares, if "yes" could be conveyed by the expressively affirmative gesture of hands held open.

Already, it seems that to speak of hedgehogs is to speak of self-preservation, and if, as Nietzsche observes, the better course of action is to save energy and react as little as possible, it may be that Derrida felt the same way, faced with the constant barrage of interviews that asked him to respond, with impossible brevity, to the weightiest questions of all. Nietzsche adds that a good parable of this sort of thing would address how one interacts with books. The scenario, here, is one of scholars wearied from constant contact with books, yearning for a day when the freshness of a thought can come—the time for this is daybreak—without having been prompted to that thought by the routine exercise of having to read tome after academic tome. Perhaps, in this light, Derrida's fatigue is akin to Nietzsche's, and the decision to respond to the prompting of an interviewer with the unexpected freshness of "poetry is a hedgehog" is one way to combat routine responses, though it is only Maurizio Ferraris who would be able to confirm whether he received Derrida's reply as one offered with open hands, or as a barbed refusal, a "no" to a question—*Che cos'è la poesia?*—Derrida found impertinent.

Another hedgehog is to be found in Schlegel, which Derrida may have remembered from reading Nancy and Lacoue-Labarthe's *The Literary Absolute*. In another essay, *Istrice 2: Ick bünn all hier*, Derrida admits that his own hedgehog may not have been a new thought (in what may be an echo of Nietzsche, Derrida speaks of a hedgehog "unique, young as on the first day of creation"[8]), since he surely read it first in *The Literary Absolute*. Perhaps the hedgehog came back to visit him like a ghost, like a *revenant*. Still, Derrida demurs. There is no automatic genealogy here, he avers, no kinship or affiliation between their *hérisson* and his own. Derrida's hedgehog is his alone, unique. In any case, Schlegel's fragment 206 reads as follows: "A fragment, like a small work of art, has to be entirely isolated from the surrounding world and be complete in itself like a hedgehog."[9] For Nancy and Lacoue-Labarthe, the "logic of the hedgehog" is a paradoxical logic where the fragment is both fragment and yet complete nonetheless. They are apparently speaking of textual fragments, but their commentary is quite prepared to bestow a considerable amount of life (and indeed, existential dignity) upon this shard of writing: "Its existential obligation [*devoir-être*], if not its existence (is it not understood that its only existence is an existential obligation and that this hedgehog is a Kantian animal?), is indeed formed by the integrity and the wholeness of the organic individual."[10] Do textual fragments have a life as we do, or only like we do? Much depends on the asseverative force of that "indeed." But it is a striking claim: it is impossible to think of the "fragmentary exigency," the fragment's compulsion to *be* a fragment, without ascribing a sort of life to it—and a rational life, a *devoir-être*, a *raison d'être*. Thus Schlegel's hedgehog-fragment is a Kantian animal, and perhaps so too, is Derrida's hedgehog-poem. Both attain the dignity of Kantian subjects, no less, if that obligation, that exigency, is as compelling for a poem or fragment as it is for those of us who exist in obedience to a life-project

characterized by the exercise of reason, and subject to the self-given impera-
tives of morality.

This elevation of poems and fragments up to the higher level apparently
reserved for "those of us," can, of course, be countered by the claim that Nancy
and Lacoue-Labarthe, if not Schlegel, are speaking metaphorically—they surely
can't be serious. Surely Derrida isn't serious either—poems just don't have
the same kind of life as animals, or human beings, or anything else that has
organic life. They don't even have the barest, merest kind of life. But remember
Benjamin, who insists that "The idea of life and afterlife in works of art should
be regarded with an entirely unmetaphorical objectivity." The challenge, here,
is to resist the presumptuous gesture that bestows life on organic forms alone.
For Benjamin, the possibility of regarding the lives and afterlives of texts with
unmetaphorical objectivity is justified by way of a concept of life that can be
awarded to anything, as long as "history" is there to endorse that life: "The concept of life is given its due only if everything that has a history of its own, and
is not merely the setting for history, is credited with life. In the final analysis,
the range of life must be determined by the standpoint of history rather than
that of nature."[11]

So perhaps history has the final say on who gets life. From that point of view,
Schlegel, Nancy, Lacoue-Labarthe, and now Derrida justify their startling positions on the putative life of texts insofar as they all inspect how it is that literary history bestows life upon texts—surely it does this by taking the long view
and speaking in terms, for instance, of *genres*. But this is what Derrida also
wishes to resist in the name of another life (the life of a singularity, of *a* poem
that belongs, but does not belong to a genre), and which the Schlegelian fragment also wishes to resist in the name of a "fragment-project" integral to that
very fragmentariness. Resistance, here, implies a spiny, hedgehog-like riposte
to a wholeness that would subsume the fragment, glue it to a greater whole.
Resistance raises its quills to ward off the depredations of genre, especially
those total genres, or the sole genre that subsumes all others into the only one
that really counts, namely Poetry, *poiesis*, or *Dichtung*.

Against this background, Benjamin comes into focus as someone who seems,
in fact, to want it both ways at once. On the one hand, "[A] translation, instead of
imitating the sense of the original, must lovingly and in detail incorporate the original's way of meaning, thus making both the original and the translation recognizable as fragments of a greater language, just as fragments are part of a vessel."[12]
To inspect a fragment is to intimate the greater whole of which it once was part. If
there is, in Benjamin, a certain nostalgia for a pre-Babelic language, somewhere

in that "intimation," there is also a forward-looking posture—a sense of eventual wholeness that motivates an *anticipation* (this is Benjamin's "messianism") of the pure language to come—the famous *reine Sprache*. On the other, fragments remain fragments—nothing can overcome this, just as Babel's splintering of the one language remains permanent. Compare Nancy and Lacoue-Labarthe: "[T]he very fragment is a project: the fragment-project does not operate as a program or prospectus but as the *immediate* projection of what it nonetheless incompletes."[13] This almost glosses Benjamin: the fragmentary translation projects—anticipates, looks forward to, hopes for—*reine Sprache*. But as a fragment, that work remains, and will forever remain undone, and indeed, it is the fragment-translation that *unworks* the eventual reconciliation of all languages into one, if it remains the case that the project of fragments is to remain as fragments. For fragments—shards of translations, in Benjamin—will always present jagged edges, hamper thereby the exercise to glue languages back together, to weld them into one.

Triangulating *Che cos'è la poesia?*, *The Literary Absolute*, and *The Task of the Translator*, as I am doing here, gives some purchase on the difficult idea that texts live, though it is perhaps only Derrida who wonders whether to gain "unmetaphporical objectivity" on such a life requires a flagrantly metaphorical format, namely the fable, parable, or allegory. It also gives a sense of the resistance of texts to what threatens them: subsumption into greater wholes. Hedgehog-poems and hedgehog-fragments bristle when their own singularity is threatened, and by undertaking the work of "incompletion," they act vigorously to fracture these menacingly greater wholes. Derrida's poematicity, that bit of poem the concept of Poem cannot quite contain, operates that incompleting, that unworking. Schlegel's fragment seems to work in much the same way to protect the "bittiness" of fragmentarity itself, if one can say such a thing. But poematicity cannot prevent us from hearing "poem"—poematicity just cannot strip "poem" out of its own formulation. Likewise, a fragment cannot refrain from intimating the whole of which it was once a part. Such is the brave futility of these kinds of resistances. Moreover, resistance can only be one part of the story, for the other part involves construing the abiding relation any part has to something greater—a singular poem to the Poem, a particular example to the generic set to which it belongs, and from which it derives at least part of its identity, a fragment that relates to what was once whole, and to which (here is the hope of Benjamin in particular) it possibly yearns to belong once more. Celebrating the spiky resistance of textual singularities is one thing, therefore, but another is taking due care not to dash the aspiration of poems, translations, and fragments to finally belong.

And this is something Derrida is mindful of. If Schlegel's fragment 206 describes the fragment as "entirely isolated from its surrounding world," it may be too complacent to declare that this is always what the fragment wants. It may wish to remain complete as a fragment, but then again, is it not cruel to deprive a text of "world"? Or to deprive a hedgehog of world, for that matter? As if one deems them beasts too poor in world, too *Weltarm*, to adopt the Heideggerian parlance, to be of much interest to philosophy when it considers being-in-the-world.

This brings us to another text where Derrida found a hedgehog. The text is Heidegger's *Identity and Difference*. In it, we find a brief reference to the brothers Grimm, and their tale of the hedgehog and the hare. A hedgehog, to be sure of victory in a race with a hare, sends his female partner ahead to the finish line, so that one or the other will always be able to declare "I am here" (Ick bünn all hier) whenever any speedy hare thinks he has beat the hedgehog to it. The tale illustrates, Derrida explains, the difficult temporalities of the "always-already-there," and the "always-already," which are temporalities vital to the way Heidegger thinks about beginning and destination, especially in view of *Dasein* when it claims to be there, always there, never anywhere, or anytime other than "there," and "then."

But, as Derrida observes, there is much to say about the couple that emerges here: is the gender difference important or not? Does *Dasein* have a gender, or a primordial genre, a sex or *Geschlecht*? Is *Dasein* indivisible? Is Being ever subject to the divisions that make for beings in their difference? The main point Derrida makes, however, is that for a hedgehog, humbly intruding into Heidegger's philosophy, it is not at all clear whether such a lowly creature could ever find a voice: could it declare "Ick," say "bünn," or ever stake his/her claim to be there, "hier," or "da"? "There is, in the end, no cogito or work for this hedgehog who cannot gather itself up or gather itself together enough to say 'Ich bin hier' or 'ergo sum,' 'immer schon da.'"[14] Some creatures forever wait to be admitted to Heidegger's, but not just Heidegger's domain where "being" is bestowed on some, but not others who live a kind of life.

Derrida's objection is ultimately that philosophy should get a little humbler. For Heidegger, philosophy can afford to ignore the hedgehog, since his thought is centered on those who are capable of posing intelligent questions to themselves about living and dying. Those who die must be capable of understanding their fatedness to die. But being-for-death is reserved for subjects, or for *Dasein*, and not, so it seems, for animals. For surely animals cannot pose such questions, animals therefore fall below a certain threshold, and enjoy only

creaturely life (and a creaturely death that is not "our" kind of death). But is
it not the case that our hedgehog is quite capable of posing questions to itself
about its impending death, and moreover, doing something about it? Think of
the hedgehog, out there on the road, curling into a self-protective ball. A futile
defense to be sure, but this is still an animal that knows what it is to anticipate
death coming upon it. "Heidegger would say: the hedgehog does not see death
coming, death does not happen to it . . . And how can one say that the hedgehog
has no apprehension of death when it rolls itself up in a ball?"[15] Rolled up tight,
the hedgehog's eyes can no longer see what is coming. Perhaps none of us need
to see death to know it is coming—remember Odysseus's old, blind dog who
welcomes him home to Ithaca, and then drops dead.

Derrida's critique of Heidegger resists the philosophical reflex that qualifies
life in terms of the peremptory discourses of hominization and animalization,
resists the apparently requisite dichotomies and implicit hierarchies—animal/
human, Being/beings. The resistance might begin here, but to persist on further
is to allow for an ethical thought that would now address matters of care and
responsibility, *Mitsein* and *Sorge*, in terms of a generous remittance of life to
things as unlikely as poems. For lest we forget, the hedgehog in question is a
poem. Derrida, as we have seen, gets to the life of a poem by way of the life of a
hedgehog, and gets to the heart of his objection to Heidegger by way of a spot
of translation: *istrice* and *Igel* would seem to be the two translations that count
here. For when Derrida responded to the question "what is poetry?" with *istrice*
and *Igel*, he perhaps meant to allow the letter "I" to make itself plain. As plain
as a pun. Certainly an English speaker confronted with *Igel* is going to think of
eagles, and perhaps, if that speaker is also familiar with German philosophy, he
or she will wonder about the loftiness of the creatures such philosophy seems to
prefer: ought philosophy pay attention to creatures—like hedgehogs—that are
much more down to earth? If *Igel*, moreover, prompts us to think of Hegel, that
proper name might stick in the craw somewhat, as it does in *Glas*: in that text,
there is always a glottal *gl* that articulates the constricted sound of a throttled
throat.

But the major point is that, with *istrice* and *Igel*, the poem now gets to say "I,"
or "Ich." Alas, the problem is that if one moves to elevate the life of a humble
hérisson above mere, creaturely life and promote it to a more dignified plane
of existence, the gesture simply exposes the hedgehog to what having a life
ultimately means—it means understanding that such a life can be lost. Death,
and not just a blithe "ceasing to be," now becomes the price Derrida asks his
hedgehog not only to pay, but also to apprehend, fearfully and with redoubtable

lucidity, as the costly meaning of being itself—Destiny, or destinality itself. As much as Derrida is concerned for the poor hedgehog-poem, thrown out there in the middle of the road, it may be that in claiming a poem has a life, Derrida has just thrown the poem under the bus. Thrownness-into-being: now the hedgehog-poem gets to feel what that is really like.

But no need to get carried away. Derrida is quite mindful that all of this is the result of a chance play of syllables and letters—a bit of chancy translation. He is also aware of the "abuse" to which he has subjected the poem, not to mention the little hedgehog: "[I]ndissolubly linked to the chance of a language and of signifiers that play the role of [a] temporary proper name (first *istrice* and then its fragile translation into *hérisson*), [it comes] into being via a letter, this 'catachrestic' *hérisson* is barely a name, it does not bear its name, it plays with syllables, but in any case it is neither a concept nor a thing."[16] Perhaps that letter "I" matters, but perhaps not. If not, then the poem subsides into a category that Derrida refuses to name—"it" is neither a concept nor a thing. Like Odradek, perhaps. We can almost hear the fading of being from the poem-hedgehog: from *istrice* and *Igel* to hedgehog, the hard "h" replaces the existential "I," but by the time we get to *hérisson*, the "h" is faint indeed. Hardly much of a sound or a word, a scanty sort of name for a poem. A nickname that *Poiesis* and *Dichtung* will swiftly move to dislodge, and forcibly rename in any case. (But speaking of proper names, will we not hear Derrida's name somewhere here? *D'herrida*—a compound name, which takes a "da" from Heidegger, *dada* Heidegger, he with whom Derrida is forever playing *Fort-Da*, plus a various syllables and letters from an *hérisson*—a little bristly, those rr's, I think). Still, Derrida bears some guilt for this catachresis. "Humble and close to the ground, it can only expose itself to accidents when it tries to save itself, and first of all to save itself from its name and to save its coming. It has no relation to itself—that is, no totalizing individuality—that does not expose it even more to death and to being-torn-apart."[17] If the peril is that a poem finds its own name unbearable, because it immediately loses its own specificity as a singular poem to Poem, becomes the token of a more general type, then the poem must save itself from its own name in order to come to be what, like Schlegel's fragment, it wants to be—complete, individual, and whole for itself, that is, not part of any genre or totality named Poem that, for its part, identifies the poem only by first dividing one poem from all others, and then forcibly reattaching it to a generic set of "all others." What it wants to be: just itself, no less and no more. This is what "poematics" tries to think, and why poematics must be differentiated from poetics, says Derrida. Yet if translation could glitch poetry and poetics by swiftly producing a chain of equivalences (*istrice, hérisson*, hedgehog, *Igel*) as a means to tack against, if not outrun, the two definitions that seem at stake—*Poiesis* and *Dichtung*—the problems remain severe. First, there is the risk of ruining the proper name the poem tries to save by exposing it to "accidents of translation"—nicknames after nicknames, the translator's callous abuse of the proper name a poem might wish to protect and defend in the name of its own self-possession, in the name of its own identity, its own "I." Second, for all that Derrida might want to prise open this self-centered, balled-up poem, open it up to the multiple names he now gives the poem, this is perhaps tantamount to tearing the poem's own integrity apart.

What to do? On the one hand, translation may be a Bad Thing. It exposes the poem to chance, and that seems to mean "accidents." Translation projects poems above and beyond whatever was once "proper" in view of the original idiom of the poem, and translation does so in only scant respect for the poem's desire to remain at home, enjoying its right and proper belonging to just one given language. On the other hand, translation may be a Good Thing, if it is the case that the distress of a poem is such that it appeals for translation. This is the distress that Kamuf wants us to hear in the stresses of that *str* in *istrice*. This distress seems to occur because poems can suffer a kind of death. I called it death by definition. For we cannot but hear in "poem" the Greek *poiesis,* and having heard this, the function of a poem has been defined already as a certain kind of "work." Or if one is speaking German, in all *Gedichte*, there is some *Dichtung*, and perhaps we will also hear *Diktat*—a dictate that tells the poem what to be, what to say, and what the import of its saying is supposed to be. And lastly, there is the noble task for poetry set by Heidegger—poetry as the setting-forth-of-truth-in-the-work. Derrida ruefully thinks of this poor poem being run down by the grand Heideggerian discourse it cannot save itself from. The road here is something like Heidegger's *Autobahn*. Referring to Heidegger's *The Origin of the Work of Art*, Derrida writes, "The poematic hedgehog crosses the highway at the risk of being run over by a great discourse that it cannot resist."[18]

The poematic: the "bit" that poetics cannot contain, the slim chance for a poem to define itself on its own terms, to resist the *Diktat* that has already named it a poem, and wedded it thereby to genericity, to a greater whole. The ruin of singularity. Here, then, is what Derrida thinks the poem says to him: "I am *a* dictation."[19] The stress on the "a" matters, for without that vital stress, we will not hear the distress of the poem. I am a dictation, says the poem, but that means the fate of a singular poem is to be dictated to—dictated to be the token of a more general type, namely the type of Poetry. A poem is dictated to be poetic, and it responds by being poetic. But what are the poem's chances to respond to the question "What is poetry?" by responding in the name of itself, as a singularity? What are the chances that a poem could offer its own singular "dict," so to speak? And dictate itself, just itself, to a reader—command that person to respond to its singular needs, dictate to a reader the nature of its need? For instance, the need of its proper name, the need of an "I" that the poem wishes saved. Could we but respond to *it* alone, we might rescue its singularity from the great definitions that have been established for Poetry. Thus says Derrida, pointedly including Benjamin: "Most of all do not let the *hérisson* be led back into the circus or the menagerie of *poiesis*: nothing to be done (*poiein*), neither 'pure poetry,' nor pure rhetoric, nor *reine Sprache*, nor 'setting-forth-of-truth-in-the-work.'"[20]

So how to rescue the poem? How to save it from generic definitions that cripple its own chance to be *a* poem, nothing more? How to save it so that a poem can make its own singular appeal, voice its own singular law, its "dict"? It would seem that the rescuers here are translators: their job is to pick this hedgehog-poem up off the road and carry it to the other side, sides, or perhaps no "side" at all. This rescue is an act of translation that rapidly redefines the poem—calls it "istrice," "hérisson," "Igel," and "hedgehog"—and hopes thereby to outrun the definitions, Greek and German, that will catch up with it.

Saving the poem

Here is the appeal of a text, anticipating its death like a prophecy: "[T]ranslate me, watch, keep me yet awhile, get going, save yourself, let's get off the autoroute."[21] It also says: "[D]estroy me, or rather render my support invisible to the outside."[22] This is where it gets complicated, and in my view, really rather beautiful. For it seems that the task of the translator is to *incorporate* the text so that it becomes invisible to the outside, untethered from the support of the page. We are speaking here of a rescue that would interiorize the text, support its inside in our insides, take the mark, trace, letter, or writ of the poem therein, and in so doing, render its textual exteriority invisible. The poem continues "Promise it: let it be disfigured, transfigured or rendered indeterminate in its *port*—and in this word you will hear the shore of departure as well as the referent toward which translation is portered. Eat, drink, swallow my letter, carry it, transport it in you, like the law of a writing become your body: *writing in (it)self.*"[23]

This is translation as a digesting, a swallowing, a taking-inward. If this is a promise as well, then the appeal of the text-as-other must come inside the body of this translator-transporter, and mark itself as the law that will be obeyed by the translator who promises. An ingestion of the law. The writ or letter of the law as a writing *in* one's own self. But also a certain inside of writing itself— writing *in* itself. "L'écriture en soi" is the original French that Kamuf renders as "*writing in (it)self.*" Perhaps, when writing, inscribed on a sheet of paper, folds in on itself, an inside and an outside is thereby produced, and thinking of this pleat or ply of the text, we have already, perforce, spoken of an it-*self*: it is indeed difficult not to bestow selfhood upon writing. In any case, this is not so far from the curl of the *hérisson* that produces an inside of itself, and in so doing, produces an outside—those spines, barbs, and quills. Once we have heard the appeal of the text, standing in desperate need of translation, and taken it into ourselves, into intimate proximity with our *for intérieur*, the self of the text and our own self meet and join in the most intimate proximity—a self next to self, or a body adjoining another body, just so, *auprès de soi* (next to (it)self). Herein, or therein, the text becomes as mobile and transportable as we are. We can now carry the body of the poem, its inside in our inside, off elsewhere—to safety, one hopes.

But this safety may depend on the hedgehog being shorn of its exterior spines—its signs? Readable letters, pointy indices of meaning. All this might have to be shed as the price of survival: the text disfigured, therefore, writing's exterior marks erased, in order that the text become amenable to this inges- tion. Disfigured in order to be transfigured into sound, resounding close by the heart, there where the rhythm of the poem is assimilated to the rhythm of breathing. Perhaps. But what of that *port*, which is italicized in both the origi- nal French, and in Kamuf's English translation? We know that translation is a transport, and that *translatio* invites us to think of maritime departures—from the home port, home shores, to foreign shores, foreign ports. But in what lan- guage might we speak and hear that *port*? In English with a hard "t," in French with a soft, inaudible "t"? What does Derrida want us to hear? I am not really sure, although "port," said in a French accent, also echoes, in me at least, with "porc." Pig, yes, but almost inevitably, I think of another spiny beast, a porcu- pine, a *porc-épic*. . . .

Epic of the porcupine, of the hedgehog? Is this the tale Derrida is telling, in and around a certain accident of translation, between French and English? I really don't know. But it is a fetching thought—almost Odyssean, or Homeric. Except that the repatriation to Ithaca is something that the epic of translation cannot confirm: the epic of translation is an anti-*Odyssey*, a tale of repatriation permanently thwarted, of a homecoming that must remain always offshore. Translations must not trespass on the home turf of "Ithaca," and if a translation ever dared, no doubt it would cringe before the slings and arrows—more quills!—loosed from the bows of the importunate suitors of the Penelope text. Well, the point, in any case, is that when the text appeals to translation, translators must promise "it," in view of an "it." A promise to indeterminacy, to neither a concept, nor a thing, to barely a text at all. The act that enacts our promise would seem to be a protective curling over the exterior surface of the poem-hedgehog, and this will assuredly be rather painful. But this curling over the poor poem is how we take the poem inside ourselves—it begins with a caring hand that cups to pick the poem up off the road.

Derrida wants this act to be a veritable taking-inside of oneself. And in that inside would we be marked by the "dict" of this singular poem—by the poem's singular law that commands the translator to this ethical duty of care. So where might this mark of the poem's singular law be inscribed? On what organ? It is the heart. For this is what the poem says to Derrida: "I am *a* dictation, pronounces poetry, learn me by heart."[24] This is the crucial, and beautiful point: it is the taking-to-heart that takes a text inside. This, then, is about an action that effectively saves the text, ensures its survival *in the memory*. German says "Erinnerung"—"innering." That's it exactly. But in French, as Derrida observes, "apprendre par coeur" has two meanings. "Apprendre" is to learn, but it is also to teach. Here is the chance of the French idiom: we *learn* the poem by heart, and this is our ethical duty, how we ensure that the poem lives on in the memory. But the poem *teaches* the translator to have a heart. Or to put it even more strikingly, the poem invents the heart itself when it comes into the body, or memory-body of the translator.

Derrida accordingly speaks of the dream of learning by heart: "Of letting your heart be traversed by the dictated dictation . . . You did not yet know the heart, you learn it thus. From this experience and from this expression I call a poem that very thing that teaches the heart, invents the heart, *that which*, finally, the word *heart* seems to mean, and which, in my language, I cannot easily discern from the word itself."[25] "You did not yet know the heart." It is such a striking thought: as if the heart is veritably invented by the incoming of the other, made known as a heart to those who have one, but who only scantly discerned its precious resource as an organ of memory. As if the heart is invented by the poem that comes into the heart, by way of the heart, "*par* le coeur." The poem advenes to the heart by inventing it.

A lovely transposition, of course, of the sort of thing that *Psyche: Inventions of the Other* addressed in such etymological detail. The incoming of the poem effects an "in-venire," an invention, and what it invents, at the moment of its advent to the reader, is precisely what the poem needs to be invented, in order to live on in the memory of the reader. It needs two things: first, it needs a reader to become a translator. When a reader responds with the heart, he or she stops being a reader and becomes a translator, because "translate me!" is what a poem, fundamentally, says to all readers. Second, it needs that we become translators in the true sense of the word, namely that we become transporters or porters of the poem's meaning because it now resides in the heart, inside of ourselves. There must be the invention of a heart, for the poem's sake, for the sake of its survival, and so the poem, with cunning and foresight, ensures that it invents one for that specific purpose. It grafts a prosthetic heart to our own, this supplementary heart serving the purpose for which the poem invented it—to keep the poem alive in the memory, so that it may live on after its demise.

This is a prosthesis that, in a sense, the reader only now discovers he or she already had. The reader discovers that heart, but now apprehends the truth of the Derridean "You did not yet know the heart, you learn it thus." You, but let us say we, *learn* the heart, thanks to the poem, and the poem, as for it, relies on us to learn it by heart. At the moment of this invention of the heart, then, a reader of poetry becomes a translator—one bidden to memory, to bear the poem in the heart, to transport the poem inside oneself. That translator becomes a porter of that poem's destiny, and, so doing, he or she assumes the ethical duty of ensuring the survival of the poem. This invention, then, is nothing short of the event of translation.

Is this heart metaphorical? Is this a heart a cardiologist might recognize? Probably not. But Derrida, of course, is quite aware that one can have prosthetic hearts, or heart transplants like his friend Jean-Luc Nancy. It is a beautiful, heartfelt thought, in any case. And if Derrida is not dead, for some of us writing in the pages of this volume, it is at least in part because, the rebarbative thickets of "theory" notwithstanding, Derrida had an extraordinary ability to articulate lovely thoughts such as these. Think of it: the heart pricked by the text, by the puncture of a command that insists something be done for the poem in mortal peril. But that prick of the ethical conscience soon gives way to the pang of loss—the stricken feeling that always accompanies those who have to remember the dead. The dead circulate in the hearts of memory, and those who have such hearts are, so Derrida seems to say, translators. Quite where a translator will take this poem, interiorized and rewritten now on the heart, *as* the heart, is not clear. The poem is now subject to the *alea* of translation. It will move to other, foreign shores, who knows where.

Mourning the poem

So let us hear what the poem fully says to Derrida: "I am *a* dictation, pronounces poetry, learn me by heart, copy me down, guard and keep me, look out for me, look at me, dictated dictation, right before your eyes: soundtrack, *wake*, trail of light, photograph of the feast in mourning."[26] Consider *wake* here, which is in English in the French version of Derrida's text. A wake in two senses, perhaps. As if the poem has a wake, or a trail of afterimages of itself, and gives us something to work with, once it is time to do the work of mourning. In doing so, the poem anticipates the mourning feast (that kind of wake), and gives us something to feast upon. The poem thereby anticipates its death, prepares us for loss, and prepares us, in advance, for the work of mourning, for the mourning feast. And besides being acoustic imprints (soundtracks), these are also visible images—a trail of light, photographs, graphic traces that rise up right before one's eyes. Consider the importance of images in mourning, since this is in fact the central focus of the essay on Louis Marin entitled "By Force of Mourning." In that text, Derrida addresses himself to Marin's account of afterimages. These are portraits of the dead that now acquire an intensity because they are all that is left of the dead person. In producing photographs and portraits, we provide ourselves afterimages to see, and we are therefore able to see death, right before our own eyes. But as for the person of the portrait, the best gift one can be given by he, she, or it, that anticipates death, is to be given the images that would be preserved by those left behind—material for the wake. Poems, Derrida seems to say, also trail themselves, leave something visible behind, in their wake, in order to be *mournable*.

Visibility therefore matters for the afterlife, for that survival on beyond death. In "Living on/Border Lines" Derrida ventures to claim that he discerns, in the French word for survival, namely "survie," not just "vie" as in "life," but also "vision," and from there, a connection can made between survival and "sur-vision." As if we need to speak of a seeing-on, as well as a living-on.[27] Thus would we inscribe the Poem into the general account Derrida gives of mourning. It is a matter of a poem that transfigures the work of death into a work that, and to quote from "By Force of Mourning," "gives and gives something to be seen."[28] Remember what the poem seems to say to Derrida—"look out for me, look at me, here I am, right before your eyes." This is the poem looking at Derrida, and Derrida's response is also a looking at the poem, a looking out for the poem. This is the visual giving of the poem, and our job is to produce after-images of the poem, postmortem—*Ça nous regarde*, ethically speaking. But if we ask where this "regard" might strike us with the compelling force of a gaze that is also an utter command, then it must be an entirely visible space—visible to the other who regards us, and asks us to regard it. No matter how recessed, interior, and concealed this space is, Derrida can still say that "[w]hen we say 'in us,' when we speak so easily and so painfully of inside and outside, we are naming space, we are speaking of a visibility of the body, a geometry of gazes, an orientation of perspectives. *We are speaking of images.*"[29]

Would we agree, therefore, to regard translation as a matter of the translator seeing the poem, and the poem seeing the translator? And indeed, agree upon the possibility that a poem does not just look at the translator, but *in* the translator? What Derrida wants us to countenance, I think, is an idea of the body of the translator as a visible body. An odd idea, to be sure, but I do wonder if it is not a matter of regarding the body of the translator—or the translator's heart—as a strangely involute space, turned inside out, opened to an exteriority, to there where it can be seen. And if this is to be a memory-body, a heart invented for the purpose of remembering, we might also have to consider remembering itself in terms of a topology of inside and outside. In *Che cos'è la poesia?* Derrida adverts to the two German words that have to do with remembering—"Erinnerung" does indeed get us to an "innering." But "by heart" in German, Derrida reminds us, is "auswendig." Turned out. And here, perhaps, is a space: the poem comes in, its trail of images comes into the inside, but to fulfill the obligation of the learning by heart, we get turned inside *out*. By our own heart.

Protecting the "poem"

We draw near, I think, to the possibility of developing a link between translation and the logic Derrida calls "invagination." Translators are turned inside out in order to be translators, and to be a translator is to be subject to the duty of "Erinnerung," to learn "auswendig," and to understand the two meanings of "apprendre par coeur." Could we speak, as Derrida does in *Glas*, of the sheath of translation? Something protective, in any case, although one would hasten to add that this is the sort of protection afforded by the heartfelt gesture of *care*. And yet it is a kind of ethics of translatory care that will have always been darkened to a certain morbidity, to a foreboding—this is the burden of all those who wish to care for a friend while alive, and care beyond the death of that same friend. For perhaps to be a translator is to be always already preparing for the death of the poem one loves as a friend. The poem is not yet dead, but the melancholy point is that all those who risk being in relations of care, friendship, or love for another, prepare for that time when that other will no longer be alive. Mourning is prospective, we prepare for it in advance by taking to heart a stock of memories of the other while alive, but upon the death of the other, we take that other yet more to the heart. "Yet more," but in a sense, completely: this is the logic that Derrida calls the Eucharistic logic of mourning, the total incorporation of the other. "Take this and eat it. Do this in memory of me." This is what learning, or taking to heart means. It is an introjection, an incorporation. A total hosting of the host and by the host. Survival is subject to the logic of parasitism, and this is not quite so far from the logic of prosthesis. But it is also the logic of a survival that kills the poem, so to speak: remember, the poem knows that to appeal for such survival is also to say "destroy me."

But we are not just speaking of poems in the generic senses we are used to. Recall that Derrida says, "I call a poem that which invents the heart." An amazing promotion of the poem: "poem" has now become a name for anything that appeals to memory, and appeals in the name of a death that thing can foresee, like a blind prophet, or hear, at least (when a hedgehog curls into a ball, it is blind to the oncoming truck, but it can assuredly hear it). Perhaps all those who respond to that appeal, then, are translators of a sort. If I suggested that translation is a work of mourning because it is concerned with the afterlife of a literary text, let us say a bit more than that. Translation is concerned not just with literary texts, but with *everything* that appeals to the heart. Thus in everything that can do this, there may yet be a little bit, or something of the Derridean poem. As if poetry, a bit of it, has got into all things that risk death, and stand needy, and ever needier for translation, asking to be granted surcease from death, or else, to live on.

Notes

1   Seamus Heaney, "Route 110," *Human Chain* (London: Faber and Faber, 2010), 58. All subsequent references to "Route 110" are to the same page.
2   Jacques Derrida, "By Force of Mourning," trans. Pascale-Anne Brault and Michael Naas, *Signature Derrida*, ed. Jay Williams (Chicago and

London: Chicago University Press, 2013), 343. Hereafter abbreviated to *Signature Derrida*.

3   Walter Benjamin, "The Task of the Translator," trans. Harry Zohn, *Walter Benjamin, Selected Writings, Volume 1, 1913–1926*, Ed. Marcus Bullock and Michael W. Jennings (Cambridge and London: The Belknap Press of Harvard University Press, 2004), 254. Hereafter abbreviated as "The Task of the Translator."

4   Jacques Derrida, *Che cos'è la poesia?*, trans. Peggy Kamuf, *Points . . . Interviews, 1974–1994*, ed. Elisabeth Weber, trans. Peggy Kamuf et al. (Stanford: Stanford University Press, 1995), 289. Hereafter abbreviated to *Points*.

5   Derrida, *Points*, 289.

6   Ibid., 475

7   Friedrich Nietzsche, *The Anti-Christ, Ecce Homo, Twilight of the Idols and Other Writings*, trans. Judith Norman, ed. Aaron Riley and Judith Norman (Cambridge: Cambridge University Press, 2005), 96.

8   Derrida, "*Istrice 2: Ick bünn all hier*," in *Points*, 301.

9   Jean-Luc Nancy and Philippe Lacoue-Labarthe, *The Literary Absolute: The Theory of Literature in German Romanticism*, trans. Philip Bernard and Cheryl Lester (Albany: SUNY Press, 1988), 43. Hereafter abbreviated to *The Literary Absolute*.

10   Nancy and Lacoue-Labarthe, *The Literary Absolute*, 43

11   Benjamin, "The Task of the Translator," 255.

12   Ibid., 260.

13   Nancy and Lacoue-Labarthe, *The Literary Absolute*, 43.

14   Derrida, *Points*, 304.

15   Ibid., 312.

16   Ibid., 303.

17   Ibid.

18   Ibid., 312.

19   Ibid., 289.

20   Ibid., 297.

21   Ibid., 295.

22   Ibid., 293.

23   Ibid.

24   Ibid., 289.

25   Ibid., 295.

26   Ibid., 289.

27   See Jacques Derrida, *Parages*, trans. Tom Conley et al., ed. John P. Leavey (Stanford: Stanford University Press, 2010), 119.

28   Derrida, *Signature Derrida*, 344.

29   Ibid., 344.

Works cited

Benjamin, Walter. "The Task of the Translator." Trans. Harry Zohn. *Walter Benjamin, Selected Writings, Volume 1, 1913–1926*. Ed. Marcus Bullock and Michael W. Jennings. Cambridge and London: The Belknap Press of Harvard University Press, 2004.

Derrida, Jacques. "By Force of Mourning." Trans. Pascale-Anne Brault and Michael Naas. *Signature Derrida*. Ed. Jay Williams. Chicago and London: Chicago University Press, 2013.

Derrida, Jacques. *Che cos'è la poesia?* Trans. Peggy Kamuf. *Points . . . Interviews, 1974–1994*. Ed. Elisabeth Weber. Trans. Peggy Kamuf et al. Stanford: Stanford University Press, 1995.

Derrida, Jacques. *Parages / Jacques Derrida*. Ed. John P. Leavey. Trans. Tom Conley, James Hulbert, John P. Leavey, and Avital Ronell. Stanford: Stanford University Press, 2011.

Derrida, Jacques. *Points . . . Interviews, 1974–1994*. Ed. Elisabeth Weber. Trans. Peggy Kamuf et al. Stanford: Stanford University Press, 1995.

Derrida, Jacques. *Psyche: Inventions of the Other, Volume 2*. Ed. Peggy Kamuf and Elizabeth Rottenberg. Stanford: Stanford University Press, 2008.

Heaney, Seamus. "Route 110." *Human Chain*. London: Faber and Faber, 2010.

Lacoue-Labarthe, Philippe, and Jean-Luc Nancy. *The Literary Absolute: The Theory of Literature in German Romanticism*. Trans. Philip Bernard and Cheryl Lester. Albany: SUNY Press, 1988.

Nietzsche, Friedrich. *The Anti-Christ, Ecce Homo, Twilight of the Idols and Other Writings*. Trans. Judith Norman. Ed. Aaron Riley and Judith Norman. Cambridge: Cambridge University Press, 2005.

7

Theory's Autoimmunity

Zahi Zalloua

In his 2009 *Valences of the Dialectic*, Fredric Jameson makes a crucial distinction between philosophy and theory. For Jameson, philosophy "is always haunted by the dream of some foolproof, self-sufficient, autonomous system, a set of inter-locking concepts which are their own cause."[1] Philosophy dreams of plenitude and mastery (this is a familiar refrain that we find in the early Derrida's critique of logocentric thought). Such is not the case for theory. Theory, however, does not simply decline to take up philosophy's timeless project. It actively works to undermine philosophy's integrity, its hermeneutic drive:

> Theory . . . has no vested interests inasmuch as it never lays claim to an absolute system, a non-ideological formulation of itself and its "truths"; indeed, always itself complicit in the being of current language, it has only the never-finished task and vocation of undermining philosophy as such, of unraveling affirmative statements and propositions of all kinds.[2]

This is not to say that theory has no concern for truth. We might even describe theory's hunger for truth as excessive or hysterical.[3] But still, theory's truth, as the Nietzschean Foucault puts it, "is a thing of the world."[4] Theory's opposition to philosophy, then, is *not* predicated on the acceptance or denial of truth. Both can be said to share a commitment to truth. Philosophy begins with curiosity or wonder—about the truth of the other, we might say—but ends, or ought to end, in knowledge. This is, after all, close to the formulation provided by Descartes in his *Passions of the Soul*, where he warns against an unhealthy excess of won-der: "Astonishment is an excess of wonder which can never be anything but bad."[5] Philosophy is about successful translation: the translation of the new into a mastered and well-digested familiar. Theory for its part does not share phi-losophy's investment in containment or sameness; rather, it seems to thrive in astonishment, in the endless, multiple, and joyful pursuit of its object.

In stark contrast to the Cartesian obsession with certainty, theory can be said to find an earlier ally in Michel de Montaigne, whose skeptical practices short-circuit philosophy's conceptual machinery. In this essay I want to pursue the question of skepticism, through an account of its most exemplary practitioner, Montaigne, and examine skepticism's relation to philosophy and theory. More precisely, I will be looking at the ways skepticism functions as a *pharmakon*—that is, how it functions as a remedy and poison for conceptualization or thinking. Toward that end, I will then turn to Derrida's notion of autoimmunity, and examine the ways its "illogical logic" makes the differences between philosophy and theory all the more visible.

The relation of skepticism to philosophy constitutes nothing short of a family drama. Skepticism and philosophy seem to be locked in an interminable dialectics:

> To conceive the *otherwise than being* requires, perhaps, as much audacity as skepticism shows, when it does not hesitate to affirm the impossibility of statement while venturing to *realize* this impossibility by the very statement of this impossibility. If, after the innumerable "irrefutable" refutations which logical thought sets against it, skepticism has the gall to return (and it always returns as philosophy's illegitimate child), it is because in the contradiction which logic sees in it the "at the same time" of the contradictories is missing, because a secret diachrony commands this ambiguous or enigmatic way of speaking, and because in general signification signifies beyond synchrony, beyond essence.[6]

Despite its perpetual undoing and overcoming by philosophy, skepticism returns as philosophy's *bastard* child. The astute Levinas commentator Robert Bernasconi has objected to the above mistranslation, which replaces legitimate with illegitimate—though he acknowledges the error is somewhat understandable:

> One might imagine that the return of skepticism is illegitimate because of the weight of the arguments against it. Indeed this impression is so striking that on the three occasions in *Otherwise than Being* when skepticism is referred to as philosophy's legitimate child, the English translator renders it as "illegitimate" ... or as "bastard" ... But skepticism is the legitimate child of philosophy insofar as the question of skepticism is still construed as a question about truth. Levinas attaches some importance to the dignity accorded to skepticism by

philosophy in spite of its refutation . . . presumably because it shows philosophy abiding by rules other than those it declares.[7]

Skepticism calls into question the very identity of philosophy. It reveals to philosophy a different way of proceeding, exposing philosophy to a different set of rules. Skepticism in its quest for truth comes to undermine the subject of philosophy, calling into question its very integrity. Skepticism always risks escaping its author's control, exceeding its authorized application; in short, skepticism always risks contaminating that which ought to be outside contamination. In the case of philosophy, the philosopher's mechanism of self-protection is arguably its universal logic, that which guarantees the smooth functioning of the economy of Sameness. Yet, as Bernasconi points out, philosophy still accepts skepticism into the fold of the family. As long as it does not devolve into a form of nihilism, skepticism will continue to be philosophy's "legitimate child." To recognize skepticism as philosophy's "legitimate child" is first and foremost an act of containment and self-protection. It seeks to foreclose the possibility of self-contamination, that is, to minimize the poison of skepticism. While Bernasconi is absolutely correct in his observation, Lingis's mistranslation exposes what it at stake in discussions of skepticism, and points to what I call philosophy's "disavowed autoimmunity."

Like skepticism, autoimmunity is a *pharmakon*, "at once remedy and poison."[8] But what does autoimmunity stand for? It is an "illogical logic"—a logic that perverts sovereignty, a logic that works to undermine the sovereign self precisely by compromising its own protection. As Derrida puts it, autoimmunization entails a process through which "a living being, in a quasi-*suicidal* fashion, 'itself' works to destroy its own protection, to immunise itself *against* its 'own' immunity."[9] Autoimmunity as such signals, then, a crisis in immunity, in the organism's mechanism of self-protection. Generalized as a condition of existence, autoimmunity compromises *from within* any claims of identity and full presence. It is a poison, unraveling the *ipseity* of the self. But Derrida also adds *that without autoimmunity nothing would happen. There would be no presence of any kind*:

> Autoimmunity is not an absolute ill or evil. It enables an exposure to the other, to *what* and to *who* comes—which means that it must remain incalculable. Without autoimmunity, with absolute immunity, nothing would ever happen or arrive; we would no longer wait, await, or expect, no longer expect one another, or expect any event.[10]

If habits constitute our lifeless or quasi-mechanical horizon, the event punctures the psychic shield that such a horizon presumably affords. In its disruption of everydayness, the event opens a space for ethics, for thinking singularity as such. Yet, Derrida also cautions against seeing the event as an ethical moment itself. The event might be better described as the "nonethical opening of ethics," as Derrida puts it in *Of Grammatology*.[11]

What becomes, then, of philosophy and theory when they are subjected to the illogical logic of autoimmunity? For Martin Hägglund, Derrida's emphasis on the "nonethical opening" is meant to stress the nonmoralizing and profoundly atheistic strain of Derridean deconstruction. It also serves as a warning against religious or ethical readings of Derrida. Simply put, there is no "ethics of alterity"; the event as such is nonethical. To be sure, Hägglund frames his reading of Derrida as analytical rather than exegetical. He is not glossing Derrida, he is clarifying his arguments, or rather, pushing them to their logical conclusion. He writes, "I not only seek to explicate what Derrida is saying; I seek to develop his arguments, fortify his logic, and pursue its implications."[12] At the heart of Hägglund's "fortification" of Derrida's logic is his desire to save Derrida from Levinas, to save deconstruction from the seductions of the transcendent other. We might also add that it attempts to save Derrida from skepticism and theory. Against the grain, Hägglund is doubtful about an "ethical turn" in Derrida, where ethics would be understood as the event of the other, as the unconditional exposure to alterity. For Hägglund, Derrida's other is strictly speaking not exclusively nor primarily another human being. The other is better understood in terms of Derrida's notion of temporality: "[the other] designates the tracing of time that makes it impossible for anything to be in itself and exposes everyone—myself as well as any other—to corruption and death."[13] Derrida associates this other—the spacing of time—with the law of autoimmunity. There is no shielding from this temporal finitude; it is unconditional. It is in Hägglund's terms an "ultratranscendental" condition, the "condition not only for everything that can be cognized and experienced, but also for everything that can be thought and desired."[14]

For Hägglund, autoimmunity is, then, first and foremost a neutral category. It describes this metaphysical exposure to temporal alterity. Accordingly, the event as something unconditional does not belong to ethics, that is, it has no "ethical status."[15] There cannot be an ethics of the event, since ethics is firmly situated in the realm of the calculable. As he puts it, "the ethical is. . . a matter of responding to alterity by making decisions and calculations, whereas the unconditional is the non-ethical opening of ethics, namely, the exposure to an undecidable other that makes it necessary to decide and calculate in the first place."[16] Hägglund is certainly right to question a conception of ethics as the blind embrace of the unconditional. There is indeed something dubious about celebrating passivity as the ethical mode of preference. But ethics as a matter of philosophical calculation simplifies matters quite a bit. Hägglund quotes the following passage from Derrida to make his point: "To be responsible in ethics and politics implies that we try to program, to anticipate, to define laws and rules."[17] The key term for me here is "try." "Try" records a certain hesitation, a skepticism; it qualifies the goals of programming, anticipating, and defining. Failure is built into the process, and failure is not merely the absence of success—there is the possibility, as Derrida says, following Beckett, of "failing well."

Trying—attempting, testing, failing—is of course at the heart of essaying. Foucault took the essay as exemplifying the philosophical enterprise itself; the essay—"the living substance of philosophy"—does not legitimate "what is already known," but rather desires to know "to what extent it might be possible to think differently."[18] It is this definition of philosophy—of philosophy as unsettling curiosity—that theory seeks to revitalize. Liberating in an oblique, rather than straightforward way, the essay works to expand thought and to create new ways of thinking: it unavoidably imposes form on thought but a kind of form that relentlessly refuses its own homogenization—its own fortification— and that tries to think beyond its own cognitive limits.

Staging philosophy's familial struggle with skepticism, Montaigne's *Essays* expose the discord between the two, pointing to new ways of conceiving of their relationship. The *Essays* open up a new path for theory and philosophy in large part by testing and foregrounding the discords and mutations of the self. In a key moment of the "Apology," Montaigne highlights his otherness and newness, portraying himself as "a new figure," as "an accidental philosopher."[19] Here we might want to substitute *accidental theorist* for *accidental philosopher*, in keeping with the use to which I have been putting these two terms here.[20] If Montaigne began as a philosopher, committed to hermeneutic self-mastery *à la* Seneca,[21] he did so only to come a full circle, taking Seneca's observation— "anything that can be added to is imperfect"[22]—as a condition for productive thinking rather than a prohibition.

To flesh out Montaigne's mutation into a theorist more fully, it might be useful to examine in more detail the contrast between his view of the self and that of Seneca, particularly since many of his early readers felt him to be a "French Seneca."[23] Seneca, one of the authors Montaigne quoted most frequently, exemplifies the cultural tradition of *philosophy-as-therapy*. In his epistolary exchange with Lucilius, the Roman Stoic constantly praises both the powers of reason and the value of self-mastery. Moreover, Seneca's letters abound with therapeutic strategies, ways to correct mistaken dispositions, aimed ultimately at *re*orienting one's precarious relation to self and relation to the world, so as to achieve a happier, more rational life. After hearing of the news that a fire had destroyed the city of Lyons, and of its devastating emotional impact on his friend Liberalis, Seneca reflects on this disastrous event and draws the moral lesson that we must perpetually envision the most tragic circumstances, thinking about them as happening to us *at this moment*. This philosophical practice of meditating on future calamities (*praemeditatio malorum*) corresponds to what Michel Foucault has called "technologies of the self," that is, techniques "which permit individuals to effect . . . a certain number of operations on their own bodies and souls, thoughts, conduct, and way of being, so as to transform themselves in order to attain a certain state of happiness, purity, wisdom, perfection, or immortality."[24] As a technique of the self, the practice of meditating on future calamities helps Seneca to attain *tranquillitas*, a state of mental tranquility resulting from the extirpation of one's most intense emotions, enabling him to fortify his psychic shield, to fashion or form a sovereign self, by limiting the affectability of the contingent world and thus reducing the self's vulnerability to chance. Despite an inherently unstable world, inner freedom and peace remain for the Roman philosopher a genuine possibility.

In his liminal essay "Of Idleness," Montaigne stages for his readers his own account of the philosophical scene, initially marked by the dream of solitary contemplation:

> Lately when I retired to my home, determined so far as possible to bother about nothing except spending the little life I have left in rest and seclusion, it seemed to me I could do my mind no greater favor than to let it entertain itself in full idleness and stay and settle in itself, which I hoped it might do more easily now, having become weightier and riper with time.[25]

Then came the recognition of his failure to simply translate old age into wisdom, into self-knowledge and self-mastery—into the ideal of *stasis*, an ideal revered by the Senecan sage:

> But I find . . . that, on the contrary, like a runaway horse, it gives itself a hundred times more trouble than it took for others, and gives birth to so many

chimeras and fantastic monsters, one after another, without order or purpose, that in order to contemplate their ineptitude and strangeness at my pleasure, I have begun to put them in writing, hoping in time to make my mind ashamed of them.[26]

Montaigne the Stoic philosopher in the pursuit of intellectual leisure suddenly mutates into Montaigne the theorist of the unruly/his unruliness. At this stage, Montaigne's ideas evoke defiance and frustration. By describing his mind as a "runaway horse" and its thoughts as "chimeras and fantastic monsters," Montaigne from the start recognizes his subject matter's profound indocility, the self's challenge to hermeneutic mastery. Not conducive to conceptuality— to the formation of concepts for the purpose of interpretive mastery—the essay pluralizes meaning; it *perverts* philosophy's quest for self-knowledge (perverts in the sense that it overturns this quest, *it turns it upside down*), exposing the inadequacies of prior models.[27]

Throughout his book, Montaigne constantly probes the "inner springs"[28] of his mind, but his meditations yield no concrete foundational knowledge. Purposive inquiry is met at every turn with textual resistance. Montaigne's *Essays* fragment and multiply the self: "Myself now and myself a while ago are indeed two."[29] They disrupt the unity of being and thinking or knowing. Indeed, an irreducible gap between intention and outcome structures the writings of the *Essays*:

I find myself more by chance encounter than by searching my judgment.[30]

But we are, I know not how, double within ourselves, with the result that we do not believe what we believe, and we cannot rid ourselves of what we condemn.[31]

Contingency rather than necessity guides the unfolding of Montaigne's *Essays*. Jacques Lacan will echo this Montaignian insight in his dismantling of the *cogito*: "I think where I am not, therefore I am where I do not think."[32] In *The Four Fundamental Concepts of Psychoanalysis*, Lacan singles out Montaigne, praising the essayist's remarkable eye for the unconscious, prefiguring, as it were, the psychoanalytic notion of the split subject:

I would show you that Montaigne is truly the one who has centred himself, not around scepticism but around the living moment of the *aphanisis* of the subject. And it is in this that he is fruitful, that he is an eternal guide, who goes beyond whatever may be represented of the moment to be defined as a historical turning-point.[33]

Catherine Belsey contextualizes Lacan's use of *aphanisis*, clarifying its psychoanalytic relevance and meaning:

> Aphanisis (disappearance) was a term first used by Ernest Jones, who argued
> that the subject's ultimate fear was that desire would disappear. Lacan appro-
> priates the term to discuss the disappearance, or sometimes the "fading," of
> the speaking subject itself, as it loses its purchase on meaning. I can disappear
> from what I am saying, and in the process make apparent the provisional char-
> acter of subjectivity.[34]

Lacan's interest in Montaigne lies in the ways he discloses the provisional character of early modern humanist subjectivity. He credits Montaigne for avoiding
both skepticism and the path of the *cogito*. The skeptics' "heroic" adherence to
the "subjective position that *one can know nothing*" and Descartes' grounding
of certainty in the self-evidence of the *cogito* result in the perpetuation of subjectivity. Montaigne offers a radical alternative: a subject paradoxically constituted by its own *aphanisis*. On Lacan's reading, what differentiates Montaigne
from the early modern skeptic is that the essayist persists in his self-undoing,
short-circuiting the skeptic's motto, "*I cannot know.*" Yet Lacan's brief assessment ignores the essayist's critical engagement with this ancient school of
thought.

   While Montaigne clearly admired the ancient skeptics, he did register a concern about their use of language:

> I can see why the Pyrrhonian philosophers cannot express their general con-
> ception in any manner of speaking; for they would need a new language. Ours
> is wholly formed of affirmative propositions, which to them are utterly repug-
> nant so that when they say "I doubt," immediately you have them by the throat
> to make them admit that at least they know and are sure of this fact, that they
> doubt.[35]

Montaigne for his part does not find himself in a "performative contradiction,"
since he acknowledges that his language is the language of affirmative propositions. But Montaigne does not stop with this rebuke of the Pyrrhonists. He
infuses his language with a singular negativity, inventing an alternative form
of skepticism: essayistic skepticism. Montaigne's comment "they would need a
new language" (the conditional "would need" underscores the irreality of this
language) functions not only as a critique of the Pyrrhonist position (their use
of language involves self-refutation) but as an incitement to imagine the possibility of a different language of skepticism: skepticism as a form of thought

inseparable from this language *à venir*. While Pyrrhonists themselves were unable to formulate their radical doubt, Montaigne's reader is *obliquely* invited to turn to Montaigne's *essay*, to his own practice of skepticism, a practice that sustains the open-endedness of the essayistic process and does not transform itself into dogmatism, or "a Pyrrhonism in an affirmative form."[36] In this light, we might think of the passing reference to this absent "new language" as describing the language of the essay, in ways that may have exceeded even Montaigne's own imagination. The newness of this skeptical language might figure as well in Montaigne's scandalous question "What do I know? [*Que sçay-je?*]"[37]

So Lacan is surely correct to distance Montaigne from those who adopt the skeptic motto, and in this respect, Lacan is arguably far more sensitive to the unsettling force of the *Essays* than Pierre Charron, one of Montaigne's early disciples, who rewrote Montaigne's motto—"What do I know?"—preferring the more measured, and philosophically friendly, skeptical claim "I don't know." Lacan, however, overstates the case against Montaigne's skepticism. If Charron violently negates Montaigne's "What do I know?" Lacan conveniently sets it aside—and neglects to take up the ethical force of the interrogative—silencing, in turn, Montaigne's skeptical voice as well.[38]

The challenge here is to apprehend what we could call the "Montaignian moment" of *aphanisis* in light of Montaigne's creative appropriation of the ancient culture of self-care: Can we think the self in Montaigne's care of the self *otherwise than being*, outside the philosophical tradition that privileges being as a knowable self-presence? Montaigne's reflections on his self, or better yet, his reflections on the psychic effects of self-study hint at such a possibility:

> I have seen no more evident monstrosity and miracle in the world than myself.
> We become habituated to anything strange by use and time; but the more I frequent myself and know myself, the more my deformity astonishes me, and the less I understand myself.[39]

Compare with Descartes' observation about his epistemological situation:

> And as I converse with myself alone and look more deeply into myself, I will attempt to render myself gradually better known and more familiar to myself. I am a thing that thinks.[40]

Whereas Descartes' self-disciplined meditations assume a teleological arc, and that "nothing in principle exceeds [their] totalising grasp,"[41] Montaigne's unruly essays record the absence of any cognitive return on his epistemic investment. Far from resulting in a privileged access to one's being, essayistic self-writing defamiliarizes and astonishes its practitioner. It insists on the "astonishing alterity"[42] of the self, disclosing reason in its utter weakness or lameness. Like a cripple, reason limps. The essay *fails well*; it fails to domesticate, to possess meaning, and to secure the foundations for self-knowledge; yet, in its failure, reason paradoxically succeeds in revealing to its author the other in him (his self as other)—his autoimmune self. As if directly responding to the surplus of meaning, to the self's internal otherness, Descartes, as we've already seen, moves to immunize himself against a pathologized, destabilizing experience of astonishment. For astonishment, according to Descartes, jeopardizes our "free will," the possibility of becoming "masters of ourselves," calling into question that which "renders us like God."[43]

Recovering the Montaignian moment for theory requires troubling such a colonization of wonder and difference, opening up a hermeneutic space to hear Montaigne's anti-Cartesian voice, his promise for a care of *the other*:

> I do not share that common error of judging another by myself. I easily believe that another man may have qualities different from mine. I more easily admit difference than resemblance between us. *I consider him simply in himself, without relations to others; I mold him to his own model.*[44]

So cognizant of his own unknowingness, of his unruliness and foreignness to himself, how can Montaigne ever assert the transparency and homogeneity of the other? Judith Butler echoes this Montaignian insight when she affirms that "my own foreignness to myself is, paradoxically, the source of my ethical connection with others."[45] To be sure, Montaigne's idealized care for the other bears the mark of its own phantasm: *the dream of a pure heterology*—the plenitude of the other prior or beyond any mediation. To some measure, the *Essays* counterbalance this logocentric impulse with their insistence on process and revision, on the endless *becoming* of interpretation: "I do not portray being: I portray passing" and "If my mind could gain a firm footing, I would not make essays, I would make decisions; but it is always in apprenticeship and on trial."[46] Still, Montaigne's dream of a pure other arguably amounts to the flip side of an ethics of self-care grounded in the integrity of the *cogito*, in the primacy of the sovereign self, who makes allowance only for what Derrida calls "conditional hospitality." In desiring to preserve the other as he or she *is*, an ethics of alterity paradoxically works to undermine itself, reifying the other's *being*, arresting his or her movement—and thus symbolically killing the other. I'm reminded here of Spivak's remark that "these days. . .only the dominant self can be problematic; the self of the Other is authentic without problem . . . This is frightening."[47] The counter to philosophy's egology does not lie in the celebration of "unconditional hospitality," which easily translates into the dangerous fascination with the other's alleged authenticity. As Derrida insists, unconditional hospitality is both indissociable from and heterogeneous to conditional hospitality.[48] Derrida's claim might serve as a reminder of the inseparability and yet incommensurability of theory and philosophy, as a warning against the lure to conflate the unconditional (openness) with theory and the conditional (closure) with philosophy. What is called for is a perpetual negotiation, a mutual interruption: theory with and against philosophy, and vice versa. In other words, theory's identity is paradoxically predicated on the contamination of the distinction between theory and philosophy: for it to be theory, theory must continually revisit its distinction from philosophy.

In this light, and this will serve as my conclusion, theory should not be understood as philosophy minus its phantasms of self-sufficiency and sovereignty. Rather, theory finds itself in Montaigne's precarious position: it desires to welcome the other unconditionally but simultaneously recognizes that it must do so within the realm of the calculable, within the realm of limits. Autoimmunity is more than an ontological fact, a constitutive necessity. The "madness of decision,"[49] as Derrida formulates it, is experienced precisely in the aporia of hospitality:

> To be hospitable is to let oneself be overtaken [*surprendre*], *to be ready to not be ready*, if such is possible, to let oneself be overtaken, to not even *let* oneself to be overtaken, to be surprised, in a fashion almost violent. . . precisely where one is not ready to receive—and not only *not yet ready* but *not ready*, *unprepared* in a mode that is not even that of the "not yet."[50]

The paradoxical injunction *"to be ready to not be ready"* is all about training the body and mind to become receptive to difference, to desire the unfamiliar. But theory must also concern itself with what happens *after* the event, *after* the encounter with the other. It is not simply a question of acknowledging and cataloguing the autoimmunity of ethics, politics, law, and so forth but to see in autoimmunity a political challenge, an ethical task, the call for a new hermeneutics, one, in short, that sustains—rather than neutralizes or fetishizes—the other as event.

Notes

1 Fredric Jameson, *Valences of the Dialectic* (New York: Verso 2009), 59.

2 Jameson, *Valences of the Dialectic*, 59.

3 See Jean-Michel Rabaté, *The Future of Theory* (Oxford: Blackwell, 2002).

4 Michel Foucault, *Power/Knowledge: Selected Interviews and Other Writings, 1972–1977*, ed. Colin Gordon (New York: Pantheon Books, 1980), 131.

5 René Descartes, *Meditations, Objections, and Replies*, ed. Roger Ariew and Donald Cress (Indianapolis: Hackett Publishing, 2006), 58.

6 Emmanuel Levinas, *Otherwise Than Being: Or Beyond Essence*, trans. Alphonso Lingis (The Hague: Martinus Nijhoff, 1981), 7.

7 Robert Bernasconi, "Skepticism in the Face of Philosophy," in *Re-Reading Levinas*, ed. Robert Bernasconi and Simon Critchley (Bloomington: Indiana University Press, 1991), 160n.10.

8 Jacques Derrida, *Philosophy in a Time of Terror: Dialogues with Jürgen Habermas and Jacques Derrida*, ed. Giovanna Borradori (Chicago: University of Chicago Press, 2003), 124. In his essay "Apology for Raymond Sebond," Montaigne considers skepticism a "*final fencer's trick,*" an "extreme remedy," and a "desperate stroke" (Michel de Montaigne, *The Essays*, trans. Donald Frame [Stanford: Stanford University Press, 1957], 418). As a *pharmakon*, skepticism functions as a "remedy" when it deflates hubris, when it demystifies reason's mystifying ways, and functions as "poison" when it becomes nihilistic, breading chaos—not only epistemic chaos but also sociopolitical chaos.

9 Giovanna Borradori, *Philosophy in a Time of Terror: Dialogues with Jürgen Habermas and Jacques Derrida* (Chicago: University of Chicago Press, 2004), 94. Derrida's autoimmunity is a particular kind of autoimmunity since in its original biological context, autoimmunity signifies a disorder, a living organism's failure to recognize that it is attacking a very part of itself. Simply put, autoimmune diseases involve attacks on the body's organs, tissues, and cells, not just the immune system.

10 Jacques Derrida, *Rogues: Two Essays on Reason*, trans. Pascale-Anne Brault and Michael Naas (Stanford: Stanford University Press, 2005), 152.

11 Jacques Derrida, *Of Grammatology*, trans. Gayatri Chakravorty Spivak (Baltimore: Johns Hopkins University Press, 1976), 140.

12 Martin Hägglund, *Radical Atheism: Derrida and the Time of Life* (Stanford: Stanford. University Press, 2008), 11.

13 Martin Hägglund, "The Non-Ethical Opening of Ethics: A Response to Derek Attridge," *Derrida Today* 3.2 (2010): 298.

14 Hägglund, *Radical Atheism*, 19

15 Hägglund, "The Non-Ethical Opening of Ethics," 302.

16 Ibid., 301.

17 Jacques Derrida, *"Perhaps or Maybe," PLI—Warwick Journal of Philosophy* 6 (1997): 6–7.

18 Michel Foucault, *The Use of Pleasure*, trans. Robert Hurley (New York: Vintage Books, 1985), 9. Thomas Flynn also has remarked of the affinities between Montaignian essayistic skepticism and the skeptical attitude informing Foucault's critique of rationality: "[Foucault's] is a skepticism more in line with Montaigne's '*Que sais-je?*' than with the obviously self-defeating form, 'I can't be certain of anything'" ("Foucault as Parrhesiast: His Last Course at Collège de France," in *The Final Foucault*, ed. James W. Bernauer and David Rasmussen [Cambridge, MA: The MIT Press, 1988], 113).

19 Montaigne, *The Essays*, 409.

20 For a more elaborate account of Montaigne's mutation from "accidental philosopher" to "accidental theorist," see Zahi Zalloua, *Reading Unruly: Interpretation and Its Ethical Demands* (Lincoln: University of Nebraska Press, 2014), 21–41.

21 While the desire for self-mastery, an aspiration originating in Plato's Socrates, is perhaps as old as philosophy itself, it is especially prevalent in ancient Stoicism. As Pierre Hadot points out, "For the Stoic . . . doing philosophy meant practicing how to 'live,' . . . giv[ing] up desiring that which does not depend on us and is beyond our control, so as to attach ourselves only to what depends on us: actions which are just and in conformity with reason" (Pierre Hadot, *Philosophy as a Way of Life: Spiritual Exercises from Socrates to Foucault*, trans. Michael Chase [New York: Blackwell, 1995], 86).

22 Seneca, *Epistles*, trans. Richard M. Gummere (Cambridge, MA: Harvard University Press, 1996), 72.7.

23 François Garasse, quoted in Olivier Millet, *La Première réception des Essais de Montaigne (1580–1640)* (Paris: Champion, 1995), 199.

24 Michel Foucault, "Technologies of the Self," in *Technologies of the Self: A Seminar With Michel Foucault*, ed. Luther H. Martin, Huck Gutman, and Patrick H. Hutton (Cambridge: MIT Press, 1988), 18.

25 Montaigne, *The Essays*, 736.

26 Ibid., 21.

27 See Dany Nobus, "Locating Perversion, Dislocating Psychoanalysis," in *Perversion: Psychoanalytic Perspectives/Perspectives on Psychoanalysis*, ed. Dany Nobus and Lisa Downing (New York: Karnac Books, 2006), 5.

28 Montaigne, *The Essays*, 481.

29 Ibid., 27.

30 Ibid.

31 Ibid., 469, emphasis added.

32 Jacques Lacan, "The Agency of the Letter in the Unconscious, or Reason since Freud," *Écrits: a Selection*, trans. Alan Sheridan (London: Tavistock, 1977), 166.

33 Jacques Lacan, *The Seminar of Jacques Lacan, Book XI: The Four Fundamental Concepts of Psychoanalysis*, ed. Jacques-Alain Miller, trans. Alan Sheridan (New York: Norton, 1977), 223–224.

34 Catherine Belsey, *Shakespeare in Theory and Practice* (Oxford: Oxford University Press, 2008), 26.

35 Montaigne, *The Essays*, 392.

36 Ibid., 376.

37 Ibid., 393.

38 Robert Eaglestone attests to the hermeneutic insatiability of the interrogative: "Unlike a statement, a question is to be interrupted: a question starts a dialogue. An idea phrased as a question resists closure and begs not only an answer but another question, an interruption" (Robert Eaglestone, *Ethical Criticism: Reading after Levinas* [Edinburgh: Edinburgh University Press, 1997], 139).

39 Montaigne, *The Essays*, 787.

40 Descartes, *Meditations*, 19.

41 Belsey, *Shakespeare in Theory and Practice*, 27.

42 Emmanuel Levinas, *Entre Nous: On Thinking-of-the Other*, trans. Michael B. Smith and Barbara Harshav (New York: Columbia University Press, 1998), 101.

43 Descartes, *Meditations*, 103.

44 Montaigne, *The Essays*, 169, emphasis added.

45 Judith Butler, *Giving an Account of Oneself* (New York: Fordham, 2005), 84.

46 Montaigne, *The Essays*, 611.

47 Gayatri Chakravorty Spivak, *The Post-Colonial Critic: Interviews, Strategies, Dialogues,* ed. Sarah Harasym (New York: Routledge, 1990), 66.

48 Jacques Derrida, *Of Hospitality: Anne Dufourmantelle Invites Jacques Derrida to Respond*, trans. Rachel Bowlby (Stanford: Stanford University Press, 2000), 27.

49 See Jacques Derrida, *The Gift of Death*, trans. David Wills (Chicago: University of Chicago Press, 1995).

50 Jacques Derrida, "*Hostipitality*," in *Acts of Religion*, ed. Gil Anidjar (New York: Routledge, 2002), 361, emphasis in the original.

Works cited

Belsey, Catherine. *Shakespeare in Theory and Practice*. Oxford: Oxford University Press, 2008.

Bernasconi, Robert. "Skepticism in the Face of Philosophy." *Re-Reading Levinas.* Ed. Robert Bernasconi and Simon Critchley. Bloomington: Indiana University Press, 1991.

Borradori, Giovanna. *Philosophy in a Time of Terror: Dialogues with Jürgen Habermas and Jacques Derrida.* Chicago: University of Chicago Press, 2004.

Butler, Judith. *Giving an Account of Oneself.* New York: Fordham, 2005.

Derrida, Jacques. *The Gift of Death.* Trans. David Wills. Chicago: University of Chicago Press, 1995.

Derrida, Jacques. *Of Grammatology.* Trans. Gayatri Chakravorty Spivak. Baltimore: Johns Hopkins University Press, 1976.

Derrida, Jacques. *Of Hospitality: Anne Dufourmantelle Invites Jacques Derrida to Respond.* Trans. Rachel Bowlby. Stanford: Stanford University Press, 2000.

Derrida, Jacques. "*Hostipitality.*" In *Acts of Religion.* Ed. Gil Anidjar. New York: Routledge, 2002. 356–420.

Derrida, Jacques. "*Perhaps or Maybe.*" *PLI—Warwick Journal of Philosophy* 6 (1997): 1–17.

Derrida, Jacques. *Philosophy in a Time of Terror: Dialogues with Jürgen Habermas and Jacques Derrida.* Ed. Giovanna Borradori. Chicago: University of Chicago Press, 2003.

Derrida, Jacques. *Rogues: Two Essays on Reason.* Trans. Pascale-Anne Brault and Michael Naas. Stanford: Stanford University Press, 2005.

Descartes, René. *Meditations, Objections, and Replies.* Ed. Roger Ariew and Donald Cress. Indianapolis: Hackett Publishing, 2006.

Eaglestone, Robert. *Ethical Criticism: Reading after Levinas.* Edinburgh: Edinburgh University Press, 1997.

Flynn, Thomas. "Foucault as Parrhesiast: His Last Course at Collège de France." *The Final Foucault.* Ed. James W. Bernauer and David Rasmussen. Cambridge, MA: The MIT Press, 1988.

Foucault, Michel. *Power/Knowledge: Selected Interviews and Other Writings, 1972–1977.* Ed. Colin Gordon. New York: Pantheon Books, 1980.

Foucault, Michel. "Technologies of the Self." *Technologies of the Self: A Seminar with Michel Foucault.* Ed. Luther H. Martin, Huck Gutman, and Patrick H. Hutton. Cambridge: MIT Press, 1988.

Foucault, Michel. *The Use of Pleasure.* Trans. Robert Hurley. New York: Vintage Books, 1985.

Hadot, Pierre. *Philosophy as a Way of Life: Spiritual Exercises from Socrates to Foucault.* Trans. Michael Chase. New York: Blackwell, 1995.

Hägglund, Martin. "The Non-Ethical Opening of Ethics: A Response to Derek Attridge." *Derrida Today* 3.2 (2010): 295–305.

Hägglund, Martin. *Radical Atheism: Derrida and the Time of Life.* Stanford: Stanford. University Press, 2008.

Jameson, Fredric. *Valences of the Dialectic.* New York: Verso 2009.

Lacan, Jacques. "The Agency of the Letter in the Unconscious, or Reason Since Freud." *Écrits: a Selection*. Trans. Alan Sheridan. London: Tavistock, 1977.

Lacan, Jacques. *The Seminar of Jacques Lacan, Book XI: The Four Fundamental Concepts of Psychoanalysis*. Ed. Jacques-Alain Miller. Trans. Alan Sheridan. New York: Norton, 1977.

Levinas, Emmanuel. *Entre Nous: On Thinking-of-the Other*. Trans. Michael B. Smith and Barbara Harshav. New York: Columbia University Press, 1998.

Levinas, Emmanuel. *Otherwise than Being: Or Beyond Essence*. Trans. Alphonso Lingis. The Hague: Martinus Nijhoff, 1981.

Millet, Olivier. *La Première réception des Essais de Montaigne (1580–1640)*. Paris: Champion, 1995.

Montaigne, Michel de. *The Essays*. Trans. Donald Frame. Stanford: Stanford University Press, 1957.

Nobus, Dany. "Locating Perversion, Dislocating Psychoanalysis." *Perversion: Psychoanalytic Perspectives/Perspectives on Psychoanalysis*. Ed. Dany Nobus and Lisa Downing. New York: Karnac Books, 2006.

Rabaté, Jean-Michel. *The Future of Theory*. Oxford: Blackwell, 2002.

Seneca. *Epistles*. Trans. Richard M. Gummere. Cambridge, MA: Harvard University Press, 1996.

Spivak, Gayatri Chakravorty. *The Post-Colonial Critic: Interviews, Strategies, Dialogues*. Ed. Sarah Harasym. New York: Routledge, 1990.

Zalloua, Zahi. *Reading Unruly: Interpretation and Its Ethical Demands*. Lincoln: University of Nebraska Press, 2014.

Part Three

Politics, Death, Theory

8

Eclipse of the Gaze: Nancy, Community, and the Death of the Other

Kir Kuiken

This chapter deliberately avoids the question of legacy or inheritance implied by the notion of "dead theory," or by the question of what comes "after" theory.[1] No doubt the place of work that is broadly conceived as "theoretical" has gradually been pushed to the margins of a variety of disciplines in the Humanities. In this case, however, the "death" implied in the term "dead theory" would be a question of the death of a field within the academy, its marginalization, or its collapse within an institution that, at one point in time, had given it life (however short-lived this life might have been). If the dispersal of theory is underway in the academy, this is for a whole set of reasons, few of which have anything to do with the "direction" theoretical inquiry in the Humanities has taken in recent years. Yet if "theory" is to have a future, whether or not it remains a "field" within academic Humanities or not, it will only be thanks to the means by which it continuously pushes up against its own internal limits, giving itself a posthumous existence by not interring itself in the tomb of endless reiteration. This is precisely why this chapter attempts to push the question of dead theory toward a different problematic: the motif of a death that lodges itself at the heart of contemporary critical theoretical questioning about some of our most basic (political) concepts, including the concept of community. Death has always been the figure of a limit for philosophy; theory has *always* been dying, one could say, from the moment of its birth. What emerges out of the problematic of dead theory is the question of how this limit must be thought not as something that befalls theory from the outside (e.g.., in the various forms of its institutional marginalization), but instead, as an event on the very interior of its corpus. Theory, in fact, lives in and on this internal limit, and it is only thanks to this limit that it still has the chance of a future. What would it mean to situate the problem of dead theory somewhat differently than as the question of its institutional demise?

In the wake of the "death of the subject," perhaps the most trenchant question to take hold of contemporary theory has been the question of what conception of community, what notion of collectivity, remains once the project of the self-recognition of the subject in the state has collapsed. Here the question of the relation to a limit is transformed into the most urgent of political questions. If death is not just a figure for the limit, but also the result of (twentieth-century) attempts to radically refound collective life, the question of what is at stake politically, ethically, or otherwise in trying to rethink the concept of community through the motif of death becomes imperative. Following Bataille, the two most significant thinkers of the relation between death and community, Jean-Luc Nancy and Maurice Blanchot, have sought to articulate their attempts to recover a conception of community no longer founded in death, precisely by reconceiving the nature of the relation between death and "being-in-common." That is, rather than attempt to radically dissociate the relation between community and death, Blanchot and Nancy instead begin by resituating the death of the other as precisely what *undoes* traditional conceptions of community founded on a shared identity. Nancy, for example, claims in *Inoperable Community* that being-in-common must be predicated on a relation to death that eschews any form of identification, or any attempt to provide a universal, collective meaning to death as the ground of collectivity. The motif of death, thus, opens us to a form of collectivity that suspends any attempt to give death meaning, to give it a sense that would transcend the *singularity* of the one who dies in the name of a value that can be shared, and around which the identity of the community can be articulated. When death is encountered as the "death of the other," as something radically not the subject's "own," Nancy contends, the impossibility of attributing a shared meaning to death interrupts the possibility of any self-presentation of the community. This interruption or "inoperability," a worklessness at the heart of the community internal to its very constitution, begins to signal a politics that no longer stems from the will to realize community as an essence or value, or as a *telos*. This "inoperability" short-circuits any form of community modeled either on a transcendence that it seeks to instantiate, or on an universal it attempts to embody.

However, it is the question of what emerges *out of* the relation to this "interruption" of the concept of community that in the end separates Blanchot and Nancy. This difference opens up two very different ways of understanding the relation between community and death. My argument in this paper concerns the way Nancy's understanding of the relation between community and the death of the other reintroduces a specular moment that, however problematized, nevertheless reinscribes a certain figurality at the heart of his rethinking of community. This specular moment, this return to a dimension of figurality (which Blanchot insistently avoids), articulates this limit internal to community as something fundamentally withdrawn from presentation, as the obverse of presentability, what Nancy will call the "eclipse of the gaze." The result is that community is always understood as the interruption of its own full self-presentation. What follows from this is a vexed problematic for contemporary critical-theoretical formulations of community: either community breaks radically with the specular logic of its own self-presentation, or it must still retain some relation to the figural that it will nonetheless constantly have to interrogate. In this sense, Nancy's theory of community as predicated on the death of the other produces a rather equivocal schematic: while attempting to fundamentally break with a tradition that gives death a founding meaning to community, it nonetheless cannot fully divest itself of a specular logic that always threatens to restore this limit as a limit *proper to* the community.

In order to arrive at this equivocation, however, it is first necessary to understand the precise form of Nancy's articulation of the constitutive limit of the death of the other as the founding condition of community. Nancy's formulations of the death of the other in *Inoperable Community* and *Being Singular Plural* (the texts where he engages most directly with this problematic) have as their background a reading of Heidegger. Focusing on the relation between *mit-sein* (or "being with," which is analyzed in chapter four of the first division of *Being and Time*) and the problematic of "being towards death,"[2] Nancy attempts to rethink the relation between them, between the limit-experience of a relation to an impossibility (my own death) and the way in which one is always already "with" others, as part of the fundamental constitution of *Dasein*. Heidegger's analysis of being-toward-death in *Being and Time* interprets death as *Dasein's* "ownmost possibility"; death is what is most proper to *Dasein*, that toward which it *alone* is authentically projected. This understanding of *Dasein's* finitude is contrasted in *Being and Time* to a relation to death that passes through what Heidegger calls the "They," which, precisely by "sharing" death, disarms it in the truism that "everyone dies," or that "one dies." In short, it forces death out of its singularization, the irreducible death of this one here. It articulates it instead as a shared "being-toward-death" that effaces its meaning entirely. For Heidegger, the dying of others is not something "we" experience in any genuine sense. And if no one can take the other's dying away from him, it is because *Dasein's* death is always singularized and singularizing, always only ever "its own." *Dasein's* relation to death, then, is fundamentally a relation to its *own* limit or finitude, its own impossibility. Yet it is precisely this relation to impossibility that gives *Dasein* back over to its "ownmost" possibilities, including the manner in which it is "with" others. That is, it is only once *Dasein* has been singularized through being-toward-death that it becomes capable of "being-with." Its relation to the death of others is never the same as its relation to its own death, and thus the collective being of *Dasein*, its "*mit-sein*," is never exposed to the limit, the impossibility and finitude of death in quite the same manner. Death and being-with remain separate issues in Heidegger.

It is precisely the traversal of this gap between being-toward-death and being-with that orchestrates surreptitiously the exchanges between Blanchot and Nancy over the difficulty of rethinking the relation between death and the problem of community. For each thinker, a relation to the death of the other facilitates a passage across this gap and reinscribes being-with at the heart of a community of mourning. They both argue that this being-with must first pass by way of another movement that seeks to interrupt the work of mourning it makes possible. In "Myth Interrupted,"[3] for instance, Nancy asks us to imagine the scene of an assembly gathered to listen to the narrative of its own formation, a story that recounts the emergence of the collective or community out of exile and loss, and into the gathered unity of a brotherhood, a people, or a city (which is the basic function of myth in his argument). Nancy's gesture regarding this fabulous scene—his attempt to rethink the question of community in relation to something other than identification with this narrative—is not to simply "demythologize" it, but to examine its *operation*, the way it entails a putting-into-work of community that immobilizes death by inaugurating myth. He seeks, in other words, to expose myth not to death "as such," since it is precisely on this that it lives and thrives, but to the *singular* death of the other. This singularity interrupts myth, becoming, as Nancy puts it, "death as the unworking that unites us because it interrupts our communication and our communion."[4] Death, at once a limit internal to philosophy, also opens up another limit, one *specific to the community*. Nancy's work thus involves a theory that invokes a "touching" of the limit, and an *inscription* of the limit, without this limit being crossed, or abolished in the fiction of a common body.

Of course, this would not be the first time that the question of community has been brought before the tribunal of death, but unlike Freud's similarly mythical scene of the totem feast,[5] Nancy pursues a question of a mourning that would attempt precisely to *avoid* identification or incorporation. For Nancy, the death of the other is neither tragic nor mythic. It is rather, as Blanchot puts it in the *Unavowable Community*, what calls the subject into question most radically:

> What, then, calls me into question most radically? Not my relation to myself as finite, or as the consciousness of being before death or for death, but my presence for another who absents himself by dying. To remain present in the proximity of another who by dying removes himself definitively, to take upon myself another's death as the only death that concerns me, this is what puts me beside myself, this is the only separation that can open me, in its very impossibility, to the Openness of a community.[6]

This "openness of a community" for Blanchot emerges out of a mourning that recuperates nothing, represents nothing. At least two forms of mourning, therefore, must be distinguished from each other, along with two different forms of being-with: the first puts death to work, giving it a meaning and a determinate sense. The second lingers over the worklessness of death, only to in turn make this worklessness the very condition for the possibility of saying "we."

What will divide Blanchot and Nancy, however, will be their relative emphasis on the transition *back* from the singular relation to the death of the other, to a being-with. At stake is not just how this transition is effectuated, but how community emerges out of it. For Blanchot what takes precedence is the ethical demand of community, an absolutely irreducible relation to the other. What is "shared" by this relation is a kind of radical dispossession of the self. As he puts it in *Unavowable Community*, the community "gives rise to an unshared though necessarily multiple speech in a way that does not let it develop itself in words: always already lost, it has no use, creates no work, and does not glorify itself in that loss."[7] Caught in the elaborate *aporia* of the need to transmit the untransmittable, to share the radical solitude of an event—the death of the other— that says nothing but radical dispossession, Blanchot's community is fundamentally "unavowable." That is, it cannot recuperate itself except in the form of an irreducible loss of sense, meaning, or signification. As Jean-Paul Madou puts it, Blanchot's community "would only be capable of being realized in the faultlines of the social fabric, in the tearing or rendering of ordinary communication. It would not be capable of being realized without being lost immediately."[8] The non-shareable secret, the unavowable secret, of the death of the other would always run the risk of becoming something that could be owned, as the "truth" or essence of the community. In the face of this possibility, Blanchot counterposes an opening to a radical inaccessibility as both the condition for, and the impossibility of, "community" in any traditional sense. What emerges then, is something closer to the fundamentally ecstatic sovereignty of Bataille, a sovereignty no longer grounded in any ipseity or autonomous subjectivity, but rather in a sort of limitless abandonment, "the accomplishment of community in that which, precisely, limits it" and a sovereignty grounded "in that which makes it absent and null, its prolongation in the only communication which henceforth suits it and which passes through literary unsuitability when the latter inscribes itself in works only to affirm the unworking that haunts them, even if they cannot reach it."[9]

Nancy, on the other hand, insists precisely on the necessity of figuration in this passage from the incommensurable death of the other to being-with. Starting from a similar experience of the death of the other as one of radical dispossession, Nancy will go on to problematize precisely the Levinasianism of Blanchot's argument, putting pressure on the way in which "the other" as an ethical category comes to (un)ground the problem of community. Emphasizing the movement *to* being-with out of the relation to the death of the other, Nancy returns to the problem that haunts Levinasian ethics: namely the problem of the encounter with the Other in the "face-to-face," the direct address of the other without intermediary. As Derrida has argued in the *Gift of Death*, the ethical formula *"tout autre est tout autre,"* or "every other (one) is every (bit) other" necessitates the question of the relation between the ground of the ethical demand, the absolute radical alterity of the Other, and the relation to *this* other, singularized: "As soon as I enter into a relation with the other, with the gaze, look, request, love, command, or call of the other, I know that I can respond only by sacrificing ethics, that is to say, by sacrificing whatever obliges me to also respond, in the same way, in the same instant, to all the others."[10] That is, what inevitably occurs in the absolute ethical demand of the Other is a sacrifice of the *same claim* upon me by so many others. My responsibility before the singularity of (the death of) the other forces a sacrifice of ethical generality. For Nancy, as for Derrida, a necessary slippage occurs between thinking an incommensurable relation to death "as such" or the Other "as such," and a relation to *this* death and *this* other.

Through the specter of a Levinasian critique of being-toward-death, and the motif of the singularity of the other in the face-to-face encounter, however, a secondary *aporia* will never cease to subject the relation between being-toward-death and being-with to an even more radical dislocation, and it is toward this that Nancy's theoretical inquiry moves. If death must be singularized through an encounter with *this* other, this singular other that addresses me directly, then this relation appears to necessitate the question of, if not *vision*, then at least *touch*, a relation to a limit that is sensed, felt, but never crossed. When Levinas casts this problem in terms of the "epiphany" of the face, it is primarily to emphasize the appeal that the nakedness of the other's gaze exerts upon me, without recourse to an image, without intermediary, in his pure nakedness. As Levinas insists:

> To manifest oneself as a face is to *impose oneself* above and beyond the manifested and purely phenomenal form, to present oneself in a mode irreducible to manifestation, the very straightforwardness of the face to face, without intermediary of any image, in one's nudity, that is, in one's destitution and hunger.[11]

There is, thus, for Levinas, likewise never a relation to the Other "as such"— only *this* other, here and now. If in Levinas, the community that emerges out of this encounter is made possible only by way of the *asymmetrical* gaze of the Other, his solicitation of me without resemblance, the point of contact that articulates our community passes by way of a gaze I do not touch, but which touches *me*, which I do not see, but which sees *me*, and through which I am solicited without communion or identification.

When Nancy examines this point of touch or contact with the other, however, he attempts both to problematize the Levinasian motif of the face-to-face, and to radicalize the asymmetry of this relation further by *withdrawing* the gaze of the other as the point of contact or address. In Levinas, it is the asymetrical "look" of the other that addresses me, and thereby instantiates the Other's hold on me. This occurs without mediation, without an image of the other who solicits me. The problematic of the death of the other, however, which Nancy situates as the radical limit internal to the concept of community, short-circuits even this address, introducing the figure of an other who no longer looks or sees. If what calls the subject to account, and opens him to an impossible being-with is no longer a gaze, or is a radically absented gaze—the look of one who is dead— then the very solicitation by the other introduces a much more problematic, and equivocal, relation to the limit that constitutes community. This limit, as we will see, begins to bifurcate, and can no longer be located solely in the gaze of the other. What Nancy introduces is an inevitable dislocation effectuated in the passage from the singularized death of the other, to a community of impossible mourning. This is due in part to a problematic decision that lies at the heart of the way the gaze of the other presents itself through the image of a look that is not returned, that does not solicit or found anything, much less a community of those who have nothing in common.[12] This look, as we will see, restages an impossible decision between *two very different relations to the incommensurable*, two relations to that which is "without relation." What follows is that there are, then, at least two possible articulations of the relation between being-toward-death and being-with. The first will insist on the asymmetry of a relation to the limit and to the other that, having nothing but this asymmetry as its ground, cannot be communicated or shared. In this case, the relation to (the death of) the other makes communion, not to mention community, impossible. The other relation to the limit that Nancy invokes passes by way of a strange kind of "image," one that does not represent, or "give" the face of the other, dead or alive, but invokes an image of the other's withdrawal from sense, an eclipse of the other's gaze who no longer solicits except through a figuration of this very eclipse. For Nancy, it is this withdrawal that initiates community, even as it remains prone to a reappropriation that gives sight back to eyes that no longer see or solicit, or that gives the other through an image, and thus sacrifices not the ethical demand that comes from the other, but his very singularity. It is this radical instability internal to the image, as we will see, that becomes for Nancy both the mark of, and threat to, a community beyond communion.

One of Nancy's more directly philosophical texts, *Being Singular Plural*, explores the question of the relation to the other most directly, developing not only a reading of a Heidegger, but of Levinas and Blanchot, around the question of being-toward-death. Nancy does not disguise his ambition to rewrite "first philosophy" by positioning what he calls the "singular plural" at its foundation, arguing in essence that the "meaning" of Being is nothing but being-with. His argument, however, consists in more than just a replay of Heideggerian fundamental ontology, oriented now around a fuller elaboration of "*mit-sein.*" For Nancy, the meaning of Being, its "signification," must first be divorced, as in Heidegger, from the notion of any content, any metaphysical claim that places "sense" or meaning somewhere outside of the world that, according to Nancy, we "share" (though precisely the meaning of this sharing requires further elaboration). In short, signification is not transcendent to the world or to the beings that constitute it; rather, the world is, for Nancy, given as their pure circulation: "We are meaning in the sense that we are the element in which significations can be produced and circulate. The least signification just as much as the most elevated (the meaning of 'nail' as well as the meaning of 'God') has no meaning in itself and, as a result, is what it is and does what it does only insofar as it is communicated, even where this communication takes place only between 'me' and 'myself.'"[13] Signification, then, begins not in presence, or in the withdrawal of presence, but in its spacing and division: "It could be expressed in the following way: Being cannot *be* anything but being-with-one-another, circulating in the *with* and as the *with* of this singularly plural coexistence. If one can put it like this, there is no other meaning than the meaning of circulation."[14] The world that we "share," then, is thus not a unified world, a common ground that preexists the "circulation" Nancy describes. Rather, the world, *as* the circulation of the "with," does not permit a position exterior to this circulation. There is thus not one world, but multiple worlds, held in tension by their circulation "with" all of the others. Nancy's gesture here, which takes the form of a claim about the nature of "world," consists in an impossible claim that is, at least at first glance, quasi-ontological. However, Nancy will go on to problematize his claim to "first philosophy" by turning some of his own constructions against themselves. Rather than offer a new interpretation of the meaning of Being à la Heidegger, Nancy instead *mirrors* what appear to be ontological claims in order to destabilize them, while proposing a reflection on the meaning of Being as already shared, divided, communicated, and so on. That is, if the meaning of Being is always already lost, and therefore always already to be mourned, it is not because Being withdraws, or because it is incommensurable to the beings that circulate around its origin. Rather, it is because beings remain *exposed* to an origin that is nothing but the spacing and intertwining of multiple singular origins—what Nancy calls the singular plural that dislocates every single, substantial *essence* of Being itself.

Thus, for Nancy, what singularizes the "otherness" of the other, and renders my relation to his death incommensurable is not his transcendence. The "origin" of Being, and the displacement of the question of its meaning is not a secret, or a withdrawal of the unpresentable, any less than it is a signification that hides itself behind a veil, waiting to be deciphered. The desire to locate the alterity of the other in the unity of transcendence is, according to Nancy,

> the desire to fix the origin, or *to give the origin to itself*, once and for all, and in one place for all, that is, always outside the world. That is why such a desire is a desire for murder, and not only murder but also for an increase of cruelty and horror, which is like the tendency toward the intensification of murder; it is mutilation, carving up, relentlessness, meticulous execution, the joy of agony. Or it is the massacre, the mass grave, massive and technological execution, the bookkeeping of the camps. It is always a matter of expediting the transformation of the other into the Other or making the Other appear in the place of the other, and, therefore, a matter of identifying the Other and the origin itself.[15]

Rather than locate the Other, as Levinas does, in places of first philosophy, Nancy attempts to expose philosophy or theory to the inappropriable dislocation that occurs in any attempt to access this origin.

In the context of Nancy's reinterpretation of the meaning of Being as a form of being-with, figuration, or the problem of the image remains latent, treated for the most part negatively, as precisely what betrays or disrupts the form of being-with Nancy is at pains to describe. Having already deconstructed the relation between figuration and identification in a variety of texts,[16] Nancy in *Being Singular Plural* seems intent on first rewriting Heidegger and clearing a certain ground, before returning to the question of what role, if any, figuration or the image might play in a transformed relationship between the community and the death of the other. If Nancy's focus so far has been on the question of the meaning of Being as the unfolding of being-with, what becomes just as apparent in *Being Singular Plural* is that this "groundless ground" acts as a screen against which can be projected what Nancy (and Lacoue-Labarthe) have called the "retreat of the political,"[17] by which they mean the retreat of every space into which, or onto which, a *figure* of community could be projected. Nancy's articulation of being-with occurs in the repetition and displacement of a Heideggerian mode of philosophizing; it therefore cannot do without the motif of something that *comes before*, is always already prior to, any form of communitarian belonging or identification. If various forms or "models" of community cannot themselves constitute the groundless supposition of community, but can only be interpreted in relation to an originary being-with, then the question remains, for Nancy, how this self-dislocating being-with is articulated, how it *un-works* models of community that attempt to erect themselves in its place. As Nancy insists, "at the right time, then, the question has to be posed as to whether being-together can do without a figure and, as a result, without an identification, if the whole of its 'substance' consists only in its spacing."[18] Or, put another way, one could frame the question thus: what is it that exposes us, a "we" or a community of whatever kind, to a being-with that cannot be transfigured into a substance or subject, whether as a homeland or a nation, promised or otherwise? What is it that, *within* this exposure to a figureless and groundless ground, allows this relation to produce a radical dispossession we "share"? In *Being Singular Plural*, Nancy defers this question. Suggesting only that there will be a "right time" to pose it, he leaves suspended the question of whether exposure to a groundless being-with still requires figuration, a passage through the image. Yet, as we will see, Nancy returns, somewhat obliquely, to this question in a later text, *Ground of the Image*, which, though not directly addressing the relation between his characterization of being-with and the image, nonetheless provides several indications that redefine his understanding of the link between community and the death of the other.

Nancy already began to gesture toward this problematic at the end of *Being Singular Plural*, where he develops an argument about the relation between death "as such" and its presentability, a distinction that introduces a "second-ary" death specific to language that further complicates the passage from the death of the other to being-with. Nancy, in short, shifts his discussion of death as a figure of the limit away from the solitude of the one who dies, toward a specifi-cally *linguistic* death that interrupts communion. It is that very interruption that introduces a tentative being-with: "Death presents the interruption of a saying of the whole and of a totality of saying: it presents the fact that the saying-of-everything is at each time an 'everything is said,' a discrete and transitory com-pleteness. This is why death does not take place 'for the subject,' but only for its representation."[19] This space of representation is the space not of the "as such" of death, but of the "with" as such. Nancy continues: "This is also why 'my death' is not swallowed up with 'me' in pure disappearance. As Heidegger says, insofar as it is the utmost possibility of existence, it exposes existence *as such*. Death takes place essentially as language; reciprocally, language always says death: it always says the interruption of meaning as its truth."[20] Language, in short, is the exposi-tion of death. It does not produce merely the representation of the death of the other, but constitutes an event that takes place in language and that allows being-with to inscribe itself in and through the incommensurable relation to those who are no longer "with us." Nancy's argument, at this point, makes explicit reference to Blanchot's claim in "Literature and the Right to Death" that this linguistic death, inscribed at the heart of language as a form of being-with, puts one into an irreducible relation with the incommensurable death of the other. In fact, this secondary death, for Nancy, *is* the very articulation of the death of the other, the very condition in which the other's death becomes shared, the open-ing of an access to the inaccessible. Nancy here cites Blanchot: "Death speaks in me. My speech is a warning that at this very moment death is loose in the world, that it has suddenly appeared between me, as I speak, and the being I address: it is there between us as the distance that separates us, but this distance is also what prevents us from being separated, because it contains the condition for all understanding."[21] This "distance," for both Nancy and Blanchot, is at once the articulation of "the death of the other" *and* its abandonment. As an "immanent and intrinsic condition of presentation in general,"[22] the death of the other takes place as a form of speech. The community is thus exposed to a radical disloca-tion through a *secondary* death, which opens up an incommensurable relation-ality that qualifies being-with, and that in turn exposes death to signification, presentation, figuration. As Nancy writes, "if the unpresentability of 'with' is not that of a hidden presence, then it is because 'with' is the unpresentability of this pre-position, that is, the unpresentability of presentation itself. 'With' does not add itself to Being, but rather creates the immanent and intrinsic condition of presentation in general."[23] Being-with is thus *already* exposure to death, defined intrinsically as exposure to the Other.

It is here, however, in Nancy, that the problem of figuration and of the image returns to interrupt the attempt to ground community on the *presentation* of the death of the other; for if being-with creates the "immanent and intrinsic condition of presentation in general," then figuration does more than present the death of the other to me (in all of its transcendence). It also *deals* death, brings death into the world, and shares it. Relying to a certain extent on a radicalization of phenomenology (through a reading of Heidegger) that still maintains a relation to what appears and to presentability more generally, Nancy extends his analysis of this secondary death in language beyond Blanchot's understanding of speech.[24] At the beginning of *Being Singular Plural*, for example, Nancy, discussing the question of an "access" to the origin as a fundamental being-with, invokes a form of relation that is neither one of pure loss, nor one of appropriation. As he insists, "We have access exactly in the mode of having access; we get there; we are on the brink, closest, at the threshold, we *touch* the origin."[25] Here, once again, Nancy describes the relation to the incommensurable not through a figure of the unpresentable "as such," but as a threshold that can be felt, if not seen, and which results in an exposure that does not cross the threshold itself. Shortly after this description, however, Nancy links this notion of access to the image, specifically photographs, which "give access" to the singularity of the death of the other: "In the singularity that he exposes, each child that is born has already concealed the access that he is 'for himself' and in which he will conceal himself 'within himself' just as he will one day hide under the final expression of a dead face. This is why we scrutinize these faces with such curiosity, in search of identification, looking to see whom the child looks like, and to see if death looks like itself. What we are looking for there, like in photographs, is not an image; it is an access."[26] Obviously, the notion of access to the incommensurable that precedes this discussion of the image has already short-circuited any notion of representations, as in Nancy's argument about a secondary linguistic death. But in this case, as with speech, the image is no longer representational not simply because it no longer presents a death that transcends it, but because it *arrests death* by once again putting it to work, giving it back over to exposition, disclosure, and revelation. The *image* of the death of the other thus cannot entirely exempt itself from the putting-to-work of death that Nancy's entire argument at this point is attempting to circumscribe. If it at once gives access to singularity, it also wrenches the singularity of the death of the other back toward, if not the space of representation, then the space of *presentation*, and of presentability in general. It thus threatens once again to do more than give access to the incommensurable, it threatens to "give" the incommensurable "as such." And if it is the gaze of the other that shows itself in the photograph, or even in the "dead face," then what remains to be thought in Nancy is the way in which this gaze presents itself as something other than Levinas's face-to-face encounter with the Other.

In *Ground of the Image*, Nancy explores this problematic of presentation by arguing that a shift in the understanding of what constitutes an image occurred in the late eighteenth and early nineteenth centuries, moving from a focus on representation to a focus on the problem of presentation. Concentrating on a reading of the Kantian "schematism"[27] Nancy elaborates a theory of the image, with Kant, as the presentation of the very conditions of presentability as such. The Kantian schematism is the famously obscure point in Kant's *Critique of Pure Reason* that draws together the conceptual and nonconceptual conditions for the possibility of objects of experience. The schema-*image* is not simply a visual representation of something conceptual, but is actually one of the *conditions* of presentation itself. It is, as Nancy argues, a gaze that operates like a performative enunciation, declaring: "this is a thing." The non-sensible image or "schema-image" is that by which the *unity* of a representation becomes possible: "What I thus give myself or what thus gives itself *before all else*—in the precise sense of these words—cannot be already an image, but must be its possibility: not *Bild*, but the *Einung* of *Bild* (Einung is an old, and rare, poetic form of Einigung, uni-fication). It is the making-one, the bringing-into-the-one of the *Bild*. It is a fore-seeing of the image, of the opening to a view in general."[28] The image in this sense is a unification that is not "opposed to multiplicity: it is the possibility that anything at all, including something multiple and fluid, may come to presence."[29] At the "ground" of the image, according the Nancy, something reveals itself as a gaze directed toward us. What presents itself in the image is a way of looking, a way of seeing: "the image makes an image by resembling a gaze."[30] The schema-image is "like" a gaze in that it simultaneously opposes itself to visibility (i.e., to a gaze or look that would be directed back towards it) *and* in that it reveals itself through what Nancy describes as a "graphic or pictorial proposition": "there is a thing only through the design of the thing, and this design gives the thing the contour of a look turned toward our vision."[31] This gaze is not the appearance of a face that solicits us. It is rather the antecedence of the image to itself, its *imaging* arrival, so to speak.

When Nancy's commentary turns to the question of the *presentation* of this gaze, his analysis focuses on the example that Heidegger uses to explicate the schema-image in his own analysis in *Kant and the Problem of Metaphysics*.[32] Heidegger illustrates the gaze of the schema-image first though a meditation on photography followed, somewhat surprisingly, by a long commentary on a death mask. Nancy remarks on the strangeness of this example, since, unlike the photograph, the death mask offers a figure that emphasizes the *blindness* inherent in the gaze that sees. In other words, its fore-seeing or projection of unity as the precondition of presentation in general withdraws in a far more abyssal manner than the "way of seeing" that the photograph articulates. This is so because the death mask divides the unity of the condition of presentation by offering two irreconcilable aspects of the gaze at the same time, through the same way of looking or seeing. For, the image of the dead man or the death mask, as Nancy insists, has both a present aspect, insofar as it *does not see*, and past one, *insofar as it looked*. Both of these aspects belong to the mask simultaneously—the first is a figure for the withdrawal of presentation that is already featured in the schema-image: a *present blindness*. The second gives us the aspect of a present-past—a "way of seeing" that no longer looks as it once did. Heidegger's example involves more than simply coming face-to-face with an irreducible blindness at the heart of the image, with a gaze that recedes from all monstration, precisely because it provides a structure for the unity that *constitutes* the gaze in the first place. "But," as Nancy suggests, "if, consequently, the *one* of the image is never anywhere but in the sketch, the fore-tracing and the fore-seeing of itself . . . if it is, in sum, an imaging that is never imagined (what Kant would call a pure image), if this imaging originates in death as the unseeing gaze face-to-face with my own gaze as it sinks in turn into its withdrawn image, then this means that the 'one' comes from the 'other," and not from an auto-intuitive self, that it comes from the other, through the other and as other, in order to return to the other."[33]

What does this gaze of the death of the other solicit, then? Clearly no recognition, interiorization, or exchange, for a blind gaze entails no reciprocity. Nor does it provide the figure of a singular incommensurability that solicits my responsibility in the asymmetry of its sheer nakedness, for the gaze also withdraws itself into a *past present*, a "having-looked" that no longer offers itself. What this "eclipse of the gaze" at the ground of the image generates is nothing but a being-with that is torn between *at least two* relations, two forms of being-with in relation to the incommensurability of the death of the other. If the eclipse of the gaze is imagined as *one*, as unitary and unified, this is possible only by eliding the demand that states that the image must also be a *self*-showing of the *unshowable*, a tracing of its own effacement, in short, a "modeling" of the absented gaze. If at the ground of every image is a secondary death, a form of a "fore-seeing" self-presentation, this secondary death nonetheless makes it possible to "present" the unity or singularity of the death of the other, giving access to this singularity through a being-with that is something other than communion. Yet if it grants this access, it also opens the threat and possibility of a gaze *without relation*—an incommensurability that cannot solicit, and that is no longer "with" in any form. If the image negotiates the passage between being-toward-death and being-with, it does so by giving access to what does not see and no longer sees in the image.

The *image* of the death of the other thus gives, in the same space, as it were, two different relations to incommensurability that cannot be dissociated. There is never, in short, a figure of being-with, or community without communion, only an *image* that attests to a task of incompletion. At the ground of the image, something inscribes itself in a disappearance no one will see, that is neither captured nor represented in or by the image, but which is nevertheless figured in and as the eclipse of a gaze that is the condition for any image. Any figure of being-with or community thus remains inevitably haunted by this gaze, which is both a threat to it, and its greatest resource. The figure of being-with offers itself, therefore, as an impossible decision, in the sketch of more than one relation to the incommensurable, more than one relation to death, more than one relation to the limit inscribed as its ground. From the incommensurable as an unmasking of the truth of death that it puts to work in the service of community, to the incommensurable as the "model" for the community of an impossible mourning, to the incommensurable that threatens the possibility of a total annihilation of any being-with whatsoever. Between all of these relations to death lies the threat and possibility of community, inscribed in the "eclipse of the gaze in the ground of the imagination itself: schema of the same in its other."[34]

Notes

1 See, for example, the collection of interviews with Jacques Derrida, Frank Kermode, Christopher Norris, and Toril Moi that comprises one of the many

volumes dealing with the question of what "comes after" theory: Michael
Payne and John Schad, eds., *Life After Theory* (New York: Continuum
Press, 2003).

2   The notion of "being-with" as a fundamental "existentiale" structure of *Dasein* is
treated in chapter four of *Being and Time*. See Martin Heidegger, *Being and Time*,
trans. John Macquarrie and Edward Robinson (San Francisco: Harper and Row
Press, 1962), 149–168. "Being-towards death" is elaborated primarily in chapter 1,
division II.

3   Jean-Luc Nancy, "Myth Interrupted" in *The Inoperative Community*, ed. Peter
Connor (Minneapolis: University of Minnesota Press, 1991), 43–70.

4   Ibid., 67.

5   Sigmund Freud, *Totem and Taboo*, trans. James Strachey (New York: W. W.
Norton, 1950).

6   Maurice Blanchot, *The Unavowable Community*, trans. Pierre Joris
(Barrytown: Station Hill Press, 1988), 9.

7   Ibid., 12.

8   Jean-Paul Madou, "The Law, the Heart: Blanchot and the Question of
Community," *Yale French Studies* 93.1 (1998), 62.

9   Blanchot, *The Unavowable Community*, 20.

10 Jacques Derrida, *The Gift of Death*, trans. David Wills (Chicago: Chicago
University Press, 2008), 69.

11 Emmanuel Levinas, *Totality and Infinity*, trans. Alphonso Lingis
(Pittsburgh: Duquesne University Press, 1969), 200.

12 I take this phrase from the title of Alphonso Lingis's study, which, from
a Levinasian perspective, examines a number of questions Nancy also
explores, particularly community, death, and the face-to-face encounter. See
Alphonso Lingis, *The Community of Those Who Have Nothing in Common*
(Bloomington: Indiana University Press, 1994).

13 Jean-Luc Nancy, *Being Singular Plural*, trans. Robert D. Richardson and Anne
E. Byrne (Stanford: Stanford University Press, 2000), 2.

14 Ibid., 3.

15 Ibid., 20.

16 See, for example, Nancy's text on Nazi mythology cowritten with Philippe
Lacoue-Labarthe. Philippe Lacoue-Labarthe and Jean-Luc Nancy, "The Nazi
Myth," *Critical Inquiry* 16.2 (Winter 1990): 291–312.

17 Philippe Lacoue-Labarthe and Jean-Luc Nancy, *Retreating the Political*, ed. Simon
Sparks (London: Routledge Press, 1997).

18 Nancy, *Being Singular Plural*, 47.

19 Ibid., 88–89.

20 Ibid.

21 Maurice Blanchot, "Literature and the Right to Death" in *The Work of Fire*, trans. Charlotte Mandel (Stanford: Stanford University Press, 1995), 323–324. Cited in Nancy, *Being Singular Plural*, 90.

22 Nancy, *Being Singular Plural*, 62.

23 Ibid.

24 For a careful analysis of Nancy's attempt to address some of Blanchot's criticisms of his conception of community, see Gregory Bird, "Community beyond Hypostasis: Nancy Responds to Blanchot" *Angelaki* 13.1 (April 2008): 3–26.

25 Nancy, *Being Singular Plural*, 13.

26 Ibid., 14.

27 The section on the "schematism" in Kant's *Critique of Pure Reason* concentrates on the conditions of presentability as such. See Immanuel Kant, *Critique of Pure Reason,* trans. Paul Guyer, "On the Schematism of the Pure Concepts of the Understanding" (Cambridge: Cambridge University Press, 1998), 271–277. For an excellent reading of what is at stake in this section (the ground of Kant's transcendental system itself), see Geoffrey Bennington, "X" in *Interrupting Derrida* (London: Routledge Press, 2000), 76–92.

28 Jean-Luc Nancy, *The Ground of the Image*, trans. Jeff Fort (New York: Fordham University Press, 2005), 83–84.

29 Ibid.

30 Ibid., 87.

31 Ibid., 89.

32 Martin Heidegger, *Kant and the Problem of Metaphysics*, trans. Richard Taft (Bloomington: Indiana University Press, 1990).

33 Nancy, *The Ground of the Image*, 97.

34 Ibid., 99.

Works cited

Bennington, Geoffrey. *Interrupting Derrida*. London: Routledge Press, 2000.

Bird, Gregory. "Community Beyond Hypostasis: Nancy Responds to Blanchot." *Angelaki* 13.1 (April 2008): 3–26.

Blanchot, Maurice. *The Unavowable Community*. Trans. Pierre Joris. Barrytown: Station Hill Press, 1988.

Blanchot, Maurice. *The Work of Fire*. Trans. Charlotte Mandel. Stanford: Stanford University Press, 1995.

Derrida, Jacques. *The Gift of Death*. Trans. David Wills. Chicago: Chicago University Press, 2008.

Freud, Sigmund. *Totem and Taboo*. Trans. James Strachey. New York: W. W. Norton, 1950.

Heidegger, Martin. *Kant and the Problem of Metaphysics*. Trans. Richard Taft. Bloomington: Indiana University Press, 1990.

Heidegger, Martin. *Being and Time*. Trans. John Macquarrie and Edward Robinson. San Francisco: Harper and Row Press, 1962.

Kant, Immanuel. *Critique of Pure Reason*. Trans. Paul Guyer. Cambridge: Cambridge University Press, 1998.

Lacoue-Labarthe, Philippe, and Jean-Luc Nancy. "The Nazi Myth." *Critical Inquiry* 16.2 (Winter 1990): 291–312.

Lacoue-Labarthe, Philippe, and Jean-Luc Nancy. *Retreating the Political*. Ed. Simon Sparks. London: Routledge Press, 1997.

Levinas, Emmanuel. *Totality and Infinity*. Trans. Alphonso Lingis. Pittsburgh: Duquesne University Press, 1969.

Lingis, Alphonso. *The Community of Those Who Have Nothing in Common*. Bloomington: Indiana University Press, 1994.

Madou, Jean-Paul. "The Law, the Heart: Blanchot and the Question of Community." *Yale French Studies* 93.1 (1998): 60–65.

Nancy, Jean-Luc. *Being Singular Plural*. Trans. Robert D. Richardson and Anne E. Byrne. Stanford: Stanford University Press, 2000.

Nancy, Jean-Luc. *The Ground of the Image*. Trans. Jeff Fort. New York: Fordham University Press, 2005.

Nancy, Jean-Luc. *The Inoperative Community*. Ed. Peter Connor. Minneapolis: University of Minnesota Press, 1991.

Payne, Michael, and John Schad, eds. *Life After Theory*. New York: Continuum Press, 2003.

9

Deleuze, Kerouac, Fascism, and Death

Hassan Melehy

When he characterizes Gilles Deleuze and Félix Guattari's 1972 *Anti-Oedipus* as "an Introduction to the Non-Fascist Life,"[1] in the preface to the 1977 English translation of the book, Michel Foucault implicitly situates it with respect to death. In an affirmation tied to his own designation at around the same time of the area of biopolitics, he speaks of *Anti-Oedipus* as an "art of living" that is "counter to all forms of fascism."[2] Foucault explains that fascism is Deleuze and Guattari's "strategic adversary": "And not only historical fascism, the fascism of Hitler and Mussolini—which was able to mobilize and use the desire of the masses so effectively—but also the fascism in us all, in our heads and in our everyday behavior, the fascism that causes us to love power, to desire the very thing that dominates and exploits us."[3] This characterization may rightly be understood as an elaboration of Foucault's enthusiastic declaration seven years earlier that "perhaps, one day, the century will be Deleuzian," in his review article on Deleuze's *Difference and Repetition* (1968) and *The Logic of Sense* (1969).[4] Hence Foucault's attribution of a life-enhancing capacity to *Anti-Oedipus* is also a declaration that the life of this philosophical work will extend beyond that of Deleuze and his coauthor Guattari, and by implication beyond their deaths. Asking the authors' forgiveness, Foucault describes *Anti-Oedipus* as not merely the most important but "the only book of ethics to be written in France in quite a long time," citing the fact that "being anti-oedipal has become a life style, a way of thinking and living."[5] That is, the work of Deleuze and Guattari already has a life beyond theirs by contributing to a powerful affirmation of life against the domination of death, and as such appears to be on its way to marking its age.

The role Foucault sees Deleuze and Guattari's work playing stems entirely from the antifascist energy that drives it. Deleuze and Guattari define fascism in its historical manifestation as very precisely a domination of death, which carries the people who embrace it to an inevitable and violent end—and this is what they ascribe to the more general phenomenon they term *fascism* throughout *Anti-Oedipus* and the second volume of *Capitalism and Schizophrenia, A Thousand Plateaus* (published in 1980, then in English translation in 1987). In the latter book, the authors follow Paul Virilio in their analysis, according to which the National Socialist state in Germany involved a rush toward death—a war machine that through the energy of desire carried the state to a violence that could only result in first an outward and then an inward destruction, collective suicide. "There is in fascism," they write, "a realized nihilism."[6] In their account, fascism is distinct from the totalitarian limitation and squelching of life that seals the flow of desire, the very movement that makes life, what they term a *line of flight* when it involves an evasion of dominant ordering power. Fascism, rather, promotes and rides on a line of flight, turns the immense energy of one current of desire against all others, and, like the subatomic particles that interact in a nuclear fission reaction, destroys itself and everything around it.

The broader scope of the advocacy of antifascism runs throughout the works Deleuze and Guattari wrote together and also Deleuze's own philosophical project. Deleuze's author studies in the history of philosophy are particularly striking for their valorization of efforts that run counter to the totalizing and unifying tendencies that have dominated Western philosophy in the form of its great systems—efforts that have always been part of the canon of philosophy. This philosophical critique addresses the present in that the philosophers topical to Deleuze—among them Spinoza, Hume, Nietzsche—in many ways take on what continue to be received habits of thinking or ideology. In *Difference and Repetition* (1968) and *The Logic of Sense* (1969), Deleuze formulates his project as a critique of representation—a critique of the conceptualization of representation that subordinates image to original, or more broadly the many to the one, selecting from among the many those that conform to the exigencies of the one. Deleuze defines this representational scheme as broadly and foundationally Platonic. In its fascist extreme, the image of the one is so energetically imposed that it destroys the very means of proliferation that it might find in the participation of at least some of the many. This critique of representation also marks Deleuze and Guattari's characterization of political fascism in *A Thousand Plateaus*, in which they note the spectacle of the Nuremberg rallies, where "the people cheered," and the "entirely ordinary Nazi speeches and conversations"[7] that presented death as a desirable spectacle. They quote the following from Klaus Mann's 1936 novel *Mephisto*: "Our beloved Führer is dragging us toward the shades of darkness and everlasting nothingness. How can we poets, we who have a special affinity for darkness and lower depths, not admire him? . . . Fires blazing on the horizon; rivers of blood in all the streets; and the frenzied dancing of the survivors, of *those who are still spared, around the bodies of the dead!*"[8] That is, the particular spectacle of Nazi power is driven by a vital energy hijacked toward immense destruction.

In *A Thousand Plateaus*, Deleuze and Guattari's critique of fascism takes on capacious proportions, seemingly involving the entirety of the West—in which, just as in the history of philosophy that is the latter's emblem, there have always run powerful currents of antifascism. It's not surprising that for these authors, as for Deleuze in all his previous books, exemplary of antifascist practices is literature, the very thing that the guardians of Plato's *Republic* regulate because of its threat to good representation. The model of antifascism with which Deleuze and Guattari open a *A Thousand Plateaus*, the rhizome that gives the introductory chapter its title, stems from literary operations: in the opening pages they mention two of their favorites, Kafka and Kleist, and soon after they mention Whitman's *Leaves of Grass*, itself a species of grass, a book that declares itself a rhizome.[9] The term *rhizome* is of course the most resonant and widely used entry in the Deleuzoguattarian lexicon, functioning as shorthand to contest all unifying hierarchies and the clearly bounded, self-identical entities that come with them. In Deleuze's own writings, apart from his collaborations with Guattari, literature is antirepresentational, neither rooted in nor an outgrowth of the reality it engages but rather forming ties with the latter. These ties push against the various drives both to confine literature to a function of mimesis and to present reality and the thinking about it in a clearly demarcated image. In contesting the representational logic that gathers vast and variegated phenomena into stabilizing images and patterns and diminishes the value and the vitality of difference—a logic that at its most energetic is fascism—literature is revolutionary.

Deleuze attributes revolutionary energy in particular to American literature in "On the Superiority of Anglo-American Literature," a text that appeared in 1977, the result of interviews Claire Parnet conducted with him for the "Dialogues" series from the Flammarion publishing house. This text dates from around the time of the first appearance of the essay "Rhizome," several years before its incorporation into *A Thousand Plateaus* as the introduction. Without using the word *rhizome*, Deleuze discusses the difference between American and European literature in terms of arborescence and rootedness, terms that he and Guattari use for processes that run counter to the rhizome. Beginning with a rather commonplace idea of America as the opening of new territory, and hence as a deterritorialization of the old, Deleuze applauds D. H. Lawrence, writing on Melville, for noting the transformative power of adventurous, exploratory travel, the refusal to be rooted. Deleuze directs this idea toward the critique of metaphysics, making a general assessment: "American literature operates along geographic lines: the flight to the West, the discovery that the true East is in the West, the meaning of the frontiers as something to cross, to push back, to surpass."[10] Deleuze illustrates with a comparison to Europe: "We don't have the equivalent in France. The French are too human, too historical, too concerned with future and past. They spend their time clarifying matters. They don't know how to become, but rather think in terms of historical past and future."[11] Moreover, he writes, "French literature is abounding in manifestos, ideologies, and theories of writing, at the same time as in personal spats, clarifications of clarifications, neurotic subservience, and narcissistic tribunals."[12] In his invective against what he presents as the drawn-out, pompous wafflings of the postwar French literary scene, Deleuze almost explicitly attributes a spontaneity to American literature, a willingness to live in the moment and not be concerned with definitions in order to find or produce something new—as opposed to the French and more generally the continental Europeans, who, he finds, must strictly root themselves according to an ordered scheme of time that moves from past to future. This is not *becoming*, not the invention of new forms, not continual obliteration of old boundaries and definitions.

This idea of American literature as spontaneity has a lot to do with why he accords rapturous praise to the main proponent of spontaneity among Anglo-American authors, Jack Kerouac, who died in 1969, just eight years before the publication of *Dialogues*, of complications of severe alcoholism. In his remarks, Deleuze is clearly aware of Kerouac's method of spontaneous prose, which involves casting a text in a quick set of motions over a short time, with minimal rewriting of the particular segment being drafted: Deleuze offers Kerouac's writing in illustration of the notion of lines of flight. Speaking of becomings, in which one form spills over into another not by way of imitating it but rather in a transformation that does away with any notion of the ontological integrity of either, Deleuze writes: "The line of flight creates these becomings. Lines of flight have no territory. Writing effects the conjunction, the transmutation of flows, by which life escapes from the *ressentiment* of persons, societies, and reigns. Kerouac's sentences are as sober as a Japanese drawing, pure lines traced freehand, crossing over eras and reigns. It took a true alcoholic to reach such sobriety."[13] This is an amazingly insightful assessment, especially given the fact that the very lengthy letters and journal entries in which Kerouac reflects on his writing method were decades away from publication. It also stands in marked contrast to most US judgments of Kerouac's prose, which typically present him as a drunken druggy who just spewed whatever onto the page. For example, "That's not writing, it's typing,"[14] said Truman Capote on TV in 1959, a little over a year after the publication of *On the Road*, the novel that to this day reductively defines Kerouac's career. Deleuze, rather, sees perfection in Kerouac's cultivated practice of casting sentences in one pass. Often quite lengthy, written not only to reflect but also to participate in the rapidity of geographic and cultural shifts in real time, as well as the cognition of these phenomena that isn't separate from but rather takes shape along with them, Kerouac wrote sentences that gather in a complex syntactical assembly a disparity of locations and vitalities. In his work, when the narrative presents a temporal or spatial border crossing, his prose provides details of the life that thrives on each side such that they become a continuity without being subordinated to cultural or political unity. Deleuze goes so far as to proclaim the accomplishment of the author's alcoholism, which even Kerouac scholars sometimes use as a reason to dismiss at least some of his writing. For Deleuze, alcohol seems to function in Kerouac's work after the fashion of sixteenth-century French author François Rabelais, to whom Kerouac regularly referred to in his writing: under certain conditions, alcohol may do away with bilious, regressive mental habits, permitting an opening of both experience and social and political borders.

The characterization of Anglo-American literature in this part of Deleuze's essay also includes the examples of Thomas Hardy, Henry Miller, and Virginia Woolf. Deleuze sees these writers as offering a confrontation with the rough challenges of the Real, and their writing as love letters to the Real insofar as said writing is part of an acceptance of death[15]—an acceptance that makes life more liveable, in firm opposition to fascism's energetic promotion of death. In this account, Deleuze accords Kerouac by far the most space. Of Kerouac's 1959 novel *The Subterraneans*, Deleuze says, "We know of no book of love more important, more stirring, more grandiose,"[16] finding in its prose the very texture of love, a writing that isn't separate from erotic experience, that transforms the writing self by opening onto the Real through textual eroticism. Deleuze has more unkind words for French literature, not naming any titles but describing it as caught in a poor and delimited humanity—its writing is for the sake of writing, not for the sake of life, and struggles with the Lacanian order of the psyche: "Oh, the misery of the imaginary and the symbolic, the real always getting put off until later."[17] Although he is not writing with Guattari here, this sentence implies the vast criticism of psychoanalysis that they make in *Anti-Oedipus* and *A Thousand Plateaus*, according to which, among many other things, acceptance of the oedipal framework imposes the very restrictions on the psyche that analysis should put itself to getting past.

In those two works, Deleuze and Guattari have many but not all of the same reasons for reserving an important place for American literature—they cite Whitman, as I've indicated, and they address the cut-up method of Kerouac's close friend and collaborator William Burroughs as a partial but limited reworking of the rooted notion of the book. The major difference between their treatment and that of Deleuze's essay is the stress they place on the fascisms that, in their view, emerge from the revolutionary energies of America and Anglo-American literature. "Strange Anglo-American literature," they write in *Anti-Oedipus*:

> from Thomas Hardy, from D. H. Lawrence to Malcolm Lowry, from Henry Miller to Allen Ginsberg and Jack Kerouac, men who know how to leave, to scramble the codes, to cause flows to circulate, to traverse the desert of the body without organs. They overcome a limit, they shatter a wall, the capitalist barrier. And of course they fail completely. The neurotic impasse again closes—the daddy-mommy of oedipalization, America, the return to the native land—or else the perversion of the exotic territorialities, then drugs, alcohol—or worse still, an old fascist dream.[18]

This is along the lines of Deleuze's notions: Anglo-American literature is "superior" because it goes deep into the de-imperialization of territories and the dehierachization of bodily functions and limits that they term the "body without organs"; Anglo-American literature thus presents the starkest challenge to capitalism itself. But the second part of the logic that Deleuze and Guattari identify here, the failure, is almost fatalist: the brand new beginning, the rebirth in complete oblivion of the ancestors, out of some necessity succumbs to the return in force of Oedipus.

Although there are probably elements in the lives of most of these authors that correspond with the steps they identify in this supposedly unceasing failure, Kerouac's life closely matches the whole pattern: living with his mother, finding a traditional greatness in sites in America where he once saw teeming transculturality, writing on marijuana, proceeding to ever-worsening stages of alcoholism. Further in *Anti-Oedipus*, they're quite explicit about this "old fascist dream": they describe Kerouac as "the artist possessing the soberest of means who took revolutionary 'flight,' but who later finds himself immersed in dreams of a Great America, and then in search of his Breton ancestors of the superior race."[19] Though the term "superior race" is a hostile epithet, this passage offers a recognizable characterization of the quest Kerouac undertook to trace his aristocratic Breton ancestry, the prehistory of his French-Canadian heritage: this project is the focus of his 1966 short novel *Satori in Paris*. In the same passage of "Rhizome" in which they speak of Whitman's grassy text, Deleuze and Guattari parenthetically cite "Kerouac going off in search of his ancestors"[20] in support of their account of the rerooting tendencies of an American literature that is otherwise intensely revolutionary.

In "On the Superiority of Anglo-American Literature," Deleuze speaks of "Kerouac's sad end," alongside Fitzgerald's alcoholism, Lawrence's discouragement, and Virginia Woolf's suicide, all examples of "a pure and simple motion of self-destructiveness" that belongs to this oppositional energy, the fact of its traversal by "a somber process of demolition, which sweeps the writer away."[21] He explains this phenomenon as follows: "Fleeing fascism, we once again find fascist concretions on the line of flight. Fleeing everything, how does one not reconstitute our country of birth, our formations of power, our alcohol, our psychoanalyses, as well as our daddy-mommies?"[22] As in his writings with Guattari, the movement Deleuze describes entails the emergence of microfascisms, resulting from the inevitability of coming across the point of origin after one completely refuses it as a reference point. However, what remains is the refusal, the total rupture, the "superiority" of the revolution that takes place in the process. "Neither the beginning nor the end are interesting," Deleuze elaborates. "[T]he beginning and the end are points. What's interesting is the middle."[23] Though Deleuze signals a certain failure of Anglo-American rebellion, his statements here are somewhat more optimistic than the characterization as downright reactionary that he and Guattari make of Anglo-American writers, especially Kerouac, in *Anti-Oedipus*. Fascism, as they say, is self-destructiveness on a grand scale; it hardly seems equivalent to the individual downfall of these three authors, or any number of others, which might well be marked by self-destructiveness but is, more than anything, sad. Of course, such failure on the part of a huge number of Anglo-American authors might take on calamitous proportions. However, in the 1977 text, Deleuze doesn't go so far as to affirm this sort of broad social failure in Anglo-American literature.

I raise this difference in order to press Deleuze and Guattari on what one might best call an insistence, a repeated claim that Anglo-American literature contains within itself the impasse to its own revolutionary success. In this trajectory Kerouac is exemplary, and *Satori in Paris* is important as the mark of failure. However, there are certain aspects of this novel that they overlook. One

major problem is that they mainly homogenize "the father," seeing only a path
of civilization from Europe to America, from the past to the future, from roots
to rhizome. Although they regularly grant a multidirectionality of growth and
movement in the rhizome—rhizomatic offshoots in the arborescent schema,
knots of arboresence in the rhizome, and so on—in this brief but important
characterization of Anglo-American literature they see revolution followed by
reaction. One of the main reasons that this pattern is problematic with respect
to *Satori in Paris* and its exemplarity is that Kerouac is closely following traditions and even archival practices belonging to Québécois culture, as well as to
the Québécois Diaspora of which he was a part: the latter is the exodus between
1840 and 1930 of half the province's population (about 900,000 in total), half of
this half, or about one quarter of all French Canadians, resettling in and around
the industrial cities of New England.[24] The genealogy that Kerouac takes up is
a product of nineteenth-century Francophone Quebec, which saw conditions
of economic, cultural, and linguistic marginalization: illustrative of these is
the explicit policy of "obliterating the nationality of the French-Canadians,"
to quote from the 1840 report by Lord Durham,[25] who regarded as necessary
for peace in Canada measures that would be classified as cultural genocide in
the twentieth century (though maybe not in the twenty-first). In these conditions, genealogy developed largely as a contestatory act. It traveled with the
migration to the United States, in response to the nineteenth-century white
Anglo-Saxon supremacy by which the French Canadians were characterized
in long-repeated phrases as "the Chinese of the Eastern States," "a horde of
industrial invaders," to quote from the 1881 official report of Carroll D. Wright,
chief of the Massachusetts Bureau of Statistics of Labor and subsequently U.S.
Commissioner of Labor. Of course, taking recourse to the fathers of Catholic,
pre-Revolutionary France, making them aristocratic when possible, as a way
to contest the embodiment of the father in the Anglo-American states raises
its own set of problems, a risk of the very fascisms against which Deleuze and
Guattari warn. However, it's not as though these problems were beyond the
awareness of the nineteenth-century Québécois and Franco-Americans, many
of whom were ambivalent as to the value of the turn to the past and the grounding of industrial-age cultural survival or *survivance* in an idealized image of the
agrarian Middle Ages.

   Although until very recently both biography and scholarship, at least in the
United States, almost completely failed to recognize that Kerouac is an heir
to these traditions, he himself was certainly aware of the problems arising in
attempting to ground identity in the ancestors. In fact, if there's a failure that

Satori in Paris attests to, it's the failure to achieve any such grounding. The novel is largely the story of encounter with bureaucracy, which Kerouac tells from the perspective of his autobiographical narrator. Although too many, when speaking of Kerouac, fail to preserve the distinction between author and narrator, doing so is essential for considering the literary construction of the novel and its difference from the reportage of memoir. This narrator, named Jean-Louis Lebris de Kérouac (the name the author received at birth),[26] also known as Jack, is in place in Paris for speaking French but out of place for speaking Québécois French; while looking for the Bibliothèque Nationale, the state archive in which he will search for his identity, he receives wrong directions from a Paris policeman, a representative of state authority; once at the library, after filling out the requisite paperwork, he learns from a librarian that the documents he is requesting were destroyed during the Second World War. On his way to Brest to continue the search, at the airport Jack misses his plane because he uses the restroom—that is, bodily functions pose an ecstatic obstacle to the bureaucratic ordering of flight schedules. In transit, he loses his bag and must further negotiate with offices. He never finds out exactly who his first French-Canadian ancestor is. Documents in the New York Public Library's Berg Collection suggest that Kerouac knew more than his narrator about the topic: this difference between real life and its fictionalization attests to the novel's status as drama with moral purpose. Kerouac plays with the idea of grounding identity in the paternal past; he demonstrates, through an adeptly ironic plot and his characteristic poetic vigor, the futility of the quest. At the end of this novel's road, in the Brittany of his ancestors, he locates a man named Lebris who might be a distant relative: the real-life man's name was Pierre Lebris, but in his fiction Kerouac chooses to call him Ulysse (the French for "Ulysses")—a name that suggests that at the end of the quest, the end of vagabondage, lies not the rocklike fixity of ancestry (as the name Pierre would suggest) but rather more wandering. Kerouac's search for roots, then, is a valorization of leaving the fathers that overtakes the need to find them. Though Kerouac affirms intimate ties with Québécois *survivance*, a set of practices promoting an extension of collective life beyond the death of individuals, he also recognizes the failure inherent in grounding oneself in a vanished past and offers the ethical alternative of recognizing the vitality available in maintaining movement in the present.[27]

This isn't a break with his earlier fiction. *On the Road*, a monument to American vagabondage and rhizomatic motion, also involves a search for fathers: a good part of the reason why narrator Sal Paradise and co-protagonist Dean Moriarty spend so much time on the road is to look for Dean's father, Old

Dean Moriarty, for the explicit purpose of grounding identity and ending the rootlessness of vagabondage. But the quest fails: Kerouac ends the novel with both a celebration of American vastness, "all that raw land that rolls in one unbelievable huge bulge over the West coast, and all that road going, all the people dreaming in the immensity," and a lamentation: "and nobody, nobody knows what's going to happen to anybody besides the forlorn rags of growing old, I think of Dean Moriarty, I even think of Old Dean Moriarty the father we never found, I think of Dean Moriarty."[28] In the course of the novel, Sal and Dean find themselves engaged in various present-day social collectives in many places in North America without the need for familial rootedness, the very idea of a homogeneous, rooted America is seriously undermined, and, in the Mexico section of the book, the ordering force of imperial thinking meets with forceful contestation. That is, the object of desire, reuniting with the father, turns out to be less important than the creative activity that the desire produces—the desire is Deleuzoguattarian, realizing itself in its own motion. Although Deleuze and Guattari characterize Kerouac as engaging in a refusal of the social and cultural order of rule by the father and then in a return to this order, for Kerouac the father is never far away, continuing to lurk: sometimes as a ghost, the father continues to lurk as a force with which to negotiate and eventually come to peace by making him one component of the vast networks of motion. Kerouac, then, is a more vigilant revolutionary than Deleuze and Guattari make him out to be. The Beat author indeed came to a sad end in the wretched sickness of alcoholism; but neither his death nor his novel about traveling to France in search of his Breton ancestors constitutes fascism in the Deleuzoguattarian sense.

The Kerouac I've described is closer to the one in Deleuze's "On the Superiority of Anglo-American Literature" than to the culprit of fascist failure that he becomes in *Anti-Oedipus* (and to be fair, less so in *A Thousand Plateaus*). Why this misreading in the latter pair of books, which then becomes a misreading of the trajectory of all of Anglo-American literature—a trajectory that isn't at work, at least not in the same way, when Deleuze speaks without Guattari of Anglo-American literature? In taking fascism as their strategic adversary, as Foucault puts it, they at times become so eagerly strategic as to place fascism where it might not otherwise be. Like the Anglo-American authors they address, in trying to leave Oedipus completely behind, they encounter him again on the road to freedom, clinging to the rootedness that their work otherwise transforms into rhizomatic motion. But differently from these authors, they aren't claiming to start completely anew—rather, at least residually remaining on the territory they're leaving, they don't manage to completely avoid capture by the very forces they criticize. That is, in order to wage a battle against Oedipus, at least provisionally one needs Oedipus, even sometimes as a straw man. Deleuze and Guattari seem intent on finding Oedipus at work even where, as in Kerouac, he's being observed at a distance—curiously, as Deleuze recognizes in his solo writing.

There is a comparable difference between Deleuze's sympathetic reading of Freud in *Difference and Repetition* and Deleuze and Guattari's targeting him as a principal perpetrator of Oedipus. In Deleuze's treatment, the Viennese doctor's notion of repetition from *Beyond the Pleasure Principle* offers an important way of reconceiving desire as, instead of negation, productive energy—though in limited fashion, stopping short of accounting for death itself as something productive.[29] In contrast, such energy is in wholesale fashion, precisely what Deleuze and Guattari, writing together, attack Freud's work for failing to effect. In the case of Kerouac, their reading misses the multiplicity of fathers in his work and the ensuing tensions that keep any of them from reaching ascendancy: Kerouac reconceives the paternal transmission of Western civilization through the scattering motion of global migration, which evades subsumption under totalizing entities like the nation-state. Essential to Deleuze and Guattari's reading is a lingering notion of nationality, evident in their designation of literatures as American and European. Moreover, they import this categorization from Deleuze's solo texts—a fact that demonstrates Deleuze's own retention of some of the restrictive forces that he otherwise opposes. None of this is to say that Deleuze or Deleuze and Guattari don't continue to offer highly valuable theoretical work in the decades following their deaths. Rather, it is to say that doing honor to them necessitates that the very kind of antifascist vigilance they advocate be brought to the reading of their work.

Notes

1   Michel Foucault, "Preface," in Gilles Deleuze and Guattari, *Anti-Oedipus: Capitalism and Schizophrenia*, trans. Robert Hurley, Mark Seem, and Helen R. Lane (Minneapolis: University of Minnesota Press, 1983), xiii.

2   Ibid.

3   Ibid.

4   Michel Foucault, "Theatrum Philosophicum," in *Language, Countermemory, Practice*, ed. Donald F. Bouchard (Ithaca: Cornell University Press, 1977), 165.

5   Deleuze and Guattari, *Anti-Oedipus*, xiii.

6   Gilles Deleuze and Félix Guattari, *A Thousand Plateaus*, trans. Brian Massumi (Minneapolis: University of Minnesota Press, 1987), 230.

7   Ibid.

8   Klaus Mann, *Mephisto*, trans. Robin Smith (New York: Random House, 1977), 202–204; qtd. in Deleuze and Guattari, *A Thousand Plateaus*, 230–231.

9   Deleuze and Guattari, *A Thousand Plateaus*, 21.

10 Gilles Deleuze and Claire Parnet, "Sur la supériorité de la littérature anglaise-américaine," in *Dialogues* (Paris: Flammarion, 1977), 48: "La littérature américaine opère d'après des lignes géographiques : la fuite vers l'Ouest, la découverte que la véritable Est est à l'Ouest, le sens des frontières comme quelque chose à franchir, à repousser, à dépasser." The translation is mine. In the English edition, "On the Superiority of Anglo-American Literature," in Gilles Deleuze and Claire Parnet, *Dialogues II*, trans. Hugh Tomlinson and Barbara Habberjam (London and New York: Continuum, 2006), which I don't quote here because of its lapses, 27–28.

11 Ibid., 48: "On n'a pas l'équivalant en France. Les Français sont trop humains, trop historiques, trop soucieux d'avenir et de passé. Ils passent leur temps à faire le point. Ils ne savent pas devenir, ils pensent en termes de passé et d'avenir historiques." English edition, 28.

12 Ibid., 61: "[L]a littérature française abonde en manifestes, en idéologies, en théories de l'écriture, en même temps qu'en querelles de personnes, en mises au point de mises au point, en complaisances névrotiques en tribunaux narcissiques." English edition, 37.

13 Ibid., 62: "La ligne de fuite est créatrice de ces devenirs. Les lignes de fuite n'ont pas de territoire. L'écriture opère la conjonction, la transmutation par des flux, par quoi la vie échappe au ressentiment des personnes, des sociétés et des règnes. Les phrases de Kérouac sont aussi sobres qu'un dessin japonais, pure ligne tracée par une main sans support, et qui traverse les âges et les règles. Il fallait un vrai alcoolique pour atteindre à cette sobriété-là." English edition, 38.

14 Stephen Battaglio, *David Susskind: A Televised Life* (New York: St. Martin's, 2010), 3; see also Dennis McNally, *Desolate Angel: Jack Kerouac, the Beat Generation, and America* (New York: Delta, 1979), 267.

15 Gilles Deleuze and Claire Parnet, *Dialogues*, 62. Somewhat enigmatically Deleuze states, "One writes only out of love—all writing is a love letter, the literature-Real. One should write only out of love, not from a tragic death." ("On n'écrit que par amour, toute écriture est une lettre d'amour: la Réel-littérature. On ne devrait écrire que par amour, et non d'une mort tragique.") English edition, 38.

16 Deleuze and Parnet, *Dialogues*, 62: "Nous ne connaissons pas de livre d'amour plus important, plus insinuant, plus grandiose que les *Souterrains* de Kérouac." English edition, 38. (Unfortunately, the translators rendered Kerouac's title as *The Underground Ones*).

17 Ibid., 63: "Ah, la misère de l'imaginaire et du symbolique, le réel étant toujours remis à demain." English edition, 38.

18 Gilles Deleuze and Félix Guattari, *Anti-Oedipus*, trans. Robert Hurley, Mark Seem, and Helen R. Lane (Minneapolis: University of Minnesota Press, 1983), 144.

19 Ibid., 305.

20 Deleuze and Guattari, *A Thousand Plateaus*, 19.

21 Deleuze and Parnet, *Dialogues*, 50: "triste fin de Kérouac," "un pur et simple mouvement d'autodestruction," "un sombre processus de démolition, qui emporte l'écrivain." English edition, 29.

22 Ibid.: "Fuyant le fascisme, nous retrouvons des concrétions fascistes sure la ligne de fuite. Fuyant tout, comment ne pas reconstituer et notre pays natal, et nos formations de pouvoir, nos alcohols, nos pyschananalyses et nos papas-mamans?" English edition, 29.

23 Ibid., 50. "Ce n'est jamais le début ni la fin qui sont intéressants, le début et la fin sont des points. L'intéressant, c'est le milieu." English edition, 29.

24 These figures are well known in Franco-American studies and histories of the migration. My main source is Yves Roby, *Histoire d'un rêve brisé? Les Canadiens français aux Etats-Unis* (Sillery, QC: Septentrion, 2007), 7, 22–27.

25 John George Lambton, Earl of Durham, *Lord Durham's Report on the Affairs of British North America*, ed. Sir C. P. Lucas (Oxford: Clarendon Press, 1912), 299.

26 Jack Kerouac, *Satori in Paris*, in *Satori in Paris and Pic* (New York: Grove Press, 1985), 4.

27 These remarks are a condensed version I make in "Kerouac's Quest for Identity: *Satori in Paris*," *Studies in American Fiction* 41.1 (Spring 2014): 49–76, and in different form in chapter five of *Kerouac: Language, Poetics, and Territory* (New York: Bloomsbury, 2016).

28 Jack Kerouac, *On the Road* (New York: Viking Press, 1957), 307.

29 Gilles Deleuze, *Difference and Repetition*, trans. Paul Patton (New York: Columbia University Press, 1994), 16–19; see also the lengthier discussion of Freud and the pleasure principle in chapter 2, especially 130–140.

Works cited

Battaglio, Stephen. *David Susskind: A Televised Life*. New York: St. Martin's, 2010.

Deleuze, Gilles. *Difference and Repetition*. Trans. Paul Patton. New York: Columbia University Press, 1994.

Deleuze, Gilles, and Claire Parnet. "Sur la Supériorité de la Littérature Anglaise-Américaine." *Dialogues*. Paris: Flammarion, 1977.

Deleuze, Gilles, and Félix Guattari. *Anti-Oedipus*. Trans. Robert Hurley, Mark Seem, and Helen R. Lane. Minneapolis: University of Minnesota Press, 1983.

Deleuze, Gilles, and Félix Guattari. *A Thousand Plateaus*. Trans. Brian Massumi. Minneapolis: University of Minnesota Press, 1987.

Foucault, Michel. "Preface." *Anti-Oedipus: Capitalism and Schizophrenia* by Gilles Deleuze and Guattari. Trans. Robert Hurley, Mark Seem, and Helen R. Lane. Minneapolis: University of Minnesota Press, 1983.

Foucault, Michel. "Theatrum Philosophicum." *Language, Countermemory, Practice*. Ed. Donald F. Bouchard. Ithaca: Cornell University Press, 1977.

Kerouac, Jack. *On the Road*. New York: Viking Press, 1957.

Kerouac, Jack. *Satori in Paris*. In *Satori in Paris and Pic: Two Novels*. New York: Grove Press, 1985.

Lambton, John George, Earl of Durham. *Lord Durham's Report on the Affairs of British North America*. Ed. Sir C. P. Lucas. Oxford: Clarendon Press, 1912.

Mann, Klaus. *Mephisto*. Trans. Robin Smith. New York: Random House, 1977.

McNally, Dennis. *Desolate Angel: Jack Kerouac, the Beat Generation, and America*. New York: Delta, 1979.

Melehy, Hassan. *Kerouac: Language, Poetics, and Territory*. New York: Bloomsbury, 2016.

Melehy, Hassan. "Kerouac's Quest for Identity: *Satori in Paris*." *Studies in American Fiction* 41.1 (Spring 2014): 49–76.

Roby, Yves. *Histoire d'un rêve brisé? Les Canadiens français aux Etats-Unis*. Sillery, QC: Septentrion, 2007.

10

Theory's Ruins

Nicole Simek

Thinking about the relationship between theory and death raises the specter of the ruin, that haunting, sublime image of destruction and survival, decay and resistant trace. The theme of "dead theory" undoubtedly first conjured up for me the image of a theory in ruins, French theory more specifically, whose decline has been repeatedly foretold or proclaimed in recent years. Those who call for theory's death often do so as well in the name of the ruin, the ruins theory allegedly leaves in its wake as it subsumes the particular into the universal, or as it supposedly destroys the pleasure and purpose of literature by breaking it apart, dissecting or vivisecting its object. But dead theory is also a theory *of* the dead, of an object that prompts reflection on theory's temporality and ethical commitments. Theory's ruins are those transient objects, those historical fragments or material traces that seem to call out for theorization, that present an alluring hermeneutic puzzle. As a precarious, endangered trace, ruins can provoke a sense of urgency, the need to preserve or recover a history on the brink of total disappearance; viewed instead as an obstinate, resilient presence, the ruin evokes defiance, perhaps defiance to theorization itself, a stumbling block that itself may prove to be theory's ruin.

Because the ruin has become associated with both reflexive contemplation and strong affective attachments, it is a site or figure that highlights particularly well the dimension of dead theory I would like to consider here, namely, theory's relationship to enchantment and disenchantment, to affective investment and critical distance. The ruin also occupies an ambiguous position in Caribbean literature and theory, the particular area through which I would like to explore this relationship. In the following pages, I will take Derek Walcott's thoughts on Caribbean ruins as a point of departure for this exploration. In a second part, I will then turn to Patrick Chamoiseau and Jean-Luc de Lagarigue's *Elmire des sept bonheurs* (published in English as *Seven Dreams of*

Elmira: A Tale of Martinique),¹ a text that serves well as an anchor and testing ground for these reflections on theory's affects and investments in the dead.

Absent ruins and broken vases

Derek Walcott famously described the Caribbean's "absence of ruins" in an early poem, and in his 1992 Nobel lecture he returned to the theme, noting, "The sigh of History rises over ruins, not over landscapes, and in the Antilles there are few ruins to sigh over, apart from the ruins of sugar estates and abandoned forts."² In his 1981 work *Caribbean Discourse*, Édouard Glissant took up this erasure of collective memory as a troubling analytical problem, the problem of making visible a "reality that is so often hidden from view." ³ Glissant points to the need to look to the landscape itself for traces of this suppressed past: "History," he writes, "is spread out beneath this surface, from the mountains to the sea, from the forest to the beaches . . . (Our landscape is its own monument: its meaning can only be traced on the underside. It is all history)."⁴ Here, the absence of the ruin does not obviate the task of excavation, but shifts the location of the surface to be probed and highlights its urgency all the more. For Glissant, "the Caribbean writer must 'dig deep' into this [collective] memory, following the latent signs that he has picked up in the everyday world."⁵

Walcott's Nobel lecture points, however, to a different sort of analytical problem, which is not so much the difficulty in piecing together a history that has been suppressed in Western accounts and also physically erased, swallowed up by tropical vegetation, but rather the problem of theorizing from the ruin, from the assumption that the present constitutes a ruin, a fragmented trace of a lost whole. Walcott's speech relates an afternoon spent in the village of Felicity, Trinidad, watching the villagers prepare for the Hindu performance of Ramleela, a festival during which the life of Lord Ram is reenacted to show the purpose of his incarnation and to celebrate the triumph of good over evil. Describing the preparations, he remarks on a particular sign he takes as a ruin:

> Under an open shed on the edge of the field, there were two huge armatures of
> bamboo that looked like immense cages. They were parts of the body of a god,
> his calves or thighs, which, fitted and reared, would make a gigantic effigy. This
> effigy would be burnt as a conclusion to the epic. The cane structures flashed
> a predictable parallel: Shelley's sonnet on the fallen statue of Ozymandias and
> his empire, that "colossal wreck" in its empty desert.⁶

This "predictable parallel" produces ironic results. Perceiving the effigy as a ruin provokes a Romantic response—a response of melancholic meditation and critical distance from the performers taking up their costumes and roles in the cane fields before him. Yet this perception comes to annul itself. Ruminating over his lack of familiarity with the epic about to be performed, Walcott comes to describe his own experience as an experience of misperception:

> It was as if, on the edge of the Central Plain, there was another plateau, a raft on which the *Ramayana* would be poorly performed in this ocean of cane, but that was my writer's view of things, and it is wrong. I was seeing the *Ramleela* at Felicity as theatre when it was faith . . . They believed in what they were playing, in the sacredness of the text, the validity of India, while I, out of the writer's habit, searched for some sense of elegy, of loss, even of degenerative mimicry in the happy faces of the boy-warriors or the heraldic profiles of the village princes . . . I was filtering the afternoon with evocations of a lost India, but why "evocations"? Why not "celebrations of a real presence"? Why should India be "lost" when none of these villagers ever really knew it, and why not "continuing," why not the perpetuation of joy . . . ? Why was I not letting my pleasure open its windows wide?[7]

Walcott frames the problem as a tension between affective dispositions, a tension between the melancholic "sigh of History" and the pleasure whose windows that sigh shuts, a pleasure described later as the ecstasy of poiesis itself. To perceive a ruin is to see with the eyes of History, with a capital H, a History that, as Walcott puts it, "can alter the eye and the moving hand to confirm a view of itself." In other words, it is to mistake an absence for a lack, to project a loss from a particular vantage point that conceives of plenitude in specific ways. Walcott's denial of his own "writer's habit" seems to go so far as to deny or reject mediation; Walcott posits that the correct reading of the scene is to read it as faith, not mediated performance—and pleasurable participation, rather than distanced melancholia, is the proper response to it. He asks himself why he, too, doesn't open his windows to pleasure.

At the same time, Walcott seeks to retain the notion of an originary fragmentation, likening the culture and creativity of the Caribbean to the glue with which one lovingly joins together the pieces of a broken vase: "Antillean art is this restoration of our shattered histories, our shards of vocabulary, our archipelago becoming a synonym for pieces broken off from the original continent." Perceiving the Antilles, and its art, becomes, then, a matter of both remembering—of mediating—and of forgetting this original moment of ruination, of attending to both pain and pleasure, or what Walcott describes as "the pain that is joy." In this sense, the ruin invites not so much a hermeneutic quest to reconstitute its original shape as an attentiveness to the present process of joining, to the qualities of the present mosaic and the forces that bind it.

Walcott describes this "gathering of broken pieces," as the work of poetry itself, the work of "abridg[ing]" without "reduc[ing]" the epic scale and vitality of the original. Here we find a common view of poetry as condensation; poetry is the work of distilling, concentrating into dense form, and in the case of the Caribbean, it is the also work of bringing together the "ill-fitting" pieces of multiple vases. The question for a theory that seeks to approach poetry then is whether the work of expansion that theory does results, ironically, in the kind of reduction that the original distillation supposedly avoided. Does theory merely break the vase apart again, or can it be poetic, creative, itself? Do the cracks it introduces merely follow and reproduce the previous lines of breakage, or do they re-fragment in new ways, prolonging the poetic act?

Ironic enchantments

I would like to turn now to *Seven Dreams of Elmira*, another work that revolves around the ruins of modernity, but that approaches the perception of loss and absence with irony.[8] *Elmira* relates the story of a Martinican rum factory in decline, one of the few actual ruins that the Caribbean offers up to the eye, as Walcott notes. The book can perhaps best be described as a collaborative photo-text, combining a mystical tale about Saint-Étienne rum with portraits of residents in the surrounding area. Written in a first-person voice said to be that of an elderly worker from the Saint-Étienne rum factory, the text tells the story of distillery workers' encounters with Elmira, a mysterious and almost divine apparition who reveals herself on rare and unforeseeable occasions to those who savor Saint-Étienne rum in just the right way. Elmira is a dazzling Creole beauty who appears slightly differently to each person who sees her. She is so enchanting that she leaves everyone who glimpses her unsuccessfully guzzling rum in a desperate attempt to experience this vision one more time, while she leaves readers suspecting that she is merely a projection of frustrated desire, a vision whose beauty hides impotence and frustration.

The particular kind of irony that *Elmira* foregrounds and that I'd like to examine here today is a self-questioning verbal irony deployed in the service of reflexivity. Reflexivity and irony are intertwined in that both rely on doubling, on the perception or attribution of an unsaid significance—irony produces doubled, or proliferating meanings, while self-reflexive fiction stages the scene of writing, doubling back on itself in order to provoke questions or critique. Both invite suspicion by suggesting that texts mean something other than what they appear to mean. Both are also commonly associated with dispassionate distancing, with a cognitive move away from taken-for-granted assumptions and absorbing sensations. It is this capacity for critical distance—an ability to produce estrangement, to unsettle meanings, and denaturalize aesthetic, political or social norms—that has allied irony and self-reflexivity to theory, and made them so appealing to modernist and postcolonial thinkers concerned with disalienation. The strength of this alliance depends, of course, on whether one views theory either as a system of abstract, generalizable concepts and methods with pretensions to universal applicability; as a "distancing mechanism . . . that propels us outside of our own subjective mode of being";[9] or as an inherently unfinished and anti-systematic mode of thought with the "task and vocation of undermining philosophy as such, of unravelling affirmative statements and propositions of all kinds."[10] The strength of the connection between irony, reflexivity, and theory also depends on the value one gives to estrangement. Linda Hutcheon has described irony as a "favored trope of the intellectual,"[11] while Rey Chow has argued that contemporary theories of reflexivity, in favoring artistic techniques of staging and estrangement, have aligned critical thought, and political progress, with rationality, while associating emotion with absorption in illusion and mystification. Reflexivity, Chow argues, has come to require "the suspension, if not evacuation, of empathetic identification in response to artistic representation."[12] Chow points out that if Walter Benjamin could still envision "emancipatory sense modalities" such as distraction, "as alienation is followed to its logical conclusion, sensuous pleasure in the form of emotional involvement becomes, increasingly, politically suspect."[13]

If, in her recent work, *Entanglements*, Chow has asked whether reflexive estrangement can still be deemed useful today "in the days of proliferating, hypermediatized screens and frames,"[14] postcolonial thinkers have raised similar questions about the progressive function of irony as a weapon of anticolonial critique when the targets of that critique have shifted from particular state actors and institutionalized discourses to more diffuse cultural flows and neoliberal economic structures. Can ironic detachment serve as a useful means for addressing what Patrick Chamoiseau has described as "silent domination" (*une domination devenue silencieuse*),[15] or what we might call, following Žižek, domination with a human face? Focusing on ironic indirection and the instability of signification in the face of colonial violence and its aftermath can appear as either an unaffordable luxury, or a threat to political progress and material change. Irony in this view competes with other critical techniques and demands, including what we might call a documentary imperative—a demand for realist or stable representations of marginalized peoples and histories, a demand for an aesthetics that can be put to the service of particular political ends.

The indeterminacy produced by ironic reflexivity competes with such a documentary imperative within *Seven Dreams of Elmira*. This competition first seems to express itself as a tension between the photographs and the written text, whose contrasting tones have struck a number of reviewers. In the original French volume, pages of text alternate with posed portraits of residents of the area, who are acknowledged as "commanders of memories" and thanked at the start of the volume.[16] The volume closes with a series of color shots of the run-down Saint-Étienne distillery and surrounding buildings. The text has been called "savory" (*savoureux*)[17] and "luscious,"[18] a "tongue-in-cheek" tale of "nirvana,"[19] while the photographs are commonly described as "striking" (*Kirkus*), "soulful, somber portraits" (Steinberg) marked by a "poignant humbleness" (*une poignante humanité*).[20] If the tale appeals to exotic appetites, the portraits seem to function, for French and American reviewers, at least, as a sort of check on guilty pleasures, drawing the reader back into somber matters and warning against the dangers of succumbing to Elmira's charms.[21] If the written tale is marked by whimsy, the somber photographic testimony creates a sort of a puzzle, clashing with the lighthearted tone and inviting archeological excavation of the type Glissant speaks in *Caribbean Discourse*.

Reading irony into the text hinges, largely, on the ways in which Elmira herself is figured in it. She is first introduced in the text as "the one absence that we all share,"[22] alerting us both to her enigmatic presence and the extent to which that presence may be an illusion. As we learn of the ways in which she embodies projected desires, she begins to look more and more like a lure, a trap, perhaps a fetishized commodity, that Chamoiseau ironizes and invites us to critique. Does the book really celebrate Elmira at all? Is the point of the text rather to move us beyond a helpless wait for alcohol-induced ecstasy? The portraits, however, would seem to trouble this nascent hermeneutics of suspicion by anchoring the narrative in the lives and beliefs of real people. In seemingly arresting ironic play by reasserting sober realities, the photographs function to encourage a hermeneutics of faith. Such an approach might read the text less as ironic lesson and rather an attempt to document or testify to Antillean ways of life, particularly those ways of life in danger of disappearing from memory. Photographer Jean-Luc de Laguarigue has endorsed such a reading of his art. A descendent of one of the economically powerful, *béké* (white minority planter) families, and one who has publically taken issue with his class' ongoing implication in economic inequality, Laguarigue characterizes his work as a "photographic quest" to "understand and render the complexity of Martinican society," and to create in its attention to memory traces what Édouard Glissant calls a "prophetic vision of the past."[23] He features interiors in much of his work, and we see people posing before the religious icons, clocks, television sets, and family photos with which they decorate their own homes. The choice of black and white for these portraits contributes to the sense that these images capture a reality that is passing away, like the fabled rum and the bygone world that produced it.

Yet keeping Walcott's reflections in mind, we can still ask how exactly the excavation of memory, or the imperative to excavate memory, unfolds in this text. What affects and modes of interpretation does the work stage or elicit? From what vantage point does one posit Elmira's absence variously as a historical, cultural loss to be mourned; as a delusion to be dismissed; or as a form of presence and plenitude to be celebrated? It is perhaps the portraits that are the lure here: while the volume includes some candid shots, the large majority are posed portraits that assume a degree of self-aware participation on the part of the residents. The subjects of the photos gaze directly at the camera, posing their hands and offering subtle smiles. Rather than merely fragments preserved from a ruined past, these portraits also function, then, as performances. These photos are staged, and what they stage is by no means self-evident. This staging invites questioning.

In thinking through staging and the particular kinds of self-awareness it implies or seeks to produce, it is important to ask what exactly is being documented, if anything, and to consider the particular cultural and material economies in which this book was produced. The book is jointly copyrighted by Gallimard, a major French press, and the Saint-Étienne Distillery itself, whose co-owner, film director Florette Hayot, is credited with conceiving the project. The Saint-Étienne plantation is one of Martinique's nine distilleries. It is a very old property that was converted from sugar to rum production in 1883. In 1994, it was purchased in a state of decline by its current owners, José and Florette Hayot, who, like the photographer Laguarigue, belong to the minority *béké* planter class. The co-owners have since sought to make of Saint-Étienne not only a productive distillery, but also to restore its architecture and transform it into a historical monument and cultural center. The site now houses a performance space inspired by poet and theorist Édouard Glissant, and a permanent photographic exhibit by Laguarigue, into which many of the Elmira works have been integrated in new forms. Glissant himself participated in dedication ceremonies there, and the center has also held events celebrating Chamoiseau's work, among others.[24]

Seen as part of the plantation's efforts to promote cultural memory, the *Elmira* volume takes on the status of an economic and cultural intervention in a society in which rum, and the plantation sites that produce rum, occupy a curious place. The plantation is at once the cradle of Creole identity, the site where various languages and ethnic affiliations came together to form a society, and at the same time the generator of persistent cleavages and social tensions within this shared Creoleness. In an economic age where local production of any sort has dwindled, and the Martinican economy depends heavily on state subsidies and employment, rum takes on a privileged status as a symbol of Martinican identity, of past and potentially future productivity. Saint-Étienne co-owner José Hayot has asserted that, "Rum is the only Martinican product that is a cultural product; rum is truly the *terroir*, the history of Martinique with all its pain and suffering. It's a product of hope, too, because Martinican society, which is a composite, Creole society, is a society of the future, and today, to be Creole is to be from the whole world, one can be from everywhere. Rum carries the somewhat universal cultural message of this Creoleness."[25]

Such a view obviously serves the commercial interests of the owners in creating a global market for the product, but within a local context, to tie rum explicitly to the pain and suffering of the past, to foreground the promotion of historical memory, and to hitch the distillery's success to a demand for local cultural production is to take a particular stance that represents a break with the white, planter class' traditional avoidance or denial of this history and denial of its own implication in oppressive economic structures. It also represents a very deliberate attempt at crossing entrenched class divisions, at creating opportunities for collaborative cultural production. Without suggesting that this sort of patronage of memory and the arts is a satisfactory solution to all conflicts over land use, unequal distribution of wealth, and *béké* planter monopolies in Martinique, I do think that keeping these particulars in mind can usefully inflect how we might read Elmira's stagings, and the curious forms of reflexivity it seems to demand.

In the acknowledgments at the start of the book, Chamoiseau attributes a sort of collective authorship to the residents of Gros-Morne, thanking these "commanders of memory" for "their willingness to share their testimony with us" (*Remerciements à ces habitants du Gros-Morne, commandeurs des souvenirs, qui ont bien voulu nous porter témoignage* [4]).[26] If we consider these residents as contributors or informants engaging with the photographer and the viewer rather than as passive objects caught unawares by the camera, their portraits function somewhat otherwise than documents conveying a particular historical content—or documents in need of a spokesperson—and more like a form of signature. To read these photos as somber and poignant—or as *only* somber and poignant—is perhaps to mistake this act of signing, or co-signing on the part of the subjects for a documentary impulse on the part of the photographer.

What exactly then might the project of the text be? My inclination is that in enlisting local residents in the creation of this tongue-in-cheek tale, the text asserts the value of ironic play in the strong sense of playful, affective engagement. In so doing, it invites us not so much to distance ourselves from the projection of desire that is Elmira, but to traverse the separation of subject and object underpinning efforts at cognitive distancing and documentary capture that the ruin inspires. In an important sense, we might say that the photos ironically authorize the whimsy of the written story, inviting us to take the story seriously, to join in the celebration of Elmira, and the pleasures of creative play.

At the end of his tale, the narrator comes to the conclusion that what he needed to understand was that:

> Elmira was in each of us, between the conscious and the unconscious, where the maps of flesh and spirit come together to suggest to each of us the *impossibility* of our lives, its trace of elevation, the star of plenitude by which we set our art, our voice, every gesture of our existence. We are all children in that regard. Gros-Morne lifts the richness of its soil above our ruined dreams. The distillery stands here, smoking out its challenges and rising up to them as it has for so many years. In our difficult wait, among the embers of hope and disenchantment that guide our will, we endeavor, in moderation, to live as best we can; and, as Elmira suggests, we try—with difficult desires, at the highest degree of impossibility—to find our quiet happiness."[27]

In this conclusion, self-reflexive theorization hinges on a capacity for play, for an affective response that might be termed an alternative rationality, a form of ironic enchantment. In such an enchantment, Elmira passes from mere laughable delusion or melancholic ruin to utopian vision, and the co-signed text takes on the dimensions of a stage in a much more literal sense: a scene on which new creative imaginations and relations of cultural production can be given space to unfold.

Notes

1   Patrick Chamoiseau, *Elmire des sept bonheurs: Confidences d'un vieux travailleur de la distillerie Saint-Étienne*. Photography by Jean-Luc de Laguarigue. Sonofa-Habitation Saint-Étienne and Éditions Gallimard, 1998; trans. Mark Polizzotti as *Seven Dreams of Elmira: A Tale of Martinique. Being the Confessions of an Old Worker at the Saint-Etienne Distillery* (Cambridge, MA: Zoland Books, 1999).

2   Derek Walcott, "Nobel Lecture: The Antilles: Fragments of Epic Memory." *Nobelprize.org.* Nobel Media AB 2013. February 2, 2014. http://www.nobelprize. org/nobel_prizes/literature/laureates/1992/walcott-lecture.html.

3   Édouard Glissant, *Caribbean Discourse*, trans. Michael Dash (Charlottesville: University Press of Virginia): 2.

4   Ibid., 11.

5   Ibid., 64.

6   Derek Walcott, "Nobel Lecture," n.p.

7   Ibid.

8   For the notion of ironic enchantment as a self-reflexive approach to modernity, I am indebted to Michael Saler's "Modernity, Disenchantment, and the Ironic Imagination," *Philosophy and Literature* 28.1 (2004): 137–149. See also Joshua A. Landy and Michael Saler, eds. *The Re-enchantment of the World: Secular Magic in a Rational Age* (Stanford: Stanford University Press, 2009).

9   Ibid., 26.

10 Fredric Jameson, *Valences of the Dialectic* (London: Verso, 2009): 59.

11 Linda Hutcheon, *Irony's Edge: The Theory and Politics of Irony* (London: Routledge, 1994), 15.

12 Rey Chow, *Entanglements, or Transmedial Thinking about Capture* (Durham: Duke University Press, 2012), 23.

13 Ibid.

14 Ibid., 25.

15 Patrick Chamoiseau, *Écrire en pays dominé* (Paris: Gallimard, 1997).

16 Chamoiseau, *Elmire des sept bonheurs*, 5.

17 A. Kwateh, "Elmire au bonheur des hommes," *Antilla* 773 (March 27, 1998), http://habitation-saint-etienne.com/art/wp-content/uploads/2012/01/Elmire-Antilla.jpg.

18 Sybil Steinberg, "Forecasts: Fiction," *Publishers Weekly* 246.30 (1999): 65.

19 *Kirkus Reviews* (August 1, 1999), LexisNexis Academic.

20 Philippe Jean Catinchi, *Le Monde* (April 24, 1998), LexisNexis Academic.

21 It is perhaps not insignificant that the French newspaper of record *Le Monde* chose some of these photos to illustrate the cover page of the special 1998 dossier commemorating the abolition of slavery in which the book review is published.

22 Chamoiseau, *Seven Dreams of Elmira*, 15.

23 "Gens de pays," blog, http://gensdepays.blogspot.com/search/label/Bio. My translation.

24 For more on the Habitation Saint-Étienne's exhibit space, Les Foudres HSE, see the page devoted to it on the distillery's website: http://www.rhumhse.com/art/foudres/.

25 Virginie Marly, "Monsieur José Hayot, Propriétaire de la Rhumerie l'Habitation Saint-Etienne en Martinique-Vinexpo 2005," *Lettre vinomedia* 162 (June 27, 2005), http://www.vin-events.com/lettre-vinomedia/archives/162/1_b3ea025d-872d-4426–863a-cd2d09e8aacd.asp?id_rubrique=1&rubrique=Les+interviews&dir=interviews&requete=&phrase=0&datecreation=undefined&absolutePage=1. My translation.

26 Chamoiseau, *Elmire des sept bonheurs*, 5. Translation modified.

27 Ibid., 29–30. Translation modified.

Works cited

Catinchi, Philippe Jean. "Livraisons." *Le Monde*. April 24, 1998. LexisNexis Academic.

Chamoiseau, Patrick. *Écrire en pays dominé*. Paris: Gallimard, 1997.

Chamoiseau, Patrick. *Elmire des sept bonheurs: Confidences d'un vieux travailleur de la distillerie Saint-Étienne*. Photography by Jean-Luc de Laguarigue. Sonofa-Habitation Saint-Étienne and Éditions Gallimard, 1998.

Chamoiseau, Patrick. *Seven Dreams of Elmira: A Tale of Martinique. Being the Confessions of an Old Worker at the Saint-Etienne Distillery*. Photography by Jean-Luc de Laguarigue. Trans. Mark Polizzotti. Cambridge, MA: Zoland Books, 1999.

Chow, Rey. *Entanglements, or Transmedial Thinking about Capture*. Durham: Duke University Press, 2012.

Glissant, Édouard. *Caribbean Discourse*. Trans. Michael Dash. Charlottesville: University Press of Virginia, 1992.

Hutcheon, Linda. *Irony's Edge: The Theory and Politics of Irony*. London: Routledge, 1994.

Jameson, Fredric. *Valences of the Dialectic*. London: Verso, 2009.

Kirkus Reviews. August, 1, 1999. LexisNexis Academic.

Kwateh, A. "Elmire au bonheur des hommes." *Antilla* 773. March 27, 1998. http://habitation-saint-etienne.com/art/wp-content/uploads/2012/01/Elmire-Antilla.jpg.

Laguarigue, Jean-Luc de. "Gens de pays." Blog. http://gensdepays.blogspot.com/
search/label/Bio.

Landy, Joshua A., and Michael Saler, eds. *The Re-enchantment of the World: Secular
Magic in a Rational Age.* Stanford: Stanford University Press, 2009.

Marly, Virginie. "Monsieur José Hayot, Propriétaire de la Rhumerie l'Habitation
Saint-Etienne en Martinique-Vinexpo 2005." *Lettre vinomedia* 162. June 27, 2005.
http://www.vin-events.com/lettre-vinomedia/archives/162/1_b3ea025d-872d-
4426–863a-cd2d09e8aacd.asp?id_rubrique=1&rubrique=Les+interviews&dir=inte
rviews&requete=&phrase=0&datecreation=undefined&absolutePage=1.

Saler, Michael. "Modernity, Disenchantment, and the Ironic Imagination." *Philosophy
and Literature* 28.1 (2004): 137–149.

Steinberg, Sybil. "Forecasts: Fiction." *Publishers Weekly* 246.30 (1999): 65.

Walcott, Derek. "Nobel Lecture: The Antilles: Fragments of Epic Memory."
Nobelprize.org. Nobel Media AB 2013. February 2, 2014. http://www.nobelprize.
org/nobel_prizes/literature/laureates/1992/walcott-lecture.html.

11

Undying Theory: Levinas, Place, and the Technology of Posthumousness

Christian Moraru

Theory, death, ethics

What is quite striking—and, to some of us, perhaps heartening—about theory in the putatively post-theoretical era is that it keeps getting another lease on life, over and over again. Repeatedly displaced by new epistemologies and sociopolitical priorities, it comes back from the dead and from another place, a place surely other to us, to threaten our intellectually cozy places and cultural comfort more broadly and thus get us going, wandering and wondering, probing and learning, anew. But, to put it bluntly, has theory—"high" or not—died to begin with? Methinks not. However, if theory is not dead, it is "deadish," as a character says in the 2004 remake of George A. Romero's 1978 *Dawn of the Dead*. Or, if theory has indeed died, it nonetheless manages somehow to return while remaining, zombie-like, quintessentially bound up with death.

It is to this nexus that I want to attend here. Doing so presupposes, as my considerations so far imply, a topological triangulation, a co-reconfiguration of the theoretical and otherworldly from the very standpoint of stand, of the point or place in the world where we may be standing, comfortably or less so, and more generally from the perspective of the world as place, of the world of places. For the place where theory happens, where it takes place by taking ours, literally and in all senses, is a site of multiple displacement, subject as it is to a certain sublime violence done to, or transactions imposed concurrently on, place and life in the name of what I would call an *ethic beyond the ethnic*: an ethic that neither erases nor discounts ethnic background and all backgrounds, grounds, and *Gründe*, but, to the contrary, one that acknowledges and honors them by working with, through, and over their contested geography, their territorially circumscribed and ethno-culturally demarcated spaces, turfs, and discourses.

This ethic, I argue, sponsors a certain posthumousness. There is nothing thanatophilic or morbid about it, though. It values or revalues death, and in that it *grounds itself under*, under or beneath our world, in this world's under and other, but it operates in and, even more so, across living places so as to place its responsibility on our lives. Thus, we must own up to it, obviously, as we are alive, during and through the decisions we make in our lives. An intimation of immortality, it tells us how to conduct them so we—theorists or not—keep on living after we have stopped doing so. Life-affirming: oddly enough, this is what death becomes within the theoretical context that I will lay out momentarily; life as a true gift of death, a gift given in Jan Patocnka's generously civic and disobedient spirit, as Derrida would probably allow; being alive, amid others, as another name of being responsible, of being ethically with them; and so, at last, life as training for death, going to the Socratic gym of life to work out an afterlife of sorts, not so much a bulk as a corpus, the one body that will last. This ethic is the keystone of my argument, one that weaves together theory, place, life, and death, and, then, self and other as their condition of possibility today more than ever. On one side, the case I am making revisits death as an environment and supreme test for theory, for what we do, and for the doers themselves, obviously. On the other side, it necessarily underscores death as life's paradoxically energizing *memento mori* while redefining life as a hereafter warm-up, a waiting room or, as a friend of mine used to say, a "home stretch" to the finish line of the after-place, of the nontopological place that takes the true measure of our ethno-geographical behavior in the world's "actually existing places."

This discussion smacks, I suppose, of postmodernism or perhaps post-postmodernism: postmodernism because erudite visitations from beyond the grave render inherently the postmodern a *postmortem* poetics,[1] an intertextual *revenant*, and also because postmodernism recuperates the biographical over and against modernism's real and perceived "impersonalism" in the Henry James-T. S. Eliot line; post-postmodernism because, if postmodernism remains marked by a discrete concept of place and a worldview in turn fashioned by a Cold War, ethno-politically disjunctive geopolitics revolving around nation-states and nation-state blocs, we are now in a totally different place, so to speak, where the world's places, more fluid and vulnerable than ever before, connect, converse, and engage each other.

Postmodernism as spectral discourse, then; its discursive ontology, a hauntology, a return of the repressed, and so an engagement, albeit ever ambiguous, with the Other, as Lawrence Hogue might aptly remind us.[2] But I will not rehearse all that. I will only note, first, that the postmodern is not only spectral but also historically coextensive with the rise and spread of our time's most popular spectral formation and possibly most popular theme, pure and simple—a theme and epitome of spectrality: the zombie; and second, that through this theme, the postmodern makes a radical effort to theorize the life-shaping and life-reshaping significance of death and of its *unheimliche* messengers. This significance foregrounds, I propose, a reasoning beyond reason, a rationality from beyond the grave. That postrationality, if you will indulge the term, makes that beyond also a place of sorts for theory as well as a location from which mundane places and their human residents can be seen—that is, can be *theorized*—in a certain way. The underworld, because it is also an otherworld, is scopogenetic. It is the darkness, and the unknown, from which gaze originates and which, by the same token, affords theory, *theoriā*, our conceptual forays into the visible of this world and, by the same movement, our ventures beyond it, into the spectacle available to the oracle's dark vision apparatus, to the *seer*.

Thinking things

Postmodernism's zombie industry forefronts such affordances. As you will recall, it has time after time reembodied figures, scenes, plot lines, and sociocultural allusions from Romero's 1960s trendsetting movies. However, in getting a "new life," the Romero films and, with them, the entire "ghoulish genre" only emulate the obstinacy of their staple character. "This thing just won't die!" the handful of humans left standing in zombie flicks invariably scream—ironically enough, an outburst itself haunted by Hamlet's undying "Rest, rest perturbed spirit!" Alas, both in Shakespeare's Denmark and in Romero's America, the "thing" does not oblige. The dead have and have not died. Literalizing an afterlife that for many of "us" remains a vaguely religious metaphor, zombies, rather than Max Brooks's readers, may be the consummate survivalists after all— *Survival of the Dead* is the title of Romero's 2009 movie. Anything but "completely and thoroughly dead,"[3] they wake in the very wake of their ambiguous demise to take up residency in the limbo of US culture and, from there, to gross out, horrify, and confound, but perhaps also "enlighten" us, tell us something about ourselves, theorize *us*.[4]

For, when read with the grain, the zombie figure does not actually speak to us. It casts a spell on us without spelling itself out. It remains "mute." Or, at most, it "tells" us what we expect or want to hear, namely, of its fundamentally inhuman essence, of that which is so unlike us, rational beings, that it cannot possibly tell us anything at all, let alone about the limits of our rationality. But, when read against its rhetorical-ideological grain, the zombie starts speaking to us despite or, better yet, by means of its unspeakably irrational appearance, thus engaging us through the very radical difference it stages so willfully. The unspeakable speaks, then, it turns out. And, a conduit of the gaze, it looks, looks in at us—of course, the scene of looking, from the outside in, is another defining moment in zombie cinema: they come from beyond the living and the visible, from beyond what the living can see, to observe us, perchance to contemplate, to peer through the fence or the kitchen window, at us sitting around the dinner table, wielding the silverware rather uncontemplatively. How is this possible?

An epitome of inhumanity, zombies are, it seems, more than simply "different" from us. The dissimilarity is total, allayed by no residual overlap, affinity, or commerce across the existential-intellectual gap between "us" and "them." This radical contrast explains why we are drawn so hypnotically to the catatonic hordes and also why they have all but supplanted vampires as our unmitigated Other in the collective imaginary.[5] Some critics claim, in effect, that zombies fascinate Americans to a degree Dracula's progeny never have. Their demonism ever part-time, dampened by the "soft" alterity built into it, the blood-sucking monsters retain a modicum of humanness because they are endowed with sentience and, more importantly, with consciousness, "twisted" as it may be. Not so zombies. As a rule, however, they have every semblance of lacking consciousness, of being atheoretical.[6] Accordingly, the zombie, being one or turning into one, performs the unadulterated difference between the inhuman in its serial and mindless form, on one side, and the human and its equivalents, the individual and the rational, on the other.

Zombies are, then, our absolute opposite. Not only that, but they are keen on *looking* absolutely opposed to how we see ourselves as living entities in general and *Homo sapiens* in particular. Preserving just the material veneer of humanness, the zombie is, and insists on appearing to the spectator or reader, as the human in its most despiritualized or a-spiritual, reified embodiment: the human as mere embodiment, the human *qua* body.[7] Except that, trading on the anatomy of "corpus" and "corpse" simultaneously, the zombie body does not have the structure of a human body either. The tautological regime of zombie phenomenality, in which how the "thing" appears to us is no more than that, an appearance, an epidermal phenomenon or "show" of deceptive layers, surfaces, and looks, holds sway over the zombified body too; the latter *presents*, quasi-theatrically, the mere façade of human physicality. This corpus no longer incorporates. In other words, it is not an organic apparatus, an anatomic-physiological system that contains and thus depends on organs with "vital" functions no less vital to the unifying, coherence-building workings of the mind, but something like a depthless, decentered, and socially decentering "body without organs."[8] Rendering thingness not inorganic but organless, this surfaciality of sorts marks a major step in the zombie body's "thing-becoming."[9]

Anima demoted to animality and its abominable kabuki theater of bodily postures and cognitive impostures, the Cartesian subject here totters before us only to cancel itself out in its dejected hypostasis of object or "thing" groping around for our flesh. The "thing" will never eat its fill, though. Its hunger for us is bottomless because, as a venerable philosophical tradition reassures us, so is the gap between the human as cogitative subject and the inhuman other as subject solely *to* our cogitations and thereby de facto object or thing. Which is to say, not only are we, humans, the sole and absolute subject, entitled to our epistemological absolutism, but the object on the other side of the human-inhuman divide is, or appears rather as, absolute too and so irredeemably hostage to the stultifying immanence of its gruesome materiality. In brief, we are a *res cogitans*, a *theorizing* subject; we are a, or better still, the "thinking thing," in which the heavily emphasized first term tones down the "thing" (*res*) in us. For, as the Cartesian dictum has it, if we think, if we are subjects—if we *are*—this happens at the expense of the thing, of the object.[10] At the same time, the only reality granted to the object of our cogitations is opaque re(s)ality, the self-imploding black hole of unthinking "thingness" or, as Lacan underscores, the twice "dumb" reality that does not speak and hence remains silent because it cannot think to begin with.[11]

Disseminating this tradition across the high- and low-brow cultures of contemporary America, the zombie plays up the object's hopelessly objectual condition by putting an "abjectual" spin on it through a tactical overdramatization of the somatic object as *ábject object* or cadaver. The underlying assumption here is that, in the "dead body," the object's destitution or, as Baudrillard says, "prostitution,"[12] its ab-jection or re-jection to the otherworld's supposedly non-subjective otherness and to its inert, a-rational thingness, is categorical and definitive *and* will be registered as such by us.[13] Thus, the object's "obscene,"[14] ignominious objectuality, the cadaveric "abjectuality" on which zombie cinema dwells so obstinately, sanctions the subject's rational downgrading to object, to a thing that, as Sartre claims, while it can be said to "exist," is not as *we* are.[15] Marked by the "accursed" ontology of subaltern beings, it *is* as tool and prosthesis, human substitute, rational ersatz; it is, bluntly put, so *we* can fully be. This fall from the rational grace of subjectivity, now a condition safely earmarked for us alone, is further compounded by the subject's "atypical" survival as zombified body: a fraudulent survival, un-whole and in that unholy, "diabolically" partial.[16] Metaphysically speaking—speaking, namely, from a simultaneously rationalist and theological position concerning what makes the subject human and under which circumstances it is "operational"—this subject would be better off if, once clinically dead, it vanished from our world without a trace and "stayed," as one of Elizabeth Kostova's characters opines, "respectably dead" instead of sticking around and appearing, in the aforementioned sense of "appearance," as thing-like body.[17] Following its "half-death"—*demi-mort*, in Lacan—and "disrespectful" of this interstitial state, the body may and does appear. But, the same tradition has it, this appearance represents, as earlier, just that, an appearance, a visual show of smoke and mirrors without substance precisely because all there seems to be to its reality is corporeality, flesh. On the face of it—the inhumanly defaced face the zombie's body turns to us—there is no subject in or with the pseudo-resurrected body that puts in an appearance. Certainly not the being in whose ontological visibility Socrates wants to bask after his death, the body is now merely a "thing" or, as Hamlet tells Rosencranz and Guildenstern, "The body is with the King, but the King is not with the body." "The King," Hamlet adds, "is a thing . . . [o]f nothing."

But is the anthropological subject the only heading under which knowledge can give itself a vehicle and a form, in short, a body? To ask the question differently: is the thing necessarily a-subjectual and a-theoretical, utterly unable to exert cogitative and articulatory functions equivalent or comparable to a living person's? And, if it is not, how exactly do zombies help us warm up to the notion of a thing's "personhood," as Barbara Johnson might say?[18]

One of Shakespeare's notoriously cryptic places, the passage above has been interpreted in a disconcerting number of ways. Most critics agree, though, that the body in question is more than meets the eye. The body, they maintain, is not, or not only, Polonius. More remarkably, we are not dealing exclusively with empirical bodies either. Along these lines, two distinct bodily formations come into play here: the King's "natural" body and the monarch's body politic.[19] One is private, physical, hence mortal. It dies and does not tarry. Or, if it does, it does not do so as such but as its metaphorically disembodied double or "spirit"—as the body's "other body." Bodying forth the law, authority, and kingship, the "somatic" body's alternate is more of a transcendental, collective-juridical concept, a signifier of political desire, of monarchic will and legitimacy. These bodily attributes of the ruler are sui generis "things" that do *not* fade away upon the death of his perishable body. They outlive his mundane exit and so can be passed on to the rightful heir or can be denied to pretenders and usurpers. In this sense, Claudius *is* a King/thing of nothing/no(-)thing. "Thingified,"[20] he looks the part but is hardly (with) "it," the real King/thing. This is why the law, which he violated when he poisoned Hamlet's father, cannot possibly be with Hamlet's uncle; it is the murdered King who retains authority even after death has degraded his physicality to nothing (physical), to the ghostly revenant. Urged by his son to "rest," the King cannot take a break because the law is still "restless," active. In or with him, power, *imperium* in Latin, remains imperative, and the first action it demands regards Claudius because his crime has reduced the law and its embodiment to a no-body, to spirit, immaterial specter.

The King's appearance is thus a "phallophany," a *phallophanie*, as Lacan writes in his seminar on desire (Book VI).[21] For, what appears (cf. Gk. *phainesthai*) or reappears, rather, in the King's phallic apparition—what steps into the visible in the enlightening *Lichtung* opened up by *Hamlet*'s revenant and what makes itself known to the Danish prince, to his spectators, and to human consciousness more generally—is the luminous essence of the phallus as *Ur*-index of relation, as "with" marker. An arch-signifier, the phallus is all about signifying, signification, and significance, *about theory*, pointing as it does to how things relate to one another, come about, signify, and overall get done in *our* world, to who is running them, that is, *with* whom "it," the law or moral-political authority, lies or should lie.

The copulative phenomenology of the "with" is here paramount. What this "with" articulates (formulates, lays down) is articulation itself as key *world operator*, as planetary *principium conjunctionis*, because the link and the aptly named "signifying chain" in which we are all enmeshed, our sociopolitical and affective-phantasmatic ties, the logical-grammatical copula and the very act of copulation make for the building blocks of worldly languages and codes, both encode this world and help decoding it semiotically and politically by revealing how bodies of people, culture, and institutions are, and must be in order to be, "with" one another.[22] Thus, on the one hand, the phallus sets up the world as sexual, cultural, political, and cultural juxtaposition, as a *with-place*—for tradition, transmitted culture, is quintessentially phallic too—and, on the other hand, assists us in parsing the world syntax accordingly. The phallus is fundamentally theoretical. Its premier function, Lacan says, is to "lift the veil"[23] from the libidinal underpinnings of cultural-political codifications and hierarchies. "With" the King, the phallus returns from the dead to unveil to the living the makeup of the symbolic. The King shows itself, becomes visible, in order to show, help us see, that which must be shown to us because we cannot discern it—we cannot be *critical* of it—on our own. The unveiling presupposes the veiled—verbalized, symbolized, disguised—status of things human, *but the mute apparition appears so that those things do not remain forever unappar-ent, unsaid, mute, and immutable to us.* It follows, then, that the "truth" the ghost conveys is both hermeneutic and critical, that it also pertains to—indeed, warrants—a certain *Kritik*. Otherwise put, this truth has to do with our world as much as with our capacity to "get" it and implicitly with the human itself, more specifically, with the critical shortcomings of human consciousness.

As Lacan insists elsewhere, this is the profound and disturbing revelation the subject experiences "in the place of the Other."[24] More basically, it is in the place occupied by the King's reappearance as apparition, as "other" to Hamlet and to us all, that we get a glimpse of some("other")thing we ordinarily do not make out from our station in the world of the living, namely, of how limited our capacity for ideological analysis and critique can be. For, if it "knows its place" in the hardened order of things mortal and immortal, human and non-human, animate and inanimate, as it usually does, the human risks not know-ing itself, and, more often than not, ignorance and its corollary, self-ignorance, are the price we pay for the entrenched cultural-metaphysical sedentariness that locks us in place and inside our *Weltanschauungen*. So, against an entire Cartesian line of thought this time around, we may conclude that we are and own up to what we are as cognitive subjects *where we normally are not*; that, perforce "beyond us," learning is an away game; that knowledge reveals itself to us, the knowing subjects, in the realm of otherness, in Montaigne's anthro-pological *ailleurs*.[25] Canvassed ad nauseam in our daily routines, the social often remains, unfortunately, a site of socio-critical, antitheoretical blind-ness: being-in-the-social, and by extension being overall, living, is a blind spot, a topo-epistemological handicap. Instead, the place where the phallus appears marks the scene where the workings of human desire, power, and ideology can be queried, made apparent, *theorized*. Returning from the otherworld in an appearance *of necessity* other to us, the King's ghost shows up, Lacan contends, "to bring to the subject's mind" [*pour . . . porter à la connaissance du sujet*][26] what in the subject's place gets in the way of his or her knowledge of the place and the world: the ideological underlays of the social terrain itself and, deeply engrained in our consciousness, the self-sufficient rationalism that blinds us to ideology's "veiled" grip over us.

And so, once again, we are not in that place, in the scopic-philosophical, theoretical sense of the onto-situation in which Socrates wants and hopes to find himself after his death. We are not in that place intellectually and theoretically speaking because, inside it, we cannot know, canot see, and thus cannot theorize our "situation"—our location *and* station. That theorization, and any other theorization and self-knowledge for that matter, knowledge and self both, only become possible relationally, as the place and the self in it are displaced, disrupted, and interpellated, "theatened" with the illuminating disintegration brought about by another (and an Other) presence and place. Far from being a space of nonexistence, of literal no-thingness, death is this place. *Death is the thing*—death is *ein Ding*—because it is in and through death that this Other presence is affirmed *and* required. For the thing/*Ding* does no more (*and* no less) than that—"its thing"—by helping us see how things connect to one another in their bigger "scheme." Here, in Heidegger's political "assembly" (*Ding*, in the Old High German),[27] things (*Dingen*) are "thinged out" (*gedungen*)—discussed, sorted out, legislated on, and other-wise "assembled" into symbolic configurations; it is to these configurations of desire, meaning, and authority that the zombie's thing-appearance alerts us on closer inspection. Revelatory and "instigative," its thingness jars us into "thinging" critically, into *theorized*, critical thinking "about things." In that, "it" is neither quiet nor stupid, regardless of how creepy, taciturn, and overall mindless its bodily performance—or precisely because this perfor-mance looks so. Supremely and necessarily amphibological, the thing's dumb show is just (for) show, a half-camouflaging, half-revelatory self-performance where performing bodies set out to "catch" *our* "conscience" by acting out *our* re(s)ality and its corollaries: objectification, instrumentalization, seriali-zation, and "massification."[28]

Place, technology, and theoretical debt

Levinas's humblingly magisterial teachings from "La mort d'autrui" are well known, and so I will not rehash them here. I only want to point out a few tightly interrelated elements relevant to my argument:

first, and this is Epicurus as summoned up by Levinas, death is not where you are; if death is here, you are not; this has both topological as well as theo-retical (scopic and contemplative) implications;

second, the place where you are, onto-theoretically speaking, the location of being and the conceptualizion thereof, are under the jurisdiction of others and other places; in death, they are the gift of an Other. For I die, phenomenologically and conceptually, only for an Other. Only an Other can see me die and can attempt to understand what is happening;

third, only an Other can see me as I am, whole, and so only he or she can constitute me scopically as such, as I emerge out of the impure shell thinkers and artists from Socrates to Henry James to David's Lodge's James—in *Phaedo*, in the 1909 essay "Is There a Life after Death," and in the 2004 novel *Author, Author*, respectively—keep talking about, the bad, "ideological" visibility we need to overcome or come out of its cocoon like the butterfly. We remember, of course, that seeing *yourself* as a whole, that image, is no more than an imago and thus the premise of *mis*recognition, both damaging and inevitable to the self's growth;

fourth, whatever cognition can occur, it is predicated on the recognition by an Other, by how he or she places me. The Other is a custodian of my wholeness, of my being, in my own death, both visually and cognitively, theoretically. I die for him or her, and both seeing and theorizing *become possible* in that death. Here, Levinas goes beyond Socrates, in that death and theory are not mechanically opposite. Death is not something to overcome theoretically. Death and theory are not incompatible at all, in fact. Death offers itself, actually, as an occasion for theory, when the latter is a triumph of *the I who finally no longer lacks an adequate, discerning eye*. On this score, Levinas and Socrates are brothers (a notion we will come back to). But there is more, for this triumph cannot be just a homerun of the ego any more, a reaffirmation of the self-reliant cogito, but a relational benefit, the gift of death as given, by an Other;

fifth, this implicitly acrrues an indebtedness, something I must pay back in kind, hence the ethical aspect of the problem at hand. If you die for somebody, before somebody's gaze and willingness to recognize you, do you not incur a debt to that entity? Self-recognition is misrecognition, *méprise*, a tautology that works as a falsely redeeming theology. As Soshana Felman reminds us in *Writing and Madness*, Lacan asks: "*Theoria*, might that not be the place in the world for the theology?" For the theology of the self, for its teleology, that is. Felman is interested in a theory of this mistake, of the radical *méprise*, in Lacan, as "essential to the very subject of theory as such." She wants to overcome the error by working out its "rhetoric."[29] What concerns me is the correction that comes from the other side, where my debt accumulates as a knowledge not originated in myself but made possible by my death, by death as debt;

sixth, honoring this debt requires the willingness to pay in kind, to die, quite literally, for that other person or to honor his or her otherness, which to me is the same thing. You leave your place behind; you become *all you can be and an all*, whole, under another's gaze; but then you have to extend the ethic of this felicitous displacement to the world's places; the territory of death is both *die Unterwelt* and the Other world, where the other things and others come from, where seeing, conceptualizing, and self-understanding, *theory*—always under the auspices and across the place of the Other—become feasible; but then life, and how you theorize it in its living places, is the place to pay off the debt.

In that sense, theory is nontopological, atopical. In the same vein, here on earth, in the world of places where, as Felman quotes Proust this time around, we commit the "perpetual error that we call, precisely, life," living has everything to do with erring and errance, place, *déplacement*, and displacement, with a certain technology of place or topotechnology, as Levinas proposes in his essay "Heidegger, Gagarin, and Us."[30] The astronaut participates in the same scopic and spatial economy as the zombie. Over and over again, from works of fiction such as Joseph McElroy's 1977 novel *Plus* to situations reenacted by the Apollo missions and by their accounts across the media in specialized venues and in the popular press alike, the astronaut in space or orbiting outside our orbit, outside the human eye, beyond the horizon, is presented as the all-embracing gaze, capable of seeing the human holistically and, implicitly, of noticing our partialities, biases, and parochialisms, in brief, the human as a symptom of ingrown culture, of fetishized place. The Soviet cosmonaut Yuri Gagarin is for Levinas—at the height of the Cold War, mind you—a kind of outsider who comes in not from the darkness of the underworld but from the brightness of the overworld to bring its clarifying gaze to bear on us. Gagarin's is a techno-logically discriminating perception of place that sets the place in motion. He comes from the dead, in a way—he will die, actually up there, as a test pilot— and he comes to instigate, for Levinas, a certain restlessness technologically. He can do so because he arrives from a place not inert, of no no-thingness, but dynamic, from a distance in turn at once distancing and de-distancing: dis-tancing insofar as it separates us from the place and thus does away with the distinction native-stranger; and de-distancing because a new togetherness becomes possible once said distinction no longer operates, a with-being that allows me, if I buy into it, to pay off the debt. I associate this technology with posthumousness because it has a lot to do with death, with the under- and over-world, but also because it is post-humus: not only post-earth, post-worldly, as popular etymology has it, but also post-soil, post-place, post-*Blut-und-Boden*, post-ethnic, post-parochial, and therefore ethical. The ethic in play is also a deontology, affording a knowledge that is simultaneously, at long last, a mastery of the world and of the self, a theorization and self-theorization and a mystery, epistemologically self-sustaining and a service to others.

In his essay, Levinas welcomes the distancing-with-de-distancing technology against Heidegger's apprehensions about the fast-growing human capabilities of "measuring and executing, for the purpose of gaining mastery over that which is as a whole."[31] As Michael Lang explains in a 2003 essay on Heidegger's "planetary discourse," for the German thinker the new, de-distancing technologies wind up supplanting human relationships. The only relationships left are technological or, in the more extreme, Pynchonian formulation from *Gravity's Rainbow*, *téchne*'s relation to itself. In the Heidegger-David Harvey line of thought, Lang demonstrates, this de-distantiation is tantamount to circumventing the human and its undergirding relatedness. Eventually, this leads to a "compression," congealing, and preordaining of everything in this world, including the material texture and the meanings of the post-Enlightenment West and of the whole globe with it, now seized mechanically and "totalistically" as a passive reflection ("globalization") of the Western model.[32]

What Levinas admires in the astronaut's "feat" is a completely different technology. This technology operates or can operate, under the right circumstances, surely still to come, ethically. It "redistricts" place planet-wide to help both the comfortably placed and the displaced to relate and come together in potentially countless ways. Less "dangerous than the spirits [*génies*] of the *Place*" that, throughout history, have placed so as to include, shelter, and help thrive, but also to exclude, control, and enslave by "splitting . . . humanity into native and strangers," this is a distancing technology liable to renew the earth as a common home. "[W]hat counts most of all, Levinas says, is that [Gagarin] left the Place," the Earth as Place. In Levinas's assessment, the cosmonaut rose "beyond any horizon" but only to open up new horizons, within which the planet's mystery, its many facets, and the faces and relations in which they are all necessarily entangled in the world at large are reaffirmed and cared for rather than fatuously mastered.[33] Or, perhaps a mastery of sorts is in play here, after all. It is the more subdued mastery of the mystery that fleetingly brushes our faces when we turn to the planet's face and to the countless faces glued together, mosaic-like, in neighborhoods, cantinas, and playgrounds. Advancing critically on the trail blazed by this technological breakthrough may allow for this mystery, for the enigma of the planet's others to persist as such, in plain sight and undefaced, protected by the very "nudity" of the face in which it comes forth. As Levinas never tires of reminding us, we are with those others in the world so that we ourselves can be and think through what this means.

Notes

1 On "postmortem" postmodernism, see Laura Savu's *Postmortem Postmodernists: The Afterlife of the Author in Recent Narratives* (Teaneck, NJ: Fairleigh Dickinson University Press, 2009).

2 W. Lawrence Hogue, *Postmodern American Literature and Its Other* (Urbana: University of Illinois Press, 2009).

3 Kyle Bishop, "Raising the Dead: Unearthing the Nonliterary Origins of Zombie Cinema," *Journal of Popular Film and Television* 33.4 (Winter 2006): 201.

4 I have developed this point in "Zombie Pedagogy: Rigor Mortis and the U.S. Body Politic," *Studies in Popular Culture* 34.2 (Spring 2012): 105–127.

5 "Although they were once human, zombies have no real connection to humanity aside from their physical form; they are the ultimate foreign Other," Bishop maintains (Bishop, "Raising the Dead," 201). At the same time, the critic argues that zombies "are in essence a metaphor for humanity itself" (ibid., 201).

6 In Laurell K. Hamilton's *The Laughing Corpse* (New York: Ace, 1994), Anita Blake runs into a zombie who regains consciousness and language after eating human flesh (257).

7 Zombies are "bodies utterly surrendered to their own physicality" (Meghan Sutherland, "Rigor/Mortis: The Industrial Life of Style in American Zombie Cinema," *Framework: The Journal of Cinema and Media* 48.1 [2007]: 64–78, 64).

8 Regarding the "body without organs," its structure, and its psychosocial role, see the locus classicus in Gilles Deleuze and Félix Guattari's *Anti-Oedipus: Capitalism and Schizophrenia*, trans. Robert Hurley, Mark Seem, and Helen R. Lane (Minneapolis: University of Minnesota Press, 1992), "The Body without Organs," chapter 2, 9–17. See too Slavoj Žižek, *Organs without Bodies: On Deleuze and Consequences* (New York: Routledge, 2004), for a discussion of the issue apropos of the zombie problem in popular culture, Lacanian psychoanalysis, and philosophy. D. Harlan Wilson applies the "body without organs" model to zombie corporeality in "Schizosophy of the Medieval Dead: Sam Raimi's *Army of Darkness*," *Journal of Popular Culture* 41.3 (2008), especially 514–515.

9 On surface, depth, and the body without organs' thing-becoming, also see Wilson's "Schizosophy of the Medieval Dead," 514–515.

10 Bill Brown, *A Sense of Things: The Object Matter of American Literature* (Chicago: University of Chicago Press, 2003), 45. For the distinction between

res cogitans and *res corporealis* and the zombie challenge to our understanding
of personhood, also see, in *The Undead and Philosophy: Chicken Soup for the
Soulless,* ed. Richard Greene and K. Silem Mohammad (Chicago: Open Court,
2006), especially William S. Larkin, essay "*Res Corporealis*: Persons, Bodies, and
Zombies," 15–26.

11   Jacques Lacan, *Le Séminaire. Livre VII: L'éthique de la psychanalyse,* texte établi
par Jacques-Alain Miller (Paris: Seuil, 1986), 68.

12   Jean Baudrillard, *Fatal Strategies* (Los Angeles: Semiotext(e), 2008), 141.

13   On the cadaver as an example of "absolute" abjection, see Julia Kristeva, *Pouvoirs
de l'horreur: Essai sur l'abjection* (Paris: Seuil, 1980), 11.

14   Baudrillard, *Fatal Strategies,* 141. On Baudrillard and the object's status in
Western thought, see Brown, *A Sense of Things,* 179.

15   Julia de Funès, *Coup de philo . . . sur les idées recues* (Paris: Michel Lafon,
2010), 33–35.

16   Jacques Lacan, *Le Désir et son interprétation. Séminaire 1958–1959. Publication
hors commerce. Document interne de l'Association freudienne internationale et
destiné à son membres.* Leçon 3 (November 26, 1958), 29.

17   Elizabeth Kostova, *The Historian* (New York: Little, Brown, 2005), 90.

18   Barbara Johnson, *Persons and Things* (Cambridge, MA: Harvard University Press,
2008), 107.

19   See Jerah Johnson, "The Concept of the 'King's Two Bodies' in *Hamlet*,"
Shakespeare Quarterly 18.4 (Fall 1967): 430–434.

20   Brown, *A Sense of Things,* 63.

21   Lacan, *Le Désir et son interpretation,* 370.

22   Jacques Lacan, *Écrits,* trans. Alan Sheridan (New York: W. W. Norton, 1977), 287.
Also see Johnson, *Persons and Things,* 212, 217.

23   Lacan, *Écrits,* 285.

24   Ibid., 288.

25   Nicole Lapierre glosses on Montaigne's dictum "Nous pensons tousjours
ailleurs" ("Our thinking always takes place elsewhere") in *Pensons ailleurs*
(Paris: Gallimard, 2006), 11–20.

26   Lacan, *Le Désir et son interpretation,* 249.

27   Michael Inwood, *A Heidegger Dictionary* (Oxford, Blackwell: 1999), 215.

28   Luigi Volta, "'Horror' nella cultura di massa: dal mito allo *zombi*," *Quaderni di
Filologia Germanica della Facolta di Lettere e Filosofia dell'Universita di Bologna* 2
(1982): 194.

29   Shoshana Felman, "Jacques Lacan: Madness and the Risks of Theory (the Use
of Misprision)," *Global Literary Theory: An Anthology,* ed. Richard J. Lane
(London: Routledge, 2013), 276.

30   Ibid., 276.

31 Martin Heidegger, *The Question Concerning Technology and Other Essays*, trans. William Lovitt (New York: Garland, 1977), 132.

32 Michael Lang, "Mapping Globalization or Globalizing the Map?: Heidegger and Planetary Discourse," *Genre* 36 (Fall/Winter 2003): 239–244.

33 Emmanuel Levinas, *Difficult Freedom: Essays on Judaism*, trans. Seán Hand (Baltimore: The Johns Hopkins University Press, 1990), 233–234. On the complex interplay of the Levinasian face and technology, see the entire issue of *Transformations*, no. 18 (2010). http://www.transformationsjournal.org/journal/issue_18/editorial.shtml.

Works cited

Baudrillard, Jean. *Fatal Strategies*. Los Angeles: Semiotext(e), 2008.

Bishop, Kyle. "Raising the Dead: Unearthing the Nonliterary Origins of Zombie Cinema." *Journal of Popular Film and Television* 33.4 (Winter 2006): 201.

Brown, Bill. *A Sense of Things: The Object Matter of American Literature.* Chicago: University of Chicago Press, 2003.

de Funès, Julia. *Coup de philo . . . sur les idées recues*. Paris: Michel Lafon, 2010.

Deleuze, Gilles, and Félix Guattari. *Anti-Oedipus: Capitalism and Schizophrenia*. Trans. Robert Hurley, Mark Seem, and Helen R. Lane. Minneapolis: University of Minnesota Press, 1992.

Felman, Shoshana. "Jacques Lacan: Madness and the Risks of Theory (The Use of Misprision)." *Global Literary Theory: An Anthology*. Ed. Richard J. Lane. London: Routledge, 2013.

Greene, Richard, and K. Silem Mohammad, eds. *The Undead and Philosophy: Chicken Soup for the Soulless*. Chicago: Open Court, 2006.

Hamilton, Laurell K. *The Laughing Corpse*. New York: Ace, 1994.

Heidegger, Martin. *The Question Concerning Technology and Other Essays*. Trans. William Lovitt. New York: Garland, 1977.

Hogue, W. Lawrence. *Postmodern American Literature and Its Other*. Urbana: University of Illinois Press, 2009.

Inwood, Michael. *A Heidegger Dictionary*. Oxford, Blackwell: 1999.

Johnson, Barbara. *Persons and Things*. Cambridge, MA: Harvard University Press, 2008.

Johnson, Jerah. "The Concept of the 'King's Two Bodies' in *Hamlet*." *Shakespeare Quarterly* 18.4 (Fall 1967): 430–434.

Kostova, Elizabeth. *The Historian*. New York: Little, Brown, 2005.

Kristeva, Julia. *Pouvoirs de l'horreur: Essai sur l'abjection*. Paris: Seuil, 1980.

Lacan, Jacques. *Écrits*. Trans. Alan Sheridan. New York: W. W. Norton, 1977.

Lacan, Jacques. *Le Désir et son interpretation: Séminaire 1958–1959. Publication hors commerce. Document interne de l'Association freudienne internationale et destiné à son membres.* Leçon 3. November 26, 1958.

Lacan, Jacques. *Le Séminaire. Livre VII: L'éthique de la psychanalyse.* Texte établi par Jacques-Alain Miller. Paris: Seuil, 1986.

Lang, Michael. "Mapping Globalization or Globalizing the Map?: Heidegger and Planetary Discourse." *Genre* 36 (Fall/Winter 2003): 239–244.

Lapierre, Nicole. *Pensons ailleurs.* Paris: Gallimard, 2006.

Larkin, William S. "*Res Corporealis*: Persons, Bodies, and Zombies." *The Undead and Philosophy: Chicken Soup for the Soulless.* Ed. Richard Greene and K. Silem Mohammad. Chicago: Open Court, 2006. 15–26.

Levinas, Emmanuel. *Difficult Freedom: Essays on Judaism.* Trans. Seán Hand. Baltimore: The Johns Hopkins University Press, 1990.

Moraru, Christian. "Zombie Pedagogy: Rigor Mortis and the U.S. Body Politic." *Studies in Popular Culture* 34.2 (Spring 2012): 105–127.

Savu, Laura. *Postmortem Postmodernists: The Afterlife of the Author in Recent Narratives.* Teaneck, NJ: Fairleigh Dickinson University Press, 2009.

Sutherland, Meghan. "Rigor/Mortis: The Industrial Life of Style in American Zombie Cinema." *Framework: The Journal of Cinema and Media* 48.1 (2007): 64–78.

Volta, Luigi. "'Horror' nella cultura di massa: dal mito allo *zombi*." *Quaderni di Filologia Germanica della Facolta di Lettere e Filosofia dell'Universita di Bologna* 2 (1982): 194.

Wilson, D. Harlan. "Schizosophy of the Medieval Dead: Sam Raimi's *Army of Darkness*." *Journal of Popular Culture* 41.3 (2008).

Žižek, Slavoj. *Organs without Bodies: On Deleuze and Consequences.* New York: Routledge, 2004.

Notes on Contributors

Jeffrey R. Di Leo is dean of the School of Arts & Sciences and professor of English and Philosophy at the University of Houston-Victoria. He is editor and publisher of *American Book Review*, and the founder and editor of *symplokē*. His most recent books include *Federman's Fictions: Innovation, Theory, and the Holocaust* (2010), *Academe Degree Zero: Reconsidering the Politics of Higher Education* (2012), *Corporate Humanities in Higher Education: Moving Beyond the Neoliberal Academy* (2013), *Turning the Page: Book Culture in the Digital Age* (2014) and *Criticism after Critique: Aesthetics, Literature, and the Political* (2014).

W. Lawrence Hogue is the John and Rebecca Moores Distinguished Professor of English at the University of Houston and the author of many books, including *The African American Male, Writing, and Difference* (2003), *Postmodern American Literature and Its Other* (2009), and *Postmodernism, Traditional Cultural Forms, and African American Narratives* (2013). He is completing a critical text on the American novel of the 1920s and 1930s, tentatively titled *Reconfiguring Modern America and Re-representing the Modern American Novel*, and a literary biography of the novelist Charles Wright. He teaches courses and seminars on contemporary American fiction, postmodern fiction, critical theory, and U.S. minority literatures.

Kir Kuiken is associate professor of English at the University at Albany, State University of New York. He is the author of *Imagined Sovereignties: Toward a New Political Romanticism* (2014), and his published work includes essays on Derrida, Heidegger, Wordsworth, Shelley, and Benjamin.

Hassan Melehy is professor of French and Francophone Studies at the University of North Carolina, Chapel Hill. His books include *Kerouac: Language, Poetics, and Territory* (2016) and *The Poetics of Literary Transfer in Early Modern France and England* (2010). He has also written numerous articles on early modern literature and philosophy, recent and contemporary critical theory, twentieth-century American literature, and film studies.

Paul Allen Miller is Vice Provost and Carolina Distinguished Professor of Classics and Comparative Literature at the University of South Carolina,

Columbia. His books include *Lyric Texts and Lyric Consciousness: The Birth of a Genre from Archaic Greece to Augustan Rome* (1994), *Latin Erotic Elegy: An Anthology and Critical Reader* (2002), *Subjecting Verses: Latin Love Elegy and the Emergence of the Real* (2004), *Latin Verse Satire: An Anthology and Critical Reader* (2005), *Postmodern Spiritual Practices: The Reception of Plato and the Construction of the Subject in Lacan, Derrida, and Foucault* (2007), and *Diotima at the Barricades: French Feminists Read Plato* (2016).

Christian Moraru is professor of English at the University of North Carolina, Greensboro, and specializes in critical theory, contemporary American literature, and comparative literature. His books include *Rewriting: Postmodern Narrative and Cultural Critique in the Age of Cloning* (2001), *Memorious Discourse: Reprise and Representation in Postmodernism* (2005), *Cosmodernism: American Narrative, Late Globalization, and the New Cultural Imaginary* (2011), and *Reading for the Planet: Toward a Geomethodology* (2015).

Brian O'Keeffe teaches French and comparative literature at Barnard College, Columbia University. He is also an associate director of the Barnard Center for Translation Studies.

Jean-Michel Rabaté is professor of English and Comparative Literature at the University of Pennsylvania. He has authored or edited thirty-five books on modernism, psychoanalysis, contemporary art, philosophy, and on writers like Beckett, Pound, and Joyce. His recent books include *Lacan Literario* (2007), *1913: The Cradle of Modernism* (2007), *The Ethic of the Lie* (2008), *Etant donnés: 1) l'art, 2) le crime* (2010), *A Handbook of Modernism Studies* (2013), *Crimes of the Future: Theory and Its Global Reproduction* (2014), *Psychoanalysis and Literature* (2014), and *1922: A Companion* (2014). His forthcoming books are *Pathos of Distance* and *Think Pig! Beckett at the Limit of the Human*.

Herman Rapaport is Reynolds Professor of English at Wake Forest University. His recent publications include, "Performativity as Ek-scription: Adonis After Derrida" in *Performatives After Deconstruction*, Ed. Mauro Senatore (2013), "Transference Love in the Age of Isms" in *Desire in Ashes*, Ed. Simon Morgan Wortham (2015), and "Is Theory a Science?" *American Literary History* 27.2 (2015).

Nicole Simek is associate professor of French and Interdisciplinary Studies at Whitman College. She specializes in French Caribbean literature and is the author of *Eating Well, Reading Well: Maryse Condé and the Ethics of Interpretation* (2008). She has coedited volumes devoted to literary cannibalism and representations of trauma in French and Francophone literature. Her wider research interests include the intersection of politics and literature in Caribbean fiction, trauma theory, and sociological approaches to literature.

Henry Sussman is visiting professor of German at Yale University. His contribution to the present volume is a companion-piece to his most recent book, *Playful Intelligence: Digitizing Tradition* (2014). Other studies relevant to his chapter in *Dead Theory* include: *The Aesthetic Contract: Statutes of Art and Intellectual Work of Modernity* (1997), *The Task of the Critic: Poetics, Philosophy, and Religion* (2005), *Idylls of the Wanderer: Outside in Literature and Theory* (2007), and *Around the Book: Systems and Literacy* (2011).

Zahi Zalloua is associate professor of French and Interdisciplinary Studies at Whitman College and editor of *The Comparatist*. He has published *Montaigne and the Ethics of Skepticism* (2005) and *Reading Unruly: Interpretation and its Ethical Demands* (2014). His forthcoming book is entitled *Beyond the Jew and the Greek: Continental Philosophy and the Palestinian Question*. He has edited two volumes on Montaigne, *Montaigne and the Question of Ethics* (2006) and *Montaigne after Theory, Theory after Montaigne* (2009), and has also published articles, edited volumes, and special journal issues on globalization, literary theory, ethical criticism, and trauma studies.

Index

Abrams, Meyer 56
Adorno, Theodor 104
affect theory 2, 41
afropolitanism 37
Agamben, Giorgio 54, 65
Althusser, Louis 26, 40, 60, 66, 67
Anidjar, Gil 32
    *The Jew, the Arab: A History of the
        Enemy* 32
Anzaldua, Gloria 37
Appiah, Anthony 37
applied ethics 5, 6, 8, 9, 13
applied philosophy 5, 7
applied theory 4–6
Arendt, Hannah 63
Aristotle 112, 119
Asensi, Manuel 83
Auerbach, Erich 61, 74
    Mimesis 74
Auster, Paul 42
    The New York Trilogy 42
autobiography,
    de Man on 112
autoimmunity,
    of theory 155–65

Badiou, Alain 3, 4, 27, 40, 54, 55,
        62, 63
    Being and Event 40
    Logics of Worlds 40
Baker, Houston A. 36
    *Blues, Ideology, and Afro-American
        Literature* 36
Balibar, Etienne 40, 54, 63, 67
    "A Point of Heresy in Western
        Marxism" 67
Ball, Mieke 54
Barish, Evelyn 6
    The Double Life of Paul de Man 6
Barthes, Roland 6, 9, 17, 26, 54, 59
Bataille, George 15, 174, 178
Bate, Walter Jackson 56

Bateson, Gregory 96
    Steps to an Ecology of Mind 96
Baudelaire, Charles 120
    Painter of Modern Life 120
Baudrillard, Jean 58, 62, 221
    "The Gulf War Did Not Take Place" 58
Beckett, Samuel 84, 159
Belsey, Catherine 162
Benjamin, Harry 106
Benjamin, Walter 54, 63, 108, 134, 135,
        139, 140, 145, 209
    "The Task of the Translator" 134, 140
Berdach, Rachel 105
    The Emperor, the Sages and Death 105
    Freud on 105
Berger, Anne-Emmanuelle 33
Bergson, Henri 54, 85
Berlant, Lauren 54
Bernasconi, Robert 156, 157
Bernstein, Charles 61
Bhabha, Homi 37, 65
Birnbaum, Jean 25, 26
Blanchot, Maurice 13, 15, 26, 53, 75, 78,
        79, 80, 81–5, 112, 116, 118, 119, 123,
        125, 126, 174–83
    "Amitié" 116, 118
    and the Sirens 82–3
    Unavowable Community 177
Bloom, Allan 27
Bricmont, Jean 27
Brooke-Rose, Christine 42
    Amalgamemnon 42
Bruckner, Pascal 26
Burroughs, William 196
Butler, Judith 35, 36, 41, 43, 45, 54, 60,
        164
    Undoing Gender 36

Calhoun, Chesire 8
Calvino, Italo 42
    Invisible Cities 42
Caputo, John D. 28

Caribbean ruins,
    Walcott and 206-8
Chamoiseau, Patrick 16, 205, 209,
    210, 212
    Elmire des sept bonheurs (with de
        Lagarigue) 205, 208-14
Chatelet, Francois 41
Cherif, Mustapha 32
    L'Islam: Tolerant ou intolerant? 32
Chow, Rey 209
    Entanglements 209
Christian, Barbara 60
Cicero 111-19, 123, 126
    De Amicitia 111, 114, 115, 118, 123
    De Republica 113
Cixous, Hélène 1, 26, 33
    The Newly Born Woman 33
Coetzee, J. M. 42
    Foe 42
Cohen, Marshall 8
Cohen, Tom 10
communitarian logic 30, 32, 44
conjunctures 66
cultural theory 2

Dasein 60, 141, 175, 176
Davis, Angela 8
de Beauvoir, Simone 63
de Certeau, Michel 60
de Chirico, Giorgio 83
de Lagarigue, Jean-Luc 16, 205, 211
    Elmire des sept bonheurs (with
        Chamoiseau) 205, 208-13
de Man, Paul 6, 9, 17, 56, 57, 59, 112, 115,
    120, 121, 122, 123, 124, 125
    "Autobiography as De-Facement" 115
de Saussure, Ferdinand 40, 44
death of theory vs. death of theorists 6-10
deconstruction,
    and feminism 34
    heirs to 25-45
    Rose's charge 35
Delany, Samuel 37
Deleuze, Gilles 1, 3, 10, 13, 16, 26, 27, 37,
    54, 60, 65, 78, 79, 80, 191-201
    A Thousand Plateaus (with
        Guattari) 192, 193, 196, 200
    Anti-Oedipus (with Guattari) 191,
        196, 200

Difference and Repetition 191, 192,
    201
    interview 193
    The Logic of Sense 191, 192
    "On the Superiority of Anglo-American
        Literature" 197
    Proust and Signs 62
Deleuze/ Guattari 86-94
    and fascism 191-2
Derrida, Jacques,
    Acts of Religion 28, 32
    Adieu: To Emmanuel Levinas 28
    The Beast and the Sovereign 28
    "By Force of Mourning" 134
    De la Grammatology 75
    death 26
    The Death Penalty 28
    For What Tomorrow...(with
        Roudinesco) 43
    Gift of Death 178
    his otherness 29
    interview 25, 28, 118
        Points 135
    Khôra 116
    "La dissémination" 62
    Learning to Live Finally 10
    "Living On/ Border Lines" 134
    Memoires for Paul de Man 112, 115,
        117, 122, 123
    Monolingualism of the Other 28
    Of Grammatology 158
    Of Hospitality 28
    *On Cosmopolitanism and
        Forgiveness* 28
    Politics of Friendship 14, 15, 111, 112,
        113, 114, 115, 116, 118, 119, 121,
        123, 124, 125
    "Racism's Last Word" 28
    Specters of Marx 14, 28, 111, 112, 116,
        118, 121, 123
    "Women in the Beehive" 29
Descartes, Rene 44, 162, 163, 164
    Passions of the Soul 155
difference 31, 35
*Differences: A Journal of Feminist Cultural
    Studies* 34-5
Donoghue, Dennis 56
Dostoyesvky, Fyodor 84
Dussel, Enrique 39

Eagleton, Terry 27, 40
eclipse of the gaze 175
Editions La Fabrique 3
Elam, Diane 35
   Feminism and Deconstruction 35
Eliot, T. S. 83, 105, 218
   "Gerontion" 105
Enlightenment, the 108
Escher, M. C. 79, 80
Evenson, Brian 42
   Fugue State 42
Everett, Percival 37

Felman, Soshana 226, 227
   Writing and Madness 226
feminism 1, 2, 12, 30, 32, 33, 34, 35, 36,
   39, 43, 57, 63
Feminist theory 41
Finkelkraut, Alain 63
Fish, Stanley 41
Fitzgerald, F. Scott 197
Florette, Hayot 211
Foucault, Michel 1, 3, 6, 10, 12, 16, 26, 27,
   37, 39, 44, 54, 59, 60, 62, 64, 112,
   116, 117, 118, 119, 120, 123, 125,
   126, 159, 160, 191, 200
Freud, Sigmund 6, 11, 14, 26, 44, 76,
   101–6, 176, 201
   Beyond the Pleasure Principle 14, 101,
     103, 104, 105, 201
   Studies on Hysteria (with Breuer) 76
   Totem and Taboo 106
Freudian deconstruction (*Abbau*)
   103
Frye, Northrop 61

Gadamer, Hans-Georg 60
Gallop, Jane 35
Gaston, Sean 10
   *The Concept of the World from Kant to
     Derrida* 10
Genet, Jean 76, 94
Glissant, Édouard 210, 211, 212
Glucksmann, Andre 26, 63
Gödel, Kurt 81
Goldman, Emma 33
governmentality 10
Graff, Gerald 56
grand theory 1

Grimes, Tom 42
   The Workshop 42
Grossberg, Lawrence 54
Grosz, Elizabeth 35
Guattari, Felix 13, 16, 60, 65, 78, 79,
   80, 191
   A Thousand Plateaus (with
     Deleuze) 192, 193, 196, 200
   Anti-Oedipus (with Deleuze) 191,
     196, 200

Habermas, Jürgen 63, 123, 124
Hägglund, Martin 158, 159
Hardy, Thomas 195
Hartman, Geoffrey 61
Hayot, Florette 211
Heaney, Seamus 133, 134
   "Route 110" 133
Hegel, Georg Wilhelm Friedrich 44, 76,
   84, 95, 142
Heidegger, Martin 6, 26, 44, 54, 56, 57, 63,
   82, 84, 101, 103, 117, 136, 141, 142,
   143, 144, 175, 176, 180, 181, 182,
   183, 184, 186, 225, 228
   Being and Time 175
   Identity and Difference 141
   *Kant and the Problem of
     Metaphysics* 186
   The Origin of the Work of Art 144
Henri-Levy, Bernard 26, 63
Henry, Michel 54
high theory 1
Hirsch, E. D. 27
Hoagland, Sarah 8
Hofstadter, Douglas 13, 74, 76, 77, 78, 79,
   80, 81, 85, 95, 96
   Gödel, Escher, Bach 77
   I Am a Strange Loop 74, 77
Hogue, W. Lawrence 12, 219
   *African American Male, Writing, and
     Difference* 37
   *Postmodern American Literature and Its
     Other* 39
Hölderlin, Friedrich 62, 84
Hollander, John 27
Homan, Margaret 35
Human Chain 133
humanism 64
Hume, David 192

Husserl, Edmund 44, 85
Hutcheon, Linda 209

idealism 1, 67
identitarian community,
    Derrida's definition 30
identitarianism 34, 61, 67
invagination 150
Irigaray, Luce 1, 35
    Speculum of the Other Woman 35
irony,
    Hutcheon on 209
Islam and the West 29
Islam-West binary opposition 31
    and Derrida 31

James, Henry 83, 218, 226
    The Wings of the Dove 83
James, William 6
Jameson, Fredric 15, 54, 155
    Valences of the Dialectic 155
Johnson, Barbara 222
Joyce, James 62, 83, 102
    Exiles 102

Kafka, Franz 82, 84, 193
Kamuf, Peggy 35, 137, 146
Kant, Immanuel 14, 44, 106, 107, 108, 117,
    118, 120, 185
    *Anthropology from a Pragmatic Point of
    View* 117
    Critique of Pure Reason 185
Kerouac, Jack 16, 191–201
Kipnis, Laura 68
Kleist, Heinrich von 193
Kofman, Sarah 26, 60
Kojève, Alexandre 82
Kostova, Elizabeth 222
Kraus, Christian Jacob 106, 107
Kristeva, Julia 1, 54, 63, 111, 116
Kuiken, Kir 15

Lacan, Jacques 1, 3, 6, 26, 37, 54, 59, 62,
    82, 104, 162, 163, 222, 223, 224
    *The Four Fundamental Concepts of
    Psychoanalysis* 161
Laclau, Ernesto 63
Lacoue-Labarthe, Philippe 138, 139,
    140, 182

Laruelle, Francois 54, 55
Latour, Bruno 54
Lawrence, D. H. 194, 197
Le Monde 43
Learning to Live Finally 25
Leitch, Vincent 1, 2
Lentriccia, Frank 56
Levi-Strauss, Claude 44
Levinas, Emmanuel 17, 26, 44, 53, 60, 179,
    180, 181, 185, 217–29, 226, 227
literary theory 2
Loraux, Nicole 122
Luhmann, Niklas 76
Lyotard, Jean-François 1, 3, 6, 26, 27, 60

McDonald, Christie 35
McElroy, Joseph 227
    Plus 227
Madou, Jean-Paul 177
Mahler, Gustav 83
Malabou, Catherine 54
Mallarmé, Stephane 62
Mann, Klaus 192
    Mephisto 192
Marin, Louis 134, 149
    "By Force of Mourning" 149
Marx, Karl 26, 44, 90, 103, 111
Marxism 1, 2, 40, 41, 62, 67, 86
Mbembe, Achille 37
Meillassoux, Quentin 54, 55
Melehy, Hassan 16
Melville, Herman 194
Miller, Henry 195
Miller, J. Hillis 83, 84
    Black Holes (with Asensi) 83
Miller, Jacques-Alain 55
Miller, Paul Allen 14
Millet, Kate 61
Miro, Joan 83
Moi, Toril 63
Montaigne, Michel de 112, 115, 118, 156,
    159, 160, 161, 162, 165, 224
    "De L'amitié" 118
    Essays 159, 163
Montalbetti, Christine 42
    Western 42
Moraru, Christian 16, 17, 39
    Cosmodernism 39
    The Planetary Turn 39

Moten, Fred 36
Mouffe, Chantal 54
mourning, Eucharistic logic of 151
Mudimbe, V. Y. 37
multiplicity 31

Nancy, Jean-Luc 15, 65, 138, 139, 140, 148,
        174, 175, 176, 177, 178, 180, 181,
        182, 183, 184, 186
    Being Singular Plural 175, 180, 182, 183
    Ground of the Image 182, 185
    Inoperable Community 175
    The Literary Absolute (with
        Lacoue-Labarthe) 138
Nelson, Cary 58
neoliberalism 10
New Criterion 28, 124
New Criticism 2, 40
New Critics 27
New Historicism 2, 41
New Materialism 41
new materialists 40
New York Times 28
Ngai, Sianne 54
Nietzsche, Friedrich 26, 32, 39, 44, 103,
        112, 119, 137, 138, 192
    Ecce Homo 137
nominalism 1
Nussbaum, Martha 13, 59, 61, 62, 65
    The Fragility of Goodness 59

object-oriented theory 41
obscurantism 1
O'Keeffe, Brian 14, 15

Paglia, Camille 27
Pavic, Milorad 42
    Dictionary of the Khazars 42
Philosophy and Public Affairs 8
Picasso, Pablo 83
Plato 74, 119, 121
    Menexenus 121, 122
Poe, Edgar Allan 62
poem, the,
    Derrida and 135–51
poematic 136, 140, 143, 144
Poesia 15, 135, 136
positivism 53, 54, 58, 67
postcolonial theory 2, 37, 39

poststructuralism 2, 40, 41, 43, 44, 59
posttheory 1, 7
Pound, Ezra 6, 55, 83
Proust, Marcel 227
psychoanalysis 2, 38, 57, 80, 82, 86, 87, 89,
        90, 91, 93, 195
    and schizoanalysis 89–90

queer theory 2, 36, 39, 43
quietism 1

Rabaté, Jean-Michel 14
Rabelais, François 195
Ramadan, Tariq 32
Rancière, Jacques 54, 63
Rapaport, Herman 13
    The Theory Mess 39
Rawls, John 8
Reagan, Ronald 66
Rich, Adrienne 56
Rilke, Rainer Maria 84
Rogers, Daniel T. 64, 67
    Age of Fracture 64, 67
Romero, George A. 217, 219
    Survival of the Dead (movie) 219
Ronell, Avital 38
Rose, Jacqueline 35
Rousseau, Jean-Jacques 44, 107
Rubin, Gayle 60
Rushdie, Salman 42
    Midnight's Children 42
Russian formalism 2

Said, Edward 37, 45
Sartre, Jean-Paul 221
Schlegel, Karl Wilhelm Friedrich 138,
        139, 140, 141, 143
Schmitt, Carl 63, 112, 114, 121, 122, 123,
        124, 125, 126
Schopenhauer, Arthur 103
Seneca 159, 160
Shakespeare, William 61, 62, 219, 222
Shattuck, Roger 27
Showalter, Elaine 35
silent domination 209
Simek, Nicole 16
Singer, Peter 5, 8
skepticism 15, 108, 156–9, 162, 163
Sloterdijk, Peter 54

Socrates 9, 68, 121, 222, 225, 226
soft philosophy 5
Sokal, Alan 27, 56, 57
Sollers, Philippe 111, 116
Sophocles 62
Spinoza, Baruch 192
Spivak, Gayatri 35, 37, 39, 41, 54, 60,
    65, 165
Steinach, Eugen 106
Steiner, George 27
Stravinsky, Igor 83
structuralism 2, 65, 86
Surface Reading 41
Sussman, Henry 13, 78

Taylor, Mark C. 37
theoreticism 1
theory,
    Kuiken on 15
    Leitch on 1, 2
    subdisciplines 2
theory renaissance 2
Thomson, Judith Jarvis 5, 8, 9
translation,
    Derrida and 133–51
Traub, Valerie 62
    *The Renaissance of Lesbianism in Early
        Modern England* 62
Tronti, Mario 67
Tsepeneag, Dumitru 42
    Vain Art of The Fugue 42

Ulrich, Johann August Heinrich 106,
    107
    Eleutheriology 106
unmetaphorical objectivity 135

Vendler, Helen 61
Virilio, Paul 192
Vizenor, Gerald 36, 37, 42
    The Heirs of Columbus 42

Wagner, Richard 6, 104
Walcott, Derek 16, 205, 206
Walker, Alice 65
    The Color Purple 65
Weissmann, Charles 102
West, Cornel 27
Whitman, Walt 193, 197
    Leaves of Grass 193
Wilden, Anthony 75, 93
Winnicott, D. W. 78
Wolin, Richard 56
Woolf, Virginia 83, 195, 197
Wordsworth, William 112, 122
    Essay upon Epitaphs 112, 122

Yeats, W. B. 106

Zalloua, Zahi 15
Žižek, Slavoj 27, 40, 54, 104, 117,
    209
zombies 219–25